Dialogue with Teacher Educators

Dialogue with Teacher Educators

Teaching Content, Modes and its Nature

R. P. Singh

SHIPRA

ISBN: 978-81-7541-491-4

First Published in India in 2010

Dialogue with Teacher Educators: Teaching Content, Modes and its Nature

SHIPRA PUBLICATIONS
H.O.: LG 18-19, Pankaj Central Market, Patparganj,
I.P. Ext., Delhi-110092, Tel: 91-11-2223 5152, 2223 6152
Br.Off.: 115, Munish Plaza, 20, Ansari Road, Darya Ganj,
New Delhi-110002, Tel: 6594 6453, 9810522367
E-mail: info@shiprapublications.com
www.shiprapublications.com

Preface

The present book, which is addressed to teacher educators, is different from all others on the subject in as much as it deals with the description of the content of teaching, presents a brief history of the development in teaching modes and lastly describes the activity called '*Teaching*' itself. The idea behind writing this book was to upgrade the information level of teacher educators and motivate them to think away from traditional knowledge and become critical in their judgments. Times are changing so must the interpretations of known facts.

For instance, when I deal with the content of teaching in *Part 1*, I am trying to correct and update the content of the present day teaching of a problem. For instance, I question the common assumption that if Macaulay had not come or written his Minutes, the teaching of English language would not have become either compulsory or popular. I have argued that it is not so. The underlying principles a popular language follows are: (a) "the language of the ruler is the language of the ruled too' and (b) "that language is more acceptable to people, which gives them their bread and butter". These principles are independent of any Macaulay. Secondly, what is not taught is the basic assumption of Macaulay that by teaching English he would Christianize India. What needs to be taught is that neither of the two assumptions was correct. The reality seldom conforms to our assumptions. Therefore, what I am trying to tell my reader is that if he or she wishes to blame Macaulay then he could be questioned on his ignorance of Indian literature and culture and even be ridiculed for his exceeding the bounds of his brief. Similarly, when we talk of Muslim backwardness in Education then we must first define 'backwardness' and compare their rates of literacy with the contemporary rates of literacy in both Bangladesh and Pakistan;

where they themselves rule, and not compare them with the Hindus and the Sikhs in India where they could be at a disadvantage. The first principle of comparison is that it should be done with the compatible variables. If we did this, the content of the 'backwardness' would be very different from what is commonly said or written.

As we look at Part 2 of the present book, we find that it deals with the modes of teaching. Indian classrooms are on the verge of being revolutionized. As it is, Technology in classroom instruction has already entered in a big way. That this poses a challenge to teachers and teaching methodology is the current hub of contemporary academic discussion. We are not sure what lies in store for both the students and teachers; but surely it makes our future ever so much uncertain and unpredictable. Thanks to India's technological revolution we have reached a stage when the concept of Country-wide Classroom can and has already become a reality. Through firm and steady steps we too have reached a stage which is comparable to the one already obtained in the advanced nations of the world. We too have our Education satellites from where we already beam instruction to our classrooms spread all over the country, and we do teach via Internet i.e. on-line and through Direct-to-Home service. This much technology we too possess. The reader is given here a brief glimpse of how and what we have already developed and the stage at which we have arrived. Even the concept of 'virtual' classroom, which was intended to be a subject merely for academic discussion or a realizable dream, has taken concrete shape in this country. The fact of the matter is that our classrooms have transformed into unrecognizable realities. The basic question therefore is; Are we ready for this change? Are we teaching our teachers on these lines? If not; then why not? Who will answer this question?—the hapless teacher or the apex body viz. the NCTE?

Part 3 of the book tries to look at the process of teaching itself. It discusses the concept and differentiates the same from all other terms that mean different things although they are used as synonyms of teaching. We all know that both pick-pocketing and History are being taught. While the first one is not considered teaching and the other one is, the reader is informed that the reason for so doing lies in the objectives of the two. In one case the Society gives its seal of approval and in the other it refuses to do so. The reader is told to remember that the two types of teaching are different. Behind the concept and practice of teaching lies the seal of social approval. The instruction becomes teaching if the objective of it all is 'social good.'

It has taken long to write such a book. I do hope that at least a few of my readers will apprcciatc thc labour that has gone into its preparation and production. However, I am willing to accept both—the criticism as well as appreciation. Now that the book is in your hands please do read. Notwithstanding the outcome of the publication, I am happy I could do what I wanted to do.

Pocket A-4/206,
Kalkaji Extension,
New Delhi 110019
Tel. 29993062
profrpsi@gmail.com

R. P. Singh

Contents

Preface v

Part 1
The Issues: Researched

1. An Object Lesson on Colonial India: The Language Policy 3
2. Caste and Education 14
3. Educational Backwardness and the Indian Muslims: A Critique of Causal Relationship 26
4. Educating the Girl Child: A Lesson for Teacher Education 36
5. Quality Assurance in Educational Research: A Quest for Possibility 49
6. Tech-Savvy Teachers: Enter 21st Century 65
7. Education as an Institutionalized Network 80

Part 2
Technology in Indian Classrooms

8. Technology in India Classroom—Introduction 107
9. Countrywide Classrooms—A Teaching Alternative: Stepping into Knowledge Society 112
10. The International Scenario: The ETV—The World Experience 121
11. The Indian Initiative 129

12. The Media Centres—EMRCs and the AVRCs: Activating Support Systems 150

13. Packaging Knowledge—Quality in Quantity: Developing Insights 157

14. The ETV in Higher Education: Reviews Within and Without 166

15. Looking Ahead: From a Vision to a Mission 194

Part 3
The Nature of Teaching

16. The Nature of Teaching—Introduction 207

17. Towards a Philosophy of Teaching 213

18. Conditions for Teaching 229

19. Conditions of Teaching: Goal-Setting 252

20. Teaching: An Analysis 266

Bibliography 278

Index 280

Part 1

The Issues: Researched

1

An Object Lesson on Colonial India: The Language Policy

"No Hindu, who has received an English education, ever remains sincerely attached to his own religion..... It is my firm belief that, if our plans of education are followed up, there will not be a single idolater among the respectable classes in Bengal thirty years hence." T. B. Macaulay, (1836).

There are several questions that need to be answered while studying India's colonial past. While a few of these questions are generic in nature, others are related to a given context. For example, why are colonies set up? The answer to this question is quite simple. Colonialism by its very nature is constituted, "as a system of controls that is constructed by the imperial powers to subordinate and to exploit their dependencies."[1] Since it is clear that by their nature colonies are set up for exploitation one should not expect much from the colonizers. The typology of the colonies has been given by Stewart C. Easton viz. (a) for the sake of conversion of religion; (b) sale of industrial goods; (c) strategic reasons; (d) for status and prestige; (e) for export of extra population or for the sake of purifying their native populations, etc. One can easily identify the reasons for colonizing India. The only condition is to remember Pt. Nehru's observation, "that the British succeeded in dominating India by a succession of fortuitous circumstances and lucky flukes", which means they had no particular model of colonization in their mind for colonizing India.

But then there are several ways of studying colonized societies. A few need to be studied on the basis of hypothetical considerations and assumptions, while for others models have to be developed. Any model developed or advanced to study a colony must discuss the nature of society the colonizer happens to have and the relationship it builds with the colony. The other parameters should include the level of education it has, its socio-economic condition and the reason why a country has been colonized.

It is possible that the British drew their inspiration from Richard Hakluyt, who had been requested by Walter Raleigh to convince Queen Elizabeth I about the importance of having colonies, who therefore wrote *Discourses of Western Planting* in which he eventually advanced these theses: (1) Her Majesty has not only the right but an obligation as Defender of the Faith to propagate her belief; (2) If she failed others will not; (3) Colonies will restore vitality to British trade; (4) Colonies will alleviate social and political unrest in the commonwealth (at that time England, Wales and Scotland) by drawing away vagrants and idlers); and (5) Thus she could thwart the ambition of Philip II of Spain.

It would be interesting to learn about the state of contemporary British economy and material progress in the British Isles as compared with France and Germany. It might interest some to learn that Britain itself continued to remain a colony of the Romans for a number of centuries starting with Caesar's in 200 B.C., and that too for strategic reasons and not for economic exploitation. The special features of English ruling class until the end of 15th century were its *alien* character and the *purchase* of 'blue' blood by those who could afford it. "In 1530 (around the time when Mughals were setting up their empire in India) the Heralds decided that any man of good reputation with free lands worth 10 pounds a year or movable goods worth 300 pounds could *buy* coat of arms—in brief, the 'blue' blood had a price tag" and until the reign of the Tudors the language of the British elite was French. That is why Chaucer's prioress spoke French:

> "....full fair and fetishly
> After the scole Starford ate Bowe."

In fact until Queen Elizabeth I, England continued to look up to the continent both for her politics and religion. It is during her reign that the powers of the nobility were reduced and the " royal monopoly of violence attained." Politically under "her rule was the East India Company, given a Charter and for the first time ever did England acquire a nationalist government and defeated the Spaniards and permitted the pirates to bring in bullion of which she was in terrible short supply."

Richard Hakluyt, a scholar of those times had advanced two basic reasons why England must: (a) secure gold and silver and (b) find new markets for her woolen cloth.

The British ruling class as already seen was mostly foreign and except for the landed aristocracy and the merchants, few had high aspirations or hopes. Daniel Defoe wrote in 1701:

"Wealth, however got, in England makes
Lords of mechanics, gentlemen of rakes:
Antiquity and birth are needless here;
'T is impudence and money that make a peer
Fate has but very small distinction set
Betwixt the counter and the coronet."

It is significant that for very personal reasons (viz lust and power) Henry VIII had severed relations with the Roman church and thus became Defender of Faith for the Church of England. This provided the British yet another reason for rivalry with the continent. Except for a few merchants and the aristocracy the life for the ordinary farmer and the factory worker was very hard indeed. It has been commented by Sir Eric Ashby (*Technology and the Academics*, p. 50) that the contribution of universities to industrial revolution in England was neglible since the first flush of industrial advancement was largely based on ordinary skills and little investments. However, the *consequence of industrialization was mass scale poverty so much so that 10 per cent of the total population constituted of paupers*. This is what justified Richard Hakluyt's thesis. E. J. Hobsbawm writes, "Behind our Industrial Revolution lay this concentration on the colonial and underdeveloped markets overseas, the successful battles to deny them to anyone else."

We must also try to understand the nature of colonolization the West gave us. Firstly, we should not forget that Britain was not the only colonizer of India. It shared India in howsoever miniscule a form with two other European colonizers viz. the French and the Portuguese. The three presidencies where the East India Company ruled did not constitute the whole of India, because the country called India even today signifies *de jure* and not *de facto* reality. For instance, we all know that today there are several parallel governments in large parts of India. Therefore when we talk of India today we make a clear distinction between de jure and de facto realities. Any generalizations based on any of the Presidencies at that time will tell only a partial reality, even as today parts of the so-called India do not stand covered in our day to day National administration.

Secondly, the language policies in all these three colonies were different. There is no reason why one should give more importance to the one against the other two. The histories of all these three colonizers are very different. The Portuguese, for instance, traded with the Mughals and brought slaves for their queens besides other delicacies. The French tried to oust the British from vast territories that they had occupied but sadly enough failed in their objects. This goes to show while the nature and purposes of colonization might not differ very greatly, that their growth eventually made a material difference.

It is important to remember that educationally too Britain was not very advanced as compared to India. In fact, we already know that they borrowed the Monitorial system from India to teach their factory workers. Until better methods were evolved the system continued to be used for factory workers in England. Gandhi had commented once that India was more literate when the British arrived, but made it largely illiterate.

The history of Indian education is marred by poor quality of assumptions that its so-called thinkers have advanced. For example, it was suggested by J. P. Nayak that the British had an obligation to teach us and indeed a few of them also thought so. This fact is not borne by any history of education where a colonizer makes provision for the education of a colony because of humanitarian reasons or considers educating the colonized as its moral obligation to do so. The Company's interest in education was limited to training a few natives who would share their administrative burden and thereby reduce financial obligations. After all, the East India Company was a business concern and not a philanthropic organization. And until 1857 the administration remained in the hands of this mercantile Company.

It would be appropriate to remember that England itself was largely an illiterate country where the masses continued to wallow in both ignorance and poverty. Its twin universities were meant to produce gentlemen, whose sole goal in life was to live off the labour of others. Hence, it would be instructive to read the letter Lord G. K. Chesterton wrote to his son while the latter embarked on his journey for Europe. The real measure of England's educational prowess or advancement could be judged by its attempts to compare its achievements in science and technology with other contemporary European powers. The fact is that until 1856 it was nowhere near the achievements in Science and Technology of either France or Germany. This came out clearly in a Science Exhibition in Paris. This exposure resulted in a lot of sole searching and it took considerable effort to set a Department of Science and Technology. A lot of heated discussions in British Parliament eventually led them to have their first Act of Education in 1870 only. This Act also did not open up its universities for the common man and the schools remained as class exclusive as before. Girls could not get admission in universities until the third decade of the 20th century. Their first comprehensive Act of Education was passed in 1944 only some 3 years before they left India. Therefore to expect a country to bother about Indian education is too far-fetched an idea to be worth consideration. Remember it was the British aristocracy and its merchants who ruled India until the last day when they left.

If this situation is compared with the then contemporary India we will notice that India was well-served by its *madrasahs* and the *tols* and the rate of literacy in India was far better than that of Great Britain That the British administration was unimaginative and heartless was the result of their cruel practices in a colony nearer home—viz. Ireland. We must not forget that colour of the skin played very insignificant role in their treatment of Indians. After all, the Irish are not coloured. One should read the literature produced by writers like Swift and Shaw to see the British in real colours.

The two surveys undertaken by Adam at the behest of William Bentick tell their own tale. While the Muslim rulers across the country provided a single type of school for everyone viz. the *Madrasah*, the Hindu subjects maintained *tols* and Sanskrit *pathsalas* for their wards. It would be interesting to go through the twin reports of Adam and read through his tables and discover caste-wise presentation of student data and also to discover where the educated Indians, particularly Hindus did go. The medium of instructions in these institutions was Persian, although for some Arabic was also taught as this is the language of the Holy Koran. (for further detail; read *History of Vernacular Education in Bengal* 1800-54 (1974) by N. L. Basak, Bharati Book Stall, Calcutta)

Then there are several assumptions by Indian scholars that are equally based on airy nothings. For instance, the British had no idea how and why India's social scene was so confusing. They took time to understand India's caste system and the animosity between the Hindus and the Muslims and social and religious practices of the Hindus like the *sati* system, child marriages, the position of women in Indian society, etc. The problems the alien rulers faced continue till this day to bother us—in their original form and remain unresolved. Why then do we expect that these alien rulers would have been able to resolve our problems when we have refused materially to change the same until this day?

I now cite a book by H. G. Rawlinson to endorse my contentions. He says: "1. England did not deprive Indians of their freedom because they hadn't any; 2. And if they were economically exploited because "Men do not found empires with philanthropic motives, and the British like the Portuguese, Dutch and French came to the East not for conquest but for trade… . The country, torn by anarchy and without sea power, would have become a French possession had not England intervened" 3. The causes of Indian poverty are to be sought, not in over-taxation and in the rain; but in the inherent social structure of Indian society i.e. caste regulation, with their drastic restrictions, are essentially uneconomic, and, combined with the conservatism of the Indian peasant, make rural prosperity unattainable; 4. over-population brought down India's prosperity line, 5, Like the Renaissance the British brought about a revolution of the mind and spirit which raised the country from the darkness of the Middle Ages to the contemporary Europe; 6, and lastly, he agrees with Lord Curzon, who said, " Our work is righteous and it shall endure."[2]

The above quote gives us an insight into what and how the British thought of their rule and, if analyzed objectively, it would approximate to the reality. The analysis would be taken up immediately after I make a reference to a book, recently read, titled: *Subject Lessons—The Western Education of Colonial India by Sanjay Seth (Duke University Press, Durham and London, 2007, pp. 264).* The present publication deals with a few issues for assessing the British impact on them and thereby on Indian society. The contents of this book are fairly well-known and the underlying assumptions too are not uncommon. It would appear as though he was breaking from the known mould. Seth discusses issues like the medium of instruction; the education of the Muslims and the education of girls, etc. but the main thrust remains focused on how Western education came to be disseminated in India, and how it was received and consumed by the local populace. He refers to the use of two terms—Western, which indicates cultural specificity; and Modern to denote its recent emergence. Macaulay and several others wanted India to learn Western education in place of mythic, superstitious and primitive education. The way Indians learnt was characterized by rote learning and uncritical acceptance of what was taught. We shall go into these issues separately, but first the conclusion of the study by Seth.

"Western knowledge arrived in India through the coercive agency of colonialism. We are told, most forthrightly by Macaulay, that this knowledge was true and that our knowledge's, like our gods, were false. I have read the discourses that western education generated as perturbations on the surface of this knowledge, half-acknowledgements that the "foundational assumptions" underpinning and enabling modern knowledge in fact could not be assumed. Nonetheless, that knowledge has now become global. There is no easy point outside it, no escape from it other than by engaging with and through it, thus I write as one of Macaulay's misbegotten offspring, working with this knowledge to contribute to the self-questioning that renews intellectual traditions and keeps them alive. There are myriad ways of doing so and I do not claim any privilege for the track I have taken. But if those who were once "subject to pedagogy" can long after they are gone, be studied in a fashion that subjects modern western education to scrutiny, there is a pleasing irony in the thought that Macaulay's bastard children will have contributed to the critical appropriation of a knowledge that was once imposed on them." [3]

THE LANGUAGE TANGLE—THE QUESTION OF MEDIUM OF INSTRUCTION

There is no other theme that is dealt with in such a cavalier manner as the colonial past of India. Take any book on India's education history we start with Macaulay and discover an assumption being advanced that had Macaulay not come to India we would not have opted for learning English or not critically examined our heritage. We are not quite sure what is it that we condemn more—Macaulay's derogatory remarks about our ancient literature and heritage or his recommendation for spending money on teaching English, doing neither of which was part of his job. While Macaulay had exceeded his portfolio specifications, his prejudices clouded his intelligence and scholarship. However if things are seen in a perspective, our conclusions would be very different. It would be preferable if policies are seen against the backdrop of colonization *per se* and not the way we have stretched the point beyond its rational domain.

The much discussed language policy during William Beatnik's tenure and the role Macaulay played in its formulation has been a fascinating topic for Indian scholars. No matter how much fresh light is thrown on this subject it has been difficult to arrive at any consensual judgment. In fact it has been extremely difficult even to decide whether any policy note was ever needed. *The Indian subjects had taken to learning English without any official persuasion or even preparation.* Long before the last of the Mughal emperors was made to relinquish his throne and even the nominal charge of the country, the cream of the local populace had anticipated future and had started preparing itself accordingly. The twin Rajas of Calcutta viz. Raja Radha Kant Deb and Raja Ram Mohun Roy had already moved into this domain long before William Bentick or T. B. Macaulay were even physically present.

It is seldom realized that almost universally people follow their innate instinct for survival. Almost every child knows in which language it can demand food and other survival kits when hungry. *The language of the ruler is the language of the ruled and is rarely true vice versa.* The academia and the bureaucracies create controversies where none needs to exist. Precisely this is what happened in the case of the not so famous Minutes of Macaulay and the joining in of the issues by T. H. Prinsep. The notoriety of the Minutes of Macaulay is largely because people lack perspective and they are generally not even aware of the limitations of scholarship or of bureaucratic norms. The rest is history and hence the following discussion from a wholly new perspective.

Language colonization is not an exotic experience for India. Conquering hordes since time immemorial have left their imprint on Indian languages, culture and life. Scholars have attempted to establish that the Rigveda itself has not been entirely free from foreign influences. The earliest record of the Indians having learnt a foreign language is that of Greek which was at one time the court language of a ruler in Gujarat.[3] Persian influence has been a little more marked not merely because once upon a time the persecuted Zoroastrians from Persia sought refuge in India, but Persian impact can be seen even otherwise till this day on Indian culture, language and among Indian Shias (a sect in Islam)... Syrian Christians of Kerala trace their lineage to the first group of Christian arrival in A.D. 1, which means along with them must have reached Indian subcontinent an alien culture and a non-indigenous language. In modern times long before the British came on the scene and tried to settle down to govern, already on the subcontinent Portuguese had made their language compulsory in 1684. While passing this order that "all Goans must learn Portuguese in three years time", the Court of Alvar had caved in to Franciscan friar's pressure that had shown a great aversion to local languages.[4] Almost a repeat of what had happened once at Nalanda, all books and written material in Goa was reduced to ashes by these missionaries. We also have traces of influence of several other oriental languages and dialects in the spoken languages of Northeast India.

Against this background the language controversy as it arose during the first few decades of 19th century of Company rule in India is indicative more of a democratic and civilized behaviour on the part of Island race than coercion. Irrespective of the terms used for their desire to carry the local population along with them in the process of language selection, the experience of both the rulers and the ruled was mutually educative. If Indians on their part showed a sense of pragmatism and acknowledged the irreversible laws of governance, the rulers, however unsure of their eventual policy framework, evinced interest in the local literature, languages and institutions. Indeed, a few even thought that it was their 'moral' obligation to preserve at least a part of Indian heritage in its pristine glory.

There are several other things that one must remember while talking of the medium of instruction in the British ruled India. Firstly, different parts of India came under foreign rule at different points in time. For instance, northern part of India was ruled over by the English monarch for less than a century but this is not true for Bengal, which remained in their economic and political control for close to over 200 years. Therefore, there is every reason to believe that no generalization is valid in this regard. Secondly, there is plenty of difference between the rule of Parliament and of the monarchy on the one hand and the rule of a business conglomerate like that of East India Company on the other. A merchant company is formed only to earn and not undertake welfare activities. The approach to governance in the case of the above two would be essentially different. Therefore, we see that the Charter Act of 1813 remained dormant (because it involved expenditure) until 1833 or so when it was decided finally that money ought to be spent only on the promotion of English language teaching in India and nothing else. But the real fillip to western education came only after 1857 when India became a responsibility of the British monarchy..

It is commonly assumed that what was being said for Bengal was true for the entire India i.e. as though India existed as a single political entity. The tragedy is that even to this day India exists only in the Indian Constitution and the political pronouncements of a few leaders. There are currently about 117 insurgent groups who owe no allegiance to this country or the government and are out to destroy both. There are several parts of the country that are waging wars against the State. Even in our so-called 'national' political parties there are groups that work for the promotion of foreign interests in India and are blind to Indian welfare. It is recorded by the media (editorially by HT, May 7, 2008) that there is no rule of law in 170 districts of India right from Nepal border to Telangana. Jails are broken with impunity, police forces are killed without remorse and taxes remain unpaid for years on end. Then in India's metropolis lives a class of people who half live in this country and behave like the westerners. Therefore, if we do not have an acceptable national identity till this day then, of which 'India' we keep making reference? It is doubtful if all those who live here owe full allegiance to the Indian Constitution till this day.

Culturally too we cannot claim to be a homogenous country. We have in this country several layers of culture, starting with aborigines to the most westernized and the urbanized. Similarly there is no word or even a group of words that can help us visualize the real state a particular tribe lives in. For instance, while the Mizo tribe is the most literate and westernized among Indians with literacy rates hovering around 92 per cent there is on the other extreme a state like Jharkhand, which happens to have areas like Abhujmand, whose tribal population shuns contact with outsiders. Also a vast section of Muslims remain alienated from the political set up and a sizable section of the same is turned militant which avowedly claims allegiance to another country/countries and is out to destroy whatever remains of India in name.. 'Unity in diversity' is a convenient slogan that we are forced to adopt in public.

The reality is that we have yet to become a Nation. Therefore, the 'India' Macaulay was talking of existed only in his imagination and not in his experience. He was not talking of the whole of India in the sense we claim we understand it today, and definitely he did not know anything about our culture or people. I am in receipt of a book titled: *Subject Lessons—The Western Education of Colonial India* by Sanjay Seth,(cited above), which offers a model to study Macaulay's legacy very differently from the way we have read this scholar thus far.

We must also remember about the nature of India's political set up when the East India Company came to open its shop here. It would be helpful to recall the type of Great Britain itself was when this Company was formed. The socio-economic condition of Britain itself has come under scanner when it set its feet in this country. A brief reference to it would suffice. We must go back to the times when the East India Company itself was being formed.

In my book *Education in an Imperial Colony* I have gone into details showing the actual condition of Great Britain at the time when East India Company was formed and the reasons why the Elizabeth 1 approved its formation.[6] While it is not possible to go into the details how and why Britain was in no position to take a high moral ground to legitimize its superiority and claim that it could give better rule to this country, I shall cite a few select pieces to show from my well-researched book cited above to support my argument.

The three main points that need to be emphasized are: the state of education in contemporary England, the British society—its composition and the economic reasons why East India Company was formed. Once we do that we can easily understand that language policies were the result of mutual convenience of the ruler and the ruled besides economic compulsions and the political will. There is nothing esoteric about such policies.

If we were to consider the present Indian language scenario, we find that English has after some interval come to occupy prime position in our educational efforts. Although a survey says that there are several language groups: such as the Indo-Aryan, Dravid, Austro-Asiatic, Tibetan-Burmese; and the Andmani. The Aryan languages constitute one third of the total and are spoken by 73 per cent of the Indians. Around 27 per cent from Dravid language groups are spoken. All this goes to show that major Indian languages continue to be spoken and remain part of Indian life. Even while the stars of English language are on the ascendance—thanks largely to the ICT, it is unlikely that it would totally replace any of the major languages either in literature or education. Whatever be the degree of our appreciation of this colonial language, we are highly unlikely to become anglicized either in dress or life-style. If Macaulay was irrelevant then, he remains equally irrelevant now We may read and write in English and even take up a job that requires adopting European manners, but an Indian remains Indian at heart and in customs. Just as an army officer wears uniform on duty, our acceptance of English language is only for a while in the course of our daily life. It neither makes us Christians nor British or American. We remain Indians—our command on a foreign language notwithstanding. A foreign language has been adopted, mastered and even made part of our daily lives, but not in the same way as our colonial masters had thought of or propagated for. The failure of their design is even more prominent the way Hindus celiberate their festivals, indulge in their rituals, undertake yatras, and keep on opening Sanskrit universities and reverting to the yoga for their well-being, Ayurveda for cure, vastu-sastra for designing buildings and the Vedas for life-sustaining inspiration.

REFERENCES

1. *Encyclopedia—Americana* (vol. 7; 1968) write up by David K. Fieldhouse of Oxford.
2. *The British Achievement in India*, William Hodge, & Co. 1948.
3. Panikkar, K. M. (1963) *Studies in Indian History*, p. 8, Asia; also see, *The Greeks in Bactria and India* (1968) by W. W. Tarn, pp. 350-408. Cambridge University Press.
4. Varde, P. S. (1977) *History of Education in Goa from 1510 to the Present-day*, p. 22, Goa Vidya Pratishthan, Panaji.
5. Sanjay, Seth (2007) *Subject Lessons—The Western Education of Colonial India* by Duke University Press, Durham and London.
6. For detail *see* Singh, R. P. (1979). *Education in an Imperial Colony*, p. 61, National Publishing House, 1979.

2

Caste and Education

"The Brahman is foremost in the society, like the head in the body. His force lies in the protection of humanity through knowledge, religion and austerity. The Kshatriya is a class amongst men. His power lies in affording happiness in humanity through justice, humility and strength. The Vaishya is another class, who amasses foodstuffs. His strength lies in becoming the lord of riches. The artisan, Shudra, is another class of men, whose strength lies in doing hard work." Yajur. Ch. XXX. 5.

Is India a Nation? If the answer is 'yes' when did we become one? This question bothers so many and the more we try to answer this question the more we get distanced from the real definition of nationhood. Nations, national governments and national pride, etc. are concepts that become real when we try to differentiate ourselves from some other people or governments. Europe gave us the definition of a Nation for the first time after Napoleonic wars. In political science, State was defined as a nation. It generally denoted "a group of people inhabiting a specific territory and living according to a common legal and political authority; a body politic or nation". In this definition, the term 'state' includes government; in another usage, the two terms are synonymous. Among types of states that developed at various times in history were the city-states of ancient Greece, in which sovereignty rested with the free citizens of an independent city. During the Middle Ages, Europe was divided politically into many small principalities, the boundaries and sovereignties which changed frequently. From this condition of political anarchy, the modern nation-state, which consists of a group of people with the same or similar nationality, inhabiting a definite territory, emerged by a gradual process, extending over centuries. The type of government has varied, first taking the form of absolute monarchies and later of constitutional monarchies or republics, some of them federations or unions of semi-independent states. In the 20th century totalitarian dictatorships, in which one ruler assumes absolute power, have been established in some states.

India somehow never became a nation despite meeting all the requirements of political definition. Even it is very doubtful whether or not we qualify to be a nation. Our identity has always remained caste. In a paper written for Times of India (April 21, 2008) Tripta Wahi talks of Identities In a Flux (particularly in medieval India). According to her when we talk of Hindus or Muslims in the medieval India it is doubtful whether such identities ever existed. For instance, when one talks of Muslims of that period they themselves identified themselves as Turks, Iranis, Afghani, Sheikh, pir, Saiyyad, Pirzadah, Dakhni etc. They also identified themselves as Lodhis, Nuhanis, Yusufzais, Afridis, etc. but seldom did they identified themselves as Muslims. For the upper caste Muslims the lower castes did not exist and if they did they were treated with contempt.

Similarly the Hindus identified themselves as a caste and not a group of Hindus. She goes on to say," Cutting across religious, caste and linguistic and ethnic identities were the distinct social identities in relation to the means of production and revenue obligations to the state. The zamindars had a distinct social identity. There were rais, ranas, choudharies, muqudams, biswadars, deshmukhs, and deshpandes. There were also khidmatis and praja. There were categories of mugrari riyaya, reza riyaya, and asamis. And of course there was a category of those who owned no means of production. and she could have as well written about the way one identified a stranger—." What is your source of eating meals? or what is your zeria-*i*-mash"

She goes on to cite a few examples in which a Hindu King was willing to pull down a temple and build a mosque in its place only if Emperor Aurangzeb agreed to make his son a ruler of a given state. It was the Muslims who opposed the imposition of zezia on the Hindus by Aurangzeb and it was withdrawn immediately after his death. The conclusion therefore is that the terms like India, Hindus and Muslims do not appear to have existed during the medieval times. The fact that all these terms exist today does not mean that they describe a reality.

The British gave us an identity of a Nation because they conquered different parts of India (merely a geographical part on the globe) at different periods of time and started ruling it from a single capital with identical rules) which even now we have not been able to convert it into a reality. The fact that Hindus have SCs and lower castes and India has STs of numerous variety and we have insurgents in all parts of the country that owe no allegiance to the State, (and there are Naxals too) only goes to show that we have a textbook identity called Indian but the ground reality is far from the claim we make. We continue to have a reality couched in caste and an individual's identity expressed in terms of his means of production and a territorial name to specify it. Beyond that it is all illusion and wishful thinking. Indian politics fully endorses the statement I have made.

Contemporary politics has vitiated the meaning and the purpose of Vedic hymns that relate to caste. Caste, as we all know, has attracted maximum attention for very narrow reasons. The case in point is the so-called caste–system and its origin besides the historic role it has played down the centuries both in the preservation and spread of our culture. On the positive side India has remained a partially literate society largely because of its caste system and the role caste has continued to play in one's academic pursuit, sacrifices and achievement. On the negative side the roots of gender bias in education and educational backwardness among several castes and communities can also be traced back to this our very own peculiar caste system and religious practices. Although it is true that caste has played a very significant role in keeping our hoary traditions intact, it has also attracted attention for its unique features. Howsoever we might condemn caste and its anachronism in the modern times but instead of diminishing in terms of importance, it keeps on increasing its stranglehold on the Indian society. Therefore, I have a hunch that the more the so-called forward classes for whom learning is important in the pursuit of their professional/caste Dharma remain glued to family traditions the greater are the chances that the literacy rates will go on moving up correspondingly. In the lower rungs of the caste ladder this awareness is bound to come because of vote bank politics.

The caste is currently undergoing a peculiar transformation. The castes that took pride in being distinct and exclusive are nowadays willing to compromise their rank and character. No caste is able to claim its superiority or is unwilling to compromise on one or the other ground. The present mini essay is part of a larger study and is meant to test the hypothesis that caste and education are historically inter-related. The dominance of particular castes in the field of education continues to show and the new entrants are finding the task of benefiting from education difficult both for social and economic reasons. The rates of literacy are more or less predictable. We know for sure who will and who will not acquire education and succeed. The intervening period of colonial rule made only an insignificant difference on the role of caste in acquiring education and to claim that the basic character of Indian society was impacted in any noticeable way by the British rule in India is only partially tenable. On the contrary the western education created a kind of resistance to change and made majority of its higher castes to start delving more and more into the past and made Indians discover advantages in retaining their past values and culture. Just as we have discovered the value of alternate medicine and reverted to the healthy practices of Yoga, we find solace in starting more Sanskrit universities and schools that in most cases do not follow the western curricula. For instance, there is a school of thought that finds Vedic mathematics more useful than the western one. We are getting more and more curious to discover our past in the name of modernity. In my opinion we are using western education only for certain category of business functions but are ever ready to reverting to past practices in the name of proven basic advantages. This is happening with both major communities—the Hindus and the Muslims. We can go a step further. We do not hesitate to start a computer center with traditional Bhumi pujan and by chanting Vedic mantras. This is how we compete and grab a western project. This basic contradiction in our behaviour and thinking does not bother us in the least.

In Indian politics since the very beginning of our known history caste has played a dominant role. The peculiar fact is that caste has survived several modern day laws, abolishing its domain areas. The truth is: the more it has been opposed and suppressed the more resistant it has become to change It is like an evergreen weed that is resistant to any and every pesticide. Today the caste- based politics has become so important that no political calculation is possible without taking it into account. For instance, India's Socialist party and its splinter group Janata Dal or Lalu faction are essentially Yadava-caste based parties without having even a remote link to anything like a political ideology of Socialism. I personally doubt whether its leaders have ever read even Ram Manohar Lohia properly, and least of all its Western advocates. It is not that we are not critical of this peculiar Indian phenomenon (read, Khushwant Singh, in his famous column Malice toward one and all, May 31, 2008) but we seem to be helpless. The Bahujan Samaj Party (BSP) is basically a Dalit group, which has acquired a clout because of its numerical strength but depending on a given exigency it also changes colours. Indian politics is as complex as Indian society itself and it is a rare genius who could unravel reality without contradicting oneself.

Caste plays an important role in the provision of education and also it continued its impact in making a difference in academic attainments. Whether one liked it or not caste plays a significant role in determining or fixing social hierarchy. In fact, every year the examination results at all levels tend merely to confirm what is commonly believed to be the role caste plays in both predicting academic attainment and deciding the dominance of a few in highly specialized jobs.. I will show here in this paper the role caste has played and continues to play till this day in education apart from the fact that even today educational institutions tend to be started and controlled for the benefit of a particular community or caste. Since these facts are known to Indians we need not go into the details to show how a particular caste or community would retain/perpetuate its hegemony, but surely I would like to show with the help of a table or two how a particular caste or community can predictably show better results than any other community or caste in either retaining their advanced status or standard.

For the inquisitive I recommend a few names of books that may be consulted with profit. (1) Andre Beteille: *Caste, class and power*; OUP, 1966; (2) Andre Beteille, *Castes: Old and new*, Asia, 1969; (3) A.D. Mddie, *The Brahmanical culture and Modernity*, Asia, 1968, 4. M. N. Srinivas, *Social Change in Modern India.*

Today whether one liked it or not even such religions that are basically egalitarian viz. Sikhism, Christianity and Islam, believe in caste and practice it openly. Muslims have their Ajlafs and the Sikh their Majhabis. The case of Christian Dalits is well-known. All these religious groups deny practicing caste dharma but in reality they are quite unwilling to marry outside their own fold. The reason why these religions have castes and nowhere else in the world is largely because majority of the members of these religious communities were at one time Hindus. They carried the Hindu customs to their respective religions even after conversion.

It is believed that castes denote profession but ever since they became hereditary, they became fossilized to denote a community that followed a profession and the respect they command is determined by the type of occupation they pursue. It is the combination of profession and political power that has given the caste a peculiar status in our society. Recent agitations in free India for declaring certain castes OBCs, ST/SC go to prove to what extent caste has been politicized. Interestingly, the caste that spurned wealth in the past for learning or power continues to maintain its community's dignity But the way politics has entered every walk of our life and impacted social behaviour has not left the Brahmins too alone.

Before we move any further let me mention that caste is common to all religions. If Muslims continue to use their past surnames or pre-fixes/ suffixes like Kunwar/Raja or some Kashmiri Hindu caste, it all goes to show the importance of the caste in India. There are certain distinct castes like the Jats and Gujjars, who inhabit only northern part of India, that have now accepted the Hindu caste system. Since Hinduism does not baptize anyone, both of these communities have fixed their caste status and consider themselves equal to the Hindu Rajputs and because of their past achievements are generally considered Martial races. They have since copied the Hindu rituals and practices. Groups of these communities are also Sikhs and Muslims but in that case they identify themselves as Jat Muslims or Jat Sikhs or Hindu Gujars or Muslim Gujars. The common element in all these groups is the stock from where they came. This aspect of caste has not been closely examined and needs further study.

When Indians talk of caste generally they talk in terms of one's occupation or the lineage. Majority of castes is occupation—based and their hierarchy is determined by the quantum of respect they enjoy, which in turn is determined by the complexity of the job one does. For instance, if the job is least complex the member of that occupation is not given entry in the household. The upward movement of a caste and its entry in the household are thus determined by the level of closeness a family feels toward it. For instance, a water carrier can enter even the kitchen and thus its caste-status is higher than that of a barber or a butcher. When occupations become family businesses they get to become castes and cease to have anything with one's origin. Those origins are then lost forever. The title 'Patel' in Gujarat reveals nothing until one announces one's full name and then alone does one come to identify whether this Patel is Hindu or Muslim, because the surname Patel denotes a designation/ownership of land and has nothing to do with a given religion, community or caste.

Before the arrival of the British in India we had no caste-based educational statistics. For the first time in India's educational history do we come across such tables and statistics in Adam's surveys, conducted at the behest of William Bentinck. Therefore for the first time we were enabled to see the role caste played in acquiring education

The Third Report of Adam (1835) shows the caste distribution in teaching community. In the common schools or the pathshalas the majority of teachers came from the Kayastha community. (The first reference to this community appears in King Sudrak's drama *Mrichchakatikam* in reference to their dominance in Judiciary. From amongst the Hindus, Kayasthas alone were very close to the Muslim rulers.) Of the 365 teachers all but 10 belonged to this caste alone. In yet another area e.g. Burdhwan, the majority came from the Brahmin community. A few teachers came from the depressed communities too like Dhoba, Bagdi, Hari, Sunri, etc. While for Adam caste functioned as no barrier to the teaching profession in Bengal but elsewhere the situation was very different. While here in Bengal "Parents of good caste did not hesitate to send their children to schools conducted by teachers of inferior castes," the situation was radically different in other parts of India. In Bengal communal relations were also fairly good and therefore it meant that Hindus sent their children to schools manned by Muslim teachers. In fact there are tabular presentation of Hindus from different castes going to Madrasahs also and their preferences in studies.

Let me show how education and caste are related. As late as 1920's i.e. about the time when Gandhiji appeared on Indian political firmament, Simon Commission had noted," The education of these classes (Harijans)* raised a question of great difficulty and importance since their children are, in many places, actually excluded from the ordinary public schools on the ground of caste alone." Nothing has changed since then. We continue to treat them worse than cattle and penalize them for what they are— although they have played no role in the accident of their birth. It is from these classes that children drop out first and therefore the midday meal scheme was made obligatory by the government of India. The figures of Sarva Shiksha Abhiyaan continue to support the contention that those who drop out of the school first or fail are the ones who come from the Harijan* community.

In the following table which I have borrowed from my own book (*Education in an Imperial Colony*, p. 75) in which I have cited Kingsley Davis for the figures of the period (1891-1931) which show educational statistics of all religious groups in India.

Table 2.1

	Muslims	*Hindu*	*Sikhs*	*Christian*	*Jain*	*Parsi*
1891	4.2	6.3	6.8	26.5	32.6	66.2
1911	5.2	7.3	8.8	28.5	34.8	82.7
1931	7.2	9.3	10.2	30.5	39.2	83.0

CENSUS FIGURES

These figures are the most reliable for the simple reason that they can not be influenced or manipulated.

The other table is based on the quinquennial Review of 1902-03.

Table 2.2

Percentage to total Population	*Percentage of pupils in sec. schools*	
Brahmins	5.1	25.3
Non- Brahmins	63.0	48.3
Muslims	23.5	15.0

* A Gandhian coinage to give some dignity to the most oppressed classes.

While these tables tell their own tales a few other studies are being cited to relate an awkward and infrequently told tale. M. N. Srinivas (writes in his book, *Social Change in Modern India*) "As far as the Hindus are concerned, there was—and to a very limited extent still is—a very broad and general correlation between traditional caste hierarchy and the new western occupational hierarchy. Thus the members of the higher castes dominated the professions, the higher level posts in government, in fact, all white collar jobs—while the lower castes provided essential services."

This reality has not changed even now. In fact one of the reasons of politicizing this issue is largely because of this kind of caste dominance. Studies after studies point out the dominance of certain castes in given professions and this is a well known reality and nothing much is likely to transform the situation. I cite a few interesting studies only to corroborate my basic contention that caste in India is an immutable reality and even politics has not been able to bring about any material change in it. A Poona study by one Richard Lambert of five factories showed that the work force of factories consisted of 15 per cent Brahmins, yet when the question of obtaining relation between caste hierarchy and factory hierarchy came up, his findings showed that" Brahmins are disproportionately represented in the clerical and supervisory classes and held the highest ranking positions within those classes. Their relative position among the P&M (non-clerical workers below the supervisory level) workers depends upon the factory, and in most factories it is not substantially higher. The backward classes are hardly represented at all."

A government of India study by Professor V. Subramanian of caste representation in the IAS up to 1965 showed that Brahmins were over-represented in it flows out of their centuries old educational tradition, their early success with western education and their entrenchment in all the occupations of the middle class."

It would be interesting to consider caste-wise dominance of certain professions in India. For instance, if the caste wise achievement of boys and girls in all examinations is taken into account it is becoming clearer that this dominant position of Brahmins is gradually getting challenged by the traditional trading class community. A study conducted by me for the NCERT way back in late 1960s (printed) had the following theoretical formulation. I tested through an empirical study the hypothesis that upper castes were most likely to go for education and continue to remain in the system as compared with the members of the other classes and communities. The study was conducted on Delhi's Government schools. The results showed that 'In spite of various measures taken by the Government like reimbursing tuition fees, scholarships, free textbooks etc. the backward and scheduled children were not enrolled in proportion to the population of their respective communities. Among 121 students, enrolled in the group studied, only 6 came from the backward and scheduled category. (Science 3, Commerce 3 and Arts 1) The population composition of the communities did not deviate much. Bearing in mind the limitation that the proportionate composition of other castes in the total population in the said localities was not determined it is found that the majority of the upper castes went for Science and Commerce streams."

It is possible to show on the basis of the past results that the challenge to the Brahmins has come largely from the trading community. Not only the Banias (Jains—though a separate religion has come to be equated with bania community) dominate in shop-keeping but in all occupations related with trading, commerce and accounting. In fact it would be interesting to count caste–wise the number of Indian business tycoons vis-à-vis other communities in India only to find that there is a rare member in that list from any other community. Similarly, the dominance of the traditional martial races in the Defense forces is equally obvious. It is not too much to say that the relationship between caste and occupation in India will take a long time to undergo a radical change.

Therefore, it could also be concluded on the basis of above analysis that education of Hindus in particular was not largely impacted by the Muslim rule in India and their single door/institution opening viz. the Madrasahs. The Hindu learning continued to flourish despite the fact the Muslims provided no secular education for anyone and it is unthinkable that for the Hindus they would have created or supported a parallel system to their own. The Brahmins and the trading community continued to learn their trade secrets from their teachers outside the Muslim provision and had not recorded any complaints either. Therefore, when the British did provide education for their selfish ends these large upper caste groups came forward to receive it with open arms. Remember not much love was lost between the two communities and there are unrecorded preferences to Company rule by the Hindus. At least this could well be concluded on the basis of the manner in which Hindus came forward to open schools with English medium across the three Presidencies.

If the British had not provided any money for imparting instruction to Indian boys they would have acquired the western education anyway. The money that was provided for the development of indigenous education had got diverted to offering western education under Company rule. Even so, this money was both inadequate and highly supervised. In Bengal and elsewhere the local populace had started schools, imparting this instruction anyway long before the arrival of Macaulay on the Indian scene.

This then is the reality. The reference to Macaulay is thus both irrelevant and out of context and his opinion not worth consideration. India's learning tradition functioned independent of who the ruler was. It is true that we owe to the Brahmins in India for protecting our heritage at considerable personal discomfort and peril because neither Muslims not the Christian missionaries ever looked kindly toward them and seldom if ever they supported them in their occupation. It is neither for money nor for any position in the power structure did they carry on with their learning tradition. Of course, part of the course-correction came from the western scholars when out of curiosity they ventured into the Brahminic domain and offered improved methods of learning and showed them how to look beyond the narrow, dusty window panes grown opaque due to time and overuse. India in general and Hindus in particular should continue to feel grateful to those communities who unmindful of the personal discomfort and hazards continued to remain glued to their caste dharma.

That the spread of education was dependent not on the provision of the schools alone but on establishing relationship with caste dharma, economic growth and personal advancement. The rates of literacy would continue to go northward in direct proportion to the caste motivation and their desire to see that their women folk should also become literate.

Those who had written about the caste and suffered the pangs of being born in Dalit families alone know the suffering the caste among the Hindus bestowed on these groups of people. One such example is that of Dr. B. R. Ambedkar and his caste fellows. Writing on untouchability Bhagwan Das—himself a dalit, says, "When the lower castes started embracing Christianity, the Hindu Mahasabha introduced the myth of Balmiki as the author of the Ramayana to uphold the caste structure. The trouble with caste is that if you try to throw it out from the front it creeps back again through the window or the back door."

THE ORIGIN OF THE CASTE

It would be interesting to read the origin of the caste in India. The truth is that present castes in India have little or no bearing whatever on the caste dharma. Not only the sources of castes have come to get mixed up, it has become impossible to match a given caste with his/her occupation.

Even the origins of the caste itself and its description have come under dispute and so has its hierarchy. The Purush Sukta of Rigveda

(X. 90), *Yajurveda's* Chapter XXXI. II and Av. XIX; 6.6 are normally cited to support what is written below:

> The Brahman became His mouth,
> Of both His arms the rajanya was made,
> His thighs became the Vaisya,
> And from His feet the Sudra was born.

Let me try to present the correct view that should have guided us. Let the Vedic text speak for itself. Historically, the varna-vyavastha or an arrangement and organization of people's lives according to their functions in life appeared in this country for the first time. Broadly speaking, the four functions in all societies are performed normally by certain class of people such as, the priests, warriors, businessmen, agriculturists and others for which the most impoverished are willing to come forward. The term Varna has been used in the same sense as 'class' is used in the West. It is the nature of work that defined one's class. It is a historical reality that over a period of time the class transformed itself into caste in India and got fossilized. In the Vedas caste and class are indistinguishable. There are numerous references in the ancient literature that the change of caste was fairly common and the two primary castes/classes continually changed their caste groups to undertake each other's social obligations. If Vishvamitra could become Bramharshi, so were others allowed joining the caste they elected for. There is a reference in which King Bharata (son of Shakuntala) asked Bharadvaj II—a Brahmin by birth to take over the reins of his empire which he accepted gladly on the condition that his progeny would be entitled to retain its original as well as the assumed caste. This gave rise to the birth a caste category called kshatropet** Brahmins. It has been pointed out that interdependence of the priest on the ruler was a necessity. But once either of the two wished to show total independence, it created tensions. This explains to some extent why open hostility and dissensions between the Kshatriyas and the Brahmins would come to the fore at the slightest pretext. This caste rivalry was largely due to the question of primacy in society, which eventually led to the birth of organized religions like Buddhism and Jainism. These religions accorded no special place to the Brahmins. Indeed they ignored the Brahmins completely and faced their backlash. Even so for a very long time caste mobility remained a recognized fact of ancient life.

** One should notice that several Brahmin and Kshatriya surnames are common in most cases such as Rawats and Gaurs are found in both communities. In the case of Gotras too the commonality is worth noting.

But read the following hymns and take your own decision:

"Thus spoke Lord God,' O Humans! This benefit –granting language of the Vedas that I am giving to the Brahmans and the Kshatriyas, it is meant for the Vaishyas, Aryas and the Sudras too. I make no distinction between ours and theirs'." —Yaj. 26/2

In the *Atharvaveda* too there is a specific mention that God makes no distinction between either castes or gender.

"The teachings of the Vedas are universal. Yajurveda 26-2 clearly enjoins upon learned persons to preach Vedic truths to all, the Brahmanas, the Kshatriyas, the Vaishyas, the Shudras, the Chandals, the degraded and the forlorn. Dwijas, the twice-born alone are not entitled to study the Vedas. The Shudras and even women are equally entitled to read the Vedas. Persons like Kavish Aylush (the seer of R. V. X. 30) a Shudra by birth, vide Aitraiya Brahmana 11-19 and women like Lopmudra were the seers of the meanings of Vedic texts and their names are from times immemorial attached to the Vedic verses. God is not partial to any one caste... or a section of people."

—Introduction to *Yajurveda*, p. 6, Devi Chand. M.A.

"O God, create a Brahman, who knows the Veda and God, for the propagation of knowledge of God and the Veda; a Kshatriya prince for the safety of kingdom; a Vaishya for rearing the cattle; a Shudra for hard labour and service. Cast aside the thief, who steals in darkness; the destroyer of heroes, who passes his days in Jail, the eunuch mentally disposed to licentiousness, the dacoit bent on looting and harming people; the harlot full of lust; and the bard disposed to abuse."

The irrelevance of the caste in modern world may be lamented by us and politicians might take advantage of its vintage but urbanization has already blurred the distinction both in terms of one's occupation and the quality of life. Education too is no longer the monopoly of the few but is available to all and all this to happen it is necessary that SSA or Sarva Shiksha Abhiyaan should succeed and all the Dalits of India unite. The day the Dalits realized their potential they would be on top of Indian society.

3

Educational Backwardness and the Indian Muslims: A Critique of Causal Relationship

"O believers, do not violate the rites of Allah, or the sacred month, or the offerings or the victims with garlands, or those that repair to the Sacred House seeking Allah's grace and pleasure. Once your pilgrimage is ended, you shall be free to go hunting."

—Sura. 1; Al-Maida, *The Holy Quran.*

Effort is made to examine whether it is true that Muslims are backward. Secondly, are the Hindus to blame for it? There seem to be inherent contradictions in such statements? But if this claim is true, it must be a typically Indian phenomenon that a community despite its seven century rule and having enjoyed all powers that make its followers rich and prosperous find themselves (sadly enough) *backward* educationally within less than a decade of their political deposition.

There is nothing new in such allegations.. The first time ever this grouse was recorded in the year 1868; i.e. exactly 11 years after the last of the Mughal Emperors was dethroned. What Sir Syed wrote in 1868 was a sort of complaint against the injustices perpetrated by the then rulers (viz. the East India Company) against Muslims, which, to say the least, resulted in their social and educational backwardness within less than a decade. What is surprising is that almost verbatim Sachar Commission has repeated this argument in 2006. Strangely enough, instead of going into the truthfulness of the grouses, generally expressed by Indian Muslims and defining 'backwardness' as a referral concept, the honorable Justice did not even examine the causal relationship between loss of power and a given community's *continu*ed backwardness in education. In fact, he should have gone into the type of efforts made by the community itself to come out of the morass they had fallen into. It is doubtful whether it is enough to keep complaining for more than a century and a half without defining their perception. *While justice may be blind, the judges are supposedly* *not.* It was expected that Justice Sachar would at least compare the literacy figures of both Pakistan and Bangladesh (both *pure-breed* Islamic countries) with India's and then decided whether or not Muslims had fallen victims of Hindu 'mischief' across political and social spectrum. But since it has not been done therefore one can easily suspect a political agenda and ulterior motives behind the Report.

Before we move into the vortex of discussion let us try to find out the meaning of 'backwardness' *per se.* This question has been dealt with in a book titled *Subject Lessons—The Western Education of Colonial India* by Sanjay Seth, Duke University Press, Durham and London, 2007. He traces the basic causes of this complaint. While the replacement of Persian with English in administration in the year 1837 halted the dominance of Muslims in administrative positions; the separation of religion from education alienated them additionally. It, in fact, blurred the nature of Muslim identity. To think of *duniya* (world) without *deen* (religion) is unacceptable to a Muslim.

"The discourse of the 'backward Muslim' not only brought into being a backwardness that was not thinkable and not seeable in pre-colonial society, but also in so doing equally abstracted from the region, class and culture that characterized the Muslims of South Asia. Thus in reconstituting the category Muslim, the discourse of backward Muslim—enabled by statistics, and representing the perspective of the governmental state, also made it available to practical consciousness, and in doing so made it possible for others to think and be Muslims in a different way. As a result education figured not only as a site where a 'colonial bourgeois subject 'was posited but also as a site where new forms of collective identity were enabled. Education proved to be transformative, but not, as modernization theory would have it, because the modern knowledge disseminated through it replaced pre-modern superstition with modern Reason, thereby transforming the 'traditional' Muslim into modern Muslim. Education proved important rather because modern, western, unlike the maktab and the madrasah, was tied up with colonial state and thus was a site for elaborating new ways of understanding and governing the 'population'." p. 127-9

Islam, which means peace, is the most codified religion in the world. Starting from conception till a Muslim dies every moment of his life has been defined and fixed. And this supervision has also to be carried out strictly by their priestly class. What Muslims will read and who will teach at what stage is all written. There is no ambiguity about it. Therefore, it is not possible to call Muslims backward or forward if they follow the tenets of Islam.

One of the reasons why Muslims look backward or forward is the scale against which one judges them While the local converts are backward. those who came from outside or converted from upper castes are not all that backward. The Ajlafs or the Muslim dalits are backward even as Christian dalits are. The dalits in India constitute a distinct category in all religious groups and this category has no equivalent anywhere in the world. The term *backward* has also to be defined particularly in relation to Islam. Islam is a world religion and does not believe in any boundaries. It is one of the most egalitarian religions and the bondage is not of blood but of the religion. Ever since the western concept of progress has come to define 'backwardness' or' forwardness' our old criteria have vitiated everything. I doubt if the West too is very sure of the attributes of progress except in terms of possession of worldly goods and the degree of comforts one enjoys in these terms. This means the orthodox Hindus or Jain would qualify to be regarded as backward because an Orthodox Hindu or Jain does not believe in worldly possessions or sets a great store by western norms—the same way as others do. The relevance of the present discourse is largely because we debate these issues without defining the parameters of the debate itself.

No one called Muslims backward during their own rule and none called the Hindus backward either. They both had defined life styles and lived within the limits of those bounded areas.

The loss of Muslim political power in India is coterminous with their being put in a separate category that defined their education and the curricula. If they studied the new curricula they had to learn those things which were not prescribed by their religion. But this does not mean that they could be called backward. However, it was a dilemma for them whether or not to go back to their prescribed religious education. The Muslim identity is definable in orthodox terms only. No one could remain a *true* Muslim without following the injunctions of the Holy Koran and Hadis and obeying the Shariat laws. Therefore to my mind Muslim backwardness can be defined only against this backdrop.

In terms of time, ever since 1857 the Muslim community has allegedly continued to remain backward educationally. This phenomenon, if true, defies all canons of logic. Firstly, historians commonly hold the view that a community that rules the roost (or, has been politically dominant) does not become backward easily. In reality, it is a proven fact that all ruling communities (be they religion-centered/caste or political entities e.g.

Communist Party of the USSR or China) benefit from the political governance at the cost of the ruled. The type of complaints the Indian Muslims, who ruled for nearly seven centuries, have gone on repeating over a century and a half should have logically emanated from the non-Muslims against a Muslim rule that had a built-in bias against Hindu learning and for which they took no step to promote or sustain. While other communities supposedly had to be at the receiving end, the rulers and their co-religionists must have benefited during the pre-British governance. This should be the stated position of any rational being. How come the Muslims are proved to be an exception to this rule?

To support my contention it could be easily shown as an example from contemporary India that the ruling castes have benefited immensely, both in UP and Bihar and perhaps in other states too. The residual positions continue to pay dividends long after the loss of political power. There is no reason to believe that this would not have been true during the Muslim rule. The Muslims have allegedly been the favourites of all political parties in ***free*** India too; therefore there is no justification for the continuance of their purported backwardness. The problem seems to be that Muslims either do not know how to benefit from the sops on offer for them or show no inclination to move forward. The only exception could be in the states, where the power has been in the hands of the ultra-rightist groups.

The main question is: Is the Muslim csomplaint of educational backwardness tenable, particularly when it is a historical fact that they ruled over Delhi for more than seven centuries? Is it not true that Muslim orthodoxy is largely responsible for this perception? Or, they have become indifferent to their 'identity' syndrome? History records the reality that the socio-economic and educational position of the rulers as compared to the ruled is always better. I am willing to showcase reality with contemporary examples and illustrate the same. Also, it is a historical fact that no Muslim ruler ever bothered to provide any separate educational system to its non-Muslim ruled community, other than the Maktabs and Madrasahs.

There is yet another reality. The language of the ruled (Hindus) and the Muslim rulers differed radically, just as this happened during the British rule. What they offered to their own wards alone was open for others too i.e. to the non-Muslims. *It means clearly that no Muslim could have complained against the provision of Islamic education or the medium of instruction to their wards*. Logically too they should also have been in an advantageous position. One could argue that if the Muslims were not educationally very advanced, they could not have been backward either (in the year 1868).

There are no data available to support either contention. If Sir Syed had a hunch, others could also base their logic on similar grounds.

It is equally strange that the Muslims continue to compare their lot with the non-Muslims even when the comparison is both unfair and also unacceptable.

What needs to be examined is this: What was the basis of the Sir Syed's complaint about the educational backwardness of Muslims only 11 years after they were dethroned? This is the principal argument to be examined. It is possible for reasons best known to the Muslim leadership that they apparently refused to come out of their *self-imposed* restrictions and chose to remain uneducated in 'modern' terms. This argument finds *an echo* in a book on Badruddin Tyabji (Publications Division) by *A. G. Noorani*, who writes about a letter that Sir Syed wrote in which he enumerated the reasons of the non-acceptance of British education by the Muslims (Remember if one does not accept something that is voluntarily offered, no complaint could be lodged by that individual of neglect) The reasons enumerated by Sir Syed are as under:

"1. A feeling of pride for the glories of their past empire,
2. Love and pride of literature of India— the Persian and the Arabic
3. A feeling that European education is antagonistic to the traditions of Islam.
4. Failure of the authorities to offer proper Islamic education to the Muslim youth.
5. Poverty among Muslims was widespread
6. A feeling that the Government of India takes no notice of their reduced status and lastly,
7. A feeling that English education was not relevant for their (Muslim) ordinary processes of life."

He (Sir Syed) then goes on to add that "We have our own languages, literature, history and religion to study, and unless we are altogether devoid of ordinary feelings of humanity, we cannot but desire that our children should possess some knowledge at least of these subjects. I must confess," he continued," that I cannot help sympathizing with them in their contempt for Muhammadan youth calling himself an educated gentleman who does not possess a decent knowledge of his religion and of Urdu and Persian literature." And then he went on to formulate four cardinal principles of Muslim nationalism: (1) Muslims and Hindus form *two separate* political entities and *'nations'*. (2) The grant of representative institutions would be detrimental to the interests of

Muslims as the population of the country is not homogenous, (3) Consequently, the Muslims should regard the paramountcy of the British as the chief safeguard of their interests, and lastly, (4) The Muslims should confine 'their attention to educational, social, and cultural development, and *avoid politics except in so far as it is necessary to counterbalance the mischief of Hindu political agitators*."

It is interesting to look at the logic of Sir Syed. On the one hand Sir Syed declares that to counter the Hindu *mischief*; the Muslims should continue to pay "attention to educational, social, and cultural development" and "should regard the paramountcy of the British as their chief safeguard" and on the other hand he has a complaint that in education Muslims are being kept deliberately backward by their masters.

Those who propose to be close to the people in power cannot advance the logic that their rivals will take more benefits than them. If Sir Syed's argument is accepted then there are only two possibilities. One, that Muslims did not pay any heed to his advice and therefore by choice elected to remain educationally backward. Secondly, the Hindu *mischief* prevented them to take an advantage so generously offered by the rulers to the Muslims. Then what happens to the arguments cited by Noorani?

Thirdly, if the Muslims had a parallel well-defined system which additionally took care of their 'identity' as well, then why complain? And complain against whom; and, for what?

The above quote at least makes one thing clear that Sir Syed considered Hindus and Muslims being distinctly different communities/and even nations. He also implied that they were rivals, if nothing else. Secondly, since Muslims had already a developed system of education there was thus no point in going in for English Education. Hindus and Muslims seemingly had 'separate' goals and their attitude toward the new rulers was also different. While the Muslims were loyal, the Hindus were mischievous. Even otherwise too it is possible to believe that Hindus and Muslims could not have had identical goals.

Before we consider any other argument let us recall that a Muslim child traditionally starts his education at the age of 4 years, 4 months and 4 days when he is supposed to go to the priest and starts learning the alphabets. If the Muslims had strictly followed their own tradition they would be the most literate people. But despite all orthodoxy the Muslims have not pursued their tradition and hence the present day backwardness. The Prophet is supposed to have encouraged his believers to travel across nations to gain knowledge. Somehow this part of the Holy command failed to be heard properly.

We come to the *second point.* While the INC was always solicitous of Muslim membership and support; and, to woo them the INC consistently refused to pass even a single Resolution against the Muslims even when it was proved that by design they had perpetrated atrocities over the Hindus; and yet the Muslim majority never accepted the INC to be their party. The percentage of Muslims joining Congress rarely went beyond 6 per cent of their total population. And these are the best figures shown in records. And all this was true from the very inception of the Congress party.

For the majority of Indian Muslims the Congress was always a Hindu Party. For example, Sir Syed had even objected to Badruddin's joining the Congress. At least this is what he had written to Badruddin Tyabji, who became Congress President in 1888. The Congress President replied in his Presidential speech, "Your objection to Congress is that it regards India as one Nation. Now I am not aware of anyone regarding *the whole of India as one nation"* (Collected Speeches of INC Presidents, Zaidi and Zaidi, Publications Division) Here lies the root of 'two' nation theory. The Congress was always hard put to please Muslims and each concession was taken as the weakness of the Congress organization.

It is difficult to reconcile the views of the Indian Muslims particularly of their leadership with the mainstream thought of others. One cannot make a reluctant horse to drink water, while water can always be made available. Quenching the thirst is the function of the horse and not of the water or its provider.

When the same argument of Muslim backwardness is raised after 150 years or so, and once again it is the Congress party and a retired Hindu judge are supportive of Sir Syed's contention. One has a legitimate point to study the reasons why this should be so.

There is yet one more reason (the third one) why a fresh and objective analysis of the reality be made. The figures collected by an organization of the present government itself contradict the reported figures of Sachar Panel. *The Hindustan Times* dated March 30, 2007 highlighted this fact and stated that the figures released by the National Sample Survey Organization (NSSO) challenged the figures given by the Sachar Panel, which were allegedly both inaccurate and exaggerated. The news item carried under the caption *"Muslims are not doing too badly"* openly ridiculed the Sachar Panel report and debunked the cited figures. For instances, the NSSO report on major religious groups shows that the unemployment rate among Muslims (4.1) and Hindus (4.4%) differs just by 0.05 per cent. For the Christians these figures were 8.6 per cent in urban areas and 4.4 per cent in rural areas. But no comment was available on these figures. Satish Deshpande of Delhi School of Economics said," The differences in these figures could be because of the methodology, "As per the NSSO methodology those who have earned any kind of remuneration for a month in a year are considered employed. Only those who have not been working for a year or are not available for work—such as pensioners, rentiers, those attending educational institutions, beggars and prostitutes—are considered unemployed."

Khushwant Singh, a veteran journalist, writing in *The Hindustan Times* (November 3, 2007) in his Malice column wrote about the main reason of the Muslim backwardness. He refers to a book written by one Dr. Zakir Naik titled *Non-Muslim Common Questions About Islam* (Madhur Sandesh Sangam) and examines four answers given by the learned doctor and says," I disagree with almost everything he has to say about misconceptions about Islam." In response to the critical comments by the doctor about the degeneration of the Western society, Khushwant Singh says, "All I can say in reply is: Dr. Naik you know next to nothing about the Western society and are talking through skull cap. People like you are making the Muslims lag behind other communities." The arguments about the superiority of Islam as compared with other religions and the extreme sensitivity of the Muslims lead one to believe that perhaps it is the question of their 'identity', which perhaps prevents them from coming out of their religious devotion and be more open, tolerant and liberal.

History is witness to the Muslim desire to lead their lives according to the sharia and the Holy Book. The rigid boundaries of Islam came to the fore when 'the believers" crossed Mediterranean, and when Ibn Sirah and Ibn Sinah wrote to the Caliphate that as they had conquered parts of Europe they had inherited its learning too. The refusal to accept Aristotle and Plato was both prompt and decisive.

In fact, this makes Muslims extra-sensitive to any discussion on their models or goals.

There is one more method to ascertain the reality behind Sachar Report. On the subcontinent there are two Islamic republics viz. Pakistan and Bangladesh. They have Muslim majority and the rulers are also Muslims. The 'mischievous' Hindus are thus denied avenues to play any adverse role in these polities. Therefore, ideally placed, Muslims should have attained higher rates of literacy than their counterparts in India. But is this so?

Now look at the UNESCO figures that came in the newspapers (November 30, 07) In terms of national educational rankings, India stood at 100 (shameful?) in 129 nations and in the same list Bangladesh was placed 107 and Pakistan, which claims to be sole representative protector of Islam second only to Saudi Arabia, touches the rock bottom i.e. 128.

This UNESCO data expose Sachar logic. There is nothing wrong if INC continues to woo Muslims and ignores all canons of logic. After all, the logic of politics is always at variance with the logic of sanity.

Additionally, one could also look at the figures of the more advanced Islamic countries and discover the reality. Here the figures published by UNESCO should function as a bulwark against any biases. One could identify at the global level models of literate or politically advanced Islamic countries. Hopefully there will emerge a Model or two, which might help our leadership to follow suit. Although not part of the basic project these additional data would be helpful in clarifying the cobwebs.

The question therefore is: How come the Government ignores the above-cited reality and sticks to an unacceptable position. Why does it believe that there is no difference in the educational position of Muslims as described by Sachar (2006), which tends to support Sir Syed (1868)? For instance, compare the languages of the two positions. "(Sir Syed) realized that the Muslims were educationally, socially, economically, culturally and politically backward" as far back as in 1868. (Ali Ahmed; p. 39) Now read Sachar Commission," The recognition of their (Muslims) educational backwardness is quite acute amongst a large section of Indian Muslims' (p. 5). The stagnation in their educational plight becomes all the more glaring and noticeable when one compares their politico-social position at two different points in time. *This precisely is the second point worth examining.* According to the Indian Constitution, the present day rule is not a Hindu rule the way the Muslim rule was during the Sultanate period or during the Mughal administration.

It would be interesting to examine yet another reason why the Muslims have gone on trying to equate themselves with the Hindus even when they regard Hindus distinctly different and whom they find neither numerically nor religion-wise compatible/comparable. The logic invariably advanced by Pakistan when dealing with the USA is of its parity with India. Since Pakistan also thinks it is as significant as India in international fora, what is wrong if Indian Muslims talk of parity with Hindu majority? Look at this position too at two different points in time.

In 1896 Rahmatullah Sayani, a distinguished Muslim, presided over the INC session. Haji Mohammad Ismail Khan, a friend of Sir Syed, suggested to the Congress President that Congress should pass a resolution to the effect that Hindus and Muslims should have *equal* number of seats in the Legislative Councils, district boards and municipalities. Sayani could not support it but Sir Syed endorsed it and wrote that "Muslims could join Congress if the INC agreed to this proposal."

Two points come out clearly: a) a large section of Muslim elites from the beginning perceived and called the Congress INC a Hindu party; and b) even the best among Muslims minced no words to declare Hindus and Muslims as 'two distinctly different entities'.

The specious logic and the preposterous claim of Muslims of being discriminated against and their claims to past glory notwithstanding did evoke a few angry reactions from the British ruling class including a lampoon or two from amongst their poets. Here is one cited by A. G. Noorani written on Lord Harris: "A Governor's Meditation"

> "They decry the Congress, the Hindus we have
> to call a turbulent race,
> Though it is reality the Muslim that we
> have had to face,
> For, though large Hindu processions may
> Go without a police escort
> Why every Friday, extra Police we have
> to resort
> to see that the congregating Muslims on
> their Sabbath day
> Break forth no fury after they have
> Ceased to pray?"

One ought to examine why the nature of logic behind Muslim argument about the reasons of their backwardness has not changed even with the passage of time. And why have the arguments of their backwardness not found a substitute?

REFERENCES

1. *Politics and National Awakening in South India* by R. Suntharalingam The Association of Asian Studies, (The University of Arizona Press,)1974
2. *Caste, Class and Power*, Andre Beteille OUP, 1969
3. *Indian Response to Colonialism in the 19th century*, editors Alok Bhalla and Sudhir Chandra, Sterling Publishers, 1993
4. *Religious Bigotry* by Madhu Limaye, Ajanta, New Delhi 1994
5. The Role of Muslims in Indian Politics, K. Sharma, Inter-India Publications, New Delhi 1985
6. *Education and the Indian Congress* R. P. Singh Scenario Publications, 1996
7. *Sir Syed on Education*, Ali Ahmad, AMU, 2006

4

Educating the Girl Child: A Lesson for Teacher Education

DUTY TOWARD WOMEN

"There is no need to control a woman's intellect. She should also be given the right to think and express her opinion because she is gifted since birth with the powers to be mentally active." Rig. 8/33/1

Report from *The Hindustan Times* (23 August, 2008)

The much repeated story of families killing a girl child to have a son next time has number now. Under the caption 'The foeticide story' following figures are shown for both Delhi and Haryana

933 girls/1000 boys	*Abortions*	*Delhi*	*Haryana*
India' sex ratio	First child	23.6 %	33.3%
868 girls/1000 boys	Second child	30.8%	50.0%
Delhi's sex ratio			
820 girls/1000 boys	Third Child	52.0%	33.3%
Haryana sex ratio	Fourth child	66.6%	50.0%

Abortions done in *private* hospitals are 81 per cent, *Government* hospitals 23 and *midwives* 16 per cent.

The Vedas are the earliest literature that we have in this country. The Vedas inform us that both boys and girls were offered education. This is, for example, what they say about the education of the girl child. "It is those girls alone that make their families happy who have been taught by lady teachers—glowing fire-like, with knowledge. Such girls speak cultured tongue, desire learned and righteous husbands, pray for readily available riches and fame, come in contact with teachers who are worth visiting, venerable and have no dearth of means." (Rig. 7/10/3) In another place we have the following information. Here we find the Rigveda.(7/15/9) talking about the methods of instruction. "O girl students! Just as intelligent teachers introduce writing and reading of letters with the help of fingers, you should know lady teachers who know innumerable subjects and possess immeasurable learning. For your balanced development such an intelligent teacher will herself make all arrangements."

Sufficient evidence is available to show that education of the girl child was considered as important as those of the boys. They too were expected to observe celibacy like the boys. There were quite a few women Rishikas mentioned by name in the Vedas. For instance, the names of Lopmudra, Ghosha, Romasa, Sikata, Nivavari, etc have come down to us by tradition. They were married only when they approved of their husbands. Her duties were well defined. In the choice of husbands they played the most crucial role of approving their husbands. "Men desirous of getting married approach women and ask for their hand, lacing the request with appreciative language. Similarly, a beautiful gentle lady of merit can also select a groom for her out of a group of eligible bachelors." (Rigveda/10/27/12) Of course, they ran their households and looked after their husbands and children. "O the housewife, who works wonderfully like the Dawn, it is you who store and look after the food grains. Please keep them in such a way so that our infants and children are well fed. "(*Yajurveda*/34/33)

The status of women in society was very different during the Vedic age. Even the Buddhists accorded them the same status as the Vedas once did. But soon after, their status started sliding down. This happened with the rise of feudalism in ancient India or during the period of the Dharmasastas. Manu smriti records this downslide very clearly. Since then no improvement in their status has been visible. The Vedas regarded women cleverer than men and also natural teachers.

Indian history is replete with glorious examples of learned, brave, fore-sighted and extraordinarily talented women. However except in the Vedas their real status in the Indian society seldom matched their potential. This somehow did not prevent a few of them from occupying positions of power and forcing the society to acknowledge their worth. While a few women did equip themselves with the latest knowledge available during the East India Company days the education of the girls remained by and large a history of sad neglect. Time was when they could hold their own against the very best of the male talent. Gradually their position got reduced to the level of a chattel in the household.

Indian hypocrisy apart in which they use all kinds of verbiage to establish that they value woman per se; (for instance, Heaven on earth is where a woman is worshipped or all the powerful deities are women like Durga and Kali, etc); but the reality has nothing to do with this. *This paper examines the position of the women during the British raj in India.* What exactly was their position during the British raj? If we went by the superstition prevalent during Sarat Chandra Chaterjee's days it was considered a sure sign for a girl to become widow if she became literate. Even a leader of the stature of Bal Gangadhar Tilak did not hesitate to declare in a public address in Pune that a girl should get married by the age of nine and that a good girl was supposedly asooryampashya i.e. one not seen even by the sun.. People like Mahatma Phule in Maharashtra and Raja Ram Mohan Roy in Bengal did take steps to teach them. One should read Sarat's novels to realize the lowly position of women in Bengal, which during those days included Assam, Bihar and Orissa. It was customary for a married woman to give some money to her husband every time she wanted to have sex. The position of women across continents and religions has not been very rosy. In Europe and particularly in England women were discriminated against in terms of admission to universities and colleges right up to the beginning of the twentieth century. For their wages they had to wait for a couple of decades more to have parity with male. It is absurd to imagine that in India alone their position was bad. The fact is that in traditional families and societies their position remains even now highly deplorable. The so-called modernity has least impacted Indian woman. It is common knowledge that even working and highly educated girls get killed every day in India. If dowry deaths are common among the educated and affluent, it is also true that their education too is neglected in the richer states like Haryana and Panjab. Modern education has failed to impact the societal attitudes toward the social position of the girl child/woman even in the so-called resurgent India. However, credit goes to the western colonizers for trying to improve their lot. For instance they banned sati, offered facilities to educate them and prohibited child marriage, etc. It is a tragedy that we remain unmoved despite all our modernity. Child marriages are reported every day from Bihar and Rajasthan. Sati system remains intact though not on a large scale. Infanticide is quite common among the rich and educated middle class. Therefore it would be interesting to examine the success of our colonial masters in trying to modernize our society.

One of the indicators of modernisation of a society is the spread of education; and the level or extent of its utilization. In that sense the efforts made by the British were both superficial and perfunctory. Their impact on Indian society was limited to few urban centres where they came across persons who were to some degree concerned with the governance or being close to their civil society that shared their interests and vision.

Table 4.1: Crude Literacy Rates 1901-to 1951

Census year	Persons	Male	Female	Persons	Male	Female
1901	5.35	9.83	0.60	N.A.	N.A.	N.A.
1911	5.92	10.56	1.05	0.57	0.73	0.45
1921	7.16	12.21	1.81	1.24	1.65	0.76
1031	9.50	15,59.00	2.93	2.34	3.38	1.12
1941	16.10	24,90.00	7.30	6.60	9.31	4.37
1951	16.67	24.95	7.93	0.57	0.05	0.63
2004-05*	63.60	78.00	51.10	9.09	14.76	5.95

Source: Census of India 2001.

*NSS 61st Round Survey Report No. 517, 2004-05, p. 57.

Table 4.2: Adult Literacy 15 Years and Above:1961-2001.

Particulars	1961	1971	1981	1991*	1996@	1998#	1999^	2001**
1. Illiteracy %								
Male	58.55	52.31	45.09	38.11	32.75	30	27.8	26.7
Female	86.85	80.64	74.30	65.91	59.33	56	56.0	52.2
Total	72.24	65.92	59.18	51.46	45.48	43	41.5	39.0
2. literacy %								
Male	41.45	47.69	54.91	61.89	67.25	70	72.2	73.3
Female	13.15	19.36	25.70	34.09	40.67	44	44.0	47.8
Total	37.76	34.08	40.82	48.54	54.32	57	58.5	61.0

Note: ** Census 2001; * excluding J&K, @NSS 05nd Round 1995-96, # NSSO Round; National Family Health Survey.

Majority of the Indian masses was indifferent to their rule unless the rule interfered with their sedate life style. Being bread earners the impact of education was more obvious on the male population than on the women folk. In India the scheduled tribes and scheduled caste women have always been hard working and undertaken the duty of being a bread earner. But the nature of their work was least complicated and did not require any degree of either innovation or sophistication, therefore their illiteracy did not appear to hinder their life-pursuits. These two communities put together constitute about half the population of the country. Except in the matriarchical societies the position of the Indian women has always been something to feel sorry about. But the British must be given credit for having started the process of modernizing India's archaic society. That they did not succeed can be ascribed to both Indian reluctance; the prevalent social taboos and the nature of unfamiliarity with the goals.

The above tables show that the rate of literacy was fairly low both in the case of men and women. Teaching a few subjects on the modern lines as the British imagined they had introduced was not enough to transform the society. In fact to a very large extent the Indian society despite all its command on modern day knowledge remains as remote from the modernization as sky is from earth.

Recently a book (*Subject Lessons—The Western Education of Colonial India (2007)* by Sanjay Seth, Duke University Press, Durham and London) has tried to examine the extent to which modern education offered by the British impacted different sections of Indian society. A look into the text of the said book should give us an idea of the extent to which our rulers went to transform our society to make it come closer to their own.

The book has a chapter titled *Gender and the Nation* which starts with a debate about whether or not Western education was good enough for the Indian girl. Interestingly, the debate per se bore no relation to the actual facilities of education on offer. The Hunter Commission (1882) recorded that only 6 girls were taking college education in the entire British India. And as late as 1913 the government confessed that "the girls' education remained to be organized." All this goes to show that until the dawn of the 20th century the education of the girls was nowhere in the reckoning. And yet female education was the subject of constant discussion. The backdrop for the discussion lay in arguing about whether or not Indians were ready for self-rule. To support the argument that Indians were basically unfit for self-rule, the rulers advanced the argument that India was not a Nation. Instead it was a conglomeration of castes, religions and races, wherein neither in reality could represent another. The second argument was that India was economically and socially so backward that it was not possible for it to join the ranks of self-governing nations. James Mill, inspired by the Scottish Enlightenment historians, wrote in his History of India. "A state of dependence more strict and humiliating than that which is ordained for the weaker sex among the Hindus cannot easily be conceived." Both the British and local converts always commented on the "wretchedness and degradation of the Indian woman." On one such occasion when K. M. Bannerji (a convert) made such an observation it invited a rebuke from Peary Chand Mitra. "There are some people who are ready at all times to find faults with everything relating to Hindus." and to pass "sweeping condemnations on our institutions respecting females." The venue of this acrimonious comment was the forum offered by the Acquisition of General Knowledge. This was not the forum where orthodoxy prevailed or people here denied the contention that there was no need to reform the situation as it existed.

However, this was the time when a group started referring to ancient Indian history; and recalled that there was a time when the position of Indian woman was not all that bad. For instance, Toru Dutt (1856-77) wrote:

> In those far–off primeval day
> Fair India's daughters were not pent
> In closed zenanas, On her ways
> Savitiri at her pleasure went
> Whither she chose,—and hour by hour
> With young companions of her age,
> She roamed the woods for fruits or flower;
> Or loitered in some hermitage,
> For to the Munis gray and old
> Her presence was as sunshine glad.
> They taught her wonders manifold
> And gave her of the best they had.

And they did not hesitate to cite the Vedas wherein it is clearly written that the girls of those times had the customary freedom to select their husbands. "On reaching puberty when a girl expresses on her own, desire to her parents for a competent, knowledgeable and renowned youth for a marriage, thereafter her guardians make a proposal to the bridegroom's side to confirm such an arrangement." Rig-Veda/5/61/9

All this constituted Bengal Renaissance. Towards the end of the 19th century rather than being an object of pity, the Indian womanhood now assumed a privileged status in nationalistic discourse. Even the reforms being suggested were to help her assume her pristine role. Tanika Sarkar is cited to elaborate the point." An icon was constructed of the patriotic subject, the good Hindu woman with her simple dress, her ritually pure conch-shelled bangles and red-vermillion mark, her happy surrender and self –immersion in the sansar (domesticity), and her endless bounty and nurture expressed by cooking and feeding. She was charged with an immense aesthetic; cultural and religious load in nationalist writings." Even Annie Besant seemed to suggest that the condition of Indian woman was largely due to decline in the Hindu religion and not because Hinduism per se was cruel and barbaric as compared with European culture or practices.

The reforms being proposed were intended to take care of the lapse on the part of Hinduism. Therefore the language used by her in her writing reflects clearly a total absence of condemnation; instead it is to recall the glorious days of Hinduism long gone by. Read for instance. "I am pleading—for a restoration to woman in India of the place that was theirs when India was the greatest."

The dialogues and controversies regarding women's education had a positive impact. A ground was gradually prepared in favour of girl's education, which included formal schooling. And all this happened in the new middle class who occupied a subordinate position in the colonial public sphere.

Seth therefore concludes that two themes dominated the pamphlets, dialogues and newspapers and magazine articles concerning female education: One, for Hindu women to receive formal education is not contrary to Hindu religion or Hindu beliefs. The Vedas and shashtras supported the argument. Two, female education will modernize and improve the existing domestic arrangements. It was commonly asserted that that educated women will make better housewives. By the late 19th century few voices were heard against women's education. Several examples could be cited to establish the veracity of this view. Both in Bengal and Maharashtra leaders came forward to support the cause of women's education like the Bramhos and Mahatma Phule.

However, Indians differentiated between offering formal education to women folks and anglicizing them. For instance, a lecturer at Calcutta University told Sadler Commission: "we do not want that women in India should continue to labour under the darkness of ignorance and superstition... But we don't want at the same time that women in Indian should be steadily anglicized." Seth concludes. "a public consensus emerged around the desirability of female education. This appears to have been reached first in Madras and Bombay and by the later 19th century in Bengal". In a way the ground work for women's education was made ready during the course of endless discussions and dialogues. But the danger continued to lurk for a long time against this education, which could convert the Indian women into a brown memsahib.

In 1925 a book titled *Mother India* written by an American lady named Katherine Mayo appeared. It created lot of stir in the country. A journalist by profession she took an extensive three month tour of India and came out with her view of the condition of women in the country. The title and the content of the book hardly matched. In the nationalist iconography India symbolized motherhood. While the content related to the woman, the title of the book referred to the Nation. This is what hurt the nationalist leadership the most. Mayo later explained the reason behind selecting this title. She had chosen the title precisely for the reason to make "inescapable the contrast between, on the one hand, florid talk of devotion and 'sacrifice' poured before an abstract figure, and, on the other hand, the consideration actually accorded to the living woman, mother of the race."

The meat of the book lay in its graphic descriptions of child bride psychologically and physically damaged by premature sex. Remember the situation has not changed one bit in certain sections of society even now in the year 2009. The interesting part of the tale is that this provoked the Indians so much that some 8 books appeared all refuting the charges and criticizing the author in no uncertain terms. Gandhi went to the extent of calling Mayo's book 'a drain Inspector's report'. Tagore also reacted in the like manner.

Seth says this reaction was rather unusual. He eventually discovered the real reason behind it. The reality was that the British were denying Indians self rule on the ground that they were unfit to govern and were criticizing the malpractices and the inhuman treatment meted out to their own countrymen from depressed castes and even ladies in their own homes. Many in England found it 'an independent' confirmation of a reality long known to them. "All who know anything about India", wrote the liberal New Statesman, "are aware, of course, of the prime evils of Hinduism, of the horrors of child marriage system, of the universality of sexual vice in its most extravagant forms, of the monstrously absurd brutalities of the caste system, of the filthy personal habits of even the most educated classes—which like the degradation of Hindu women, are unequalled even among the most primitive African or Australian savages—of the universal cruelty to animals, and of the equally universal prevalence of laziness, untruthfulness, cowardice and personal corruption."

Although each word written a century or so back remains true till this day and yet the nation had risen up then in arms against the truth, which it is extremely hard to deny even now. Therefore, it is legitimate to conclude as Seth does that "in claiming to show that the very area over which nationalism claimed exclusive sway was one where 'backwardness' and ' medievalism' continued to reign, and thus those who claimed to lead and remake the nation had not the will to even remake their women and their own homes." After six decades of freedom we are still planning for the education of the girls from all strata of society and yet the rate of success in this direction has been deplorable. The latest measure adopted by the

Government of India is to focus on the SC/ST girls under the SSA by depositing some money which they could claim on the successful completion of their High School examination.

In the past couple of decades some progress has been made the world over. It would appear that we have been left behind in the race and unless we make some Herculean efforts we are likely to remain lagging behind the others. Some of these efforts are related here.

The UNESCO General Conference of 1960 adopted a declaration for education without any distinction of sex. In 1975, the Conference held at Mexico City pointed out the importance of equal educational opportunity for effective role of women in social development. The year 1975 was also observed as International Women's Year to focus attention of the nations towards women. In 1979, the Declaration on the Elimination of Discrimination on Women was adopted by the U. N. General Assembly. hoping that all appropriate measures would be taken by the nations to eliminate discrimination against women in order to ensure to them equal rights with men in the field of education and also to eliminate any stereotyped concept of the roles of men and women at all levels. The decade 1976-85 was observed as the decade for women. During the decade, in the year 1980, elimination of all forms of Discrimination against Women was proclaimed by the U. N. General Assembly. The International Conference on Population and Development highlighted importance of women, stating that:

> "Advancing gender equality and equity and the empowerment of women, and the elimination of all kinds of violence against women, and ensuring women's ability to control their own fertility, are cornerstones of population related programmes. The human rights of the women and the girl child are inalienable, integral and indivisible part of universal human rights. The full and equal participation of women in civil, cultural, economic, political and social life, at the national, regional and international levels, and the eradication of all forms of discrimination on grounds of sex, are priority objectives of the international community"
>
> —UN 1995, Principle 4, p. 9

Bad practices include: female genital mutilation, early marriage, more stress on the role of male persons in the family, preference for sons over daughters, prevalence of female infanticide, heavier manual work at home, etc. Declining sex ratio has been a concern in the country. The sex ratio in 1901 was 1000: 972. This came down to 927 in 1991 and 933 in 2001. The worst position is found in Daman & Diu (710), followed by

Chandigarh (777), Dadar & NH (812) and Delhi (821), Haryana (861), Sikkim (875), Punjab (876), etc. The ratio is the highest in case of Chhattisgarh, followed by Manipur, Andhra Pradesh and Orissa, etc.

Since independence, efforts have been made to safeguard the interest of girls and women and to improve their status. Some of these are: Special Marriage Act 1954—that prohibits marriage of girls before 18 years of age; Hindu Marriage Act 1955—that prohibits polygamy and providing adequate grounds for women to seek divorce; The Citizenship Act of 1955 providing for adult suffrage of women at par with men; Hindu Adoption and Maintenance Act 1956—giving right for adoption of a daughter and right to unmarried, widow or divorced women to adopt; Hindu Succession Act 1956—giving the right of inheritance to women heirs; Suppression of Immoral Traffic in Women and Girls Act 1956—to check seduction, exploitation and commercialisation of women 1956/1978/1986; Maternity Benefit Act 1961/1976;Equal Remuneration Act 1976; Factories Act 1976; Family Courts Act 1984; Dowry Prohibition Act 1984. Other steps include: Reservation of Seats for Women in Panchayats; National Commission for Women Act 1990, Functioning of National Commission for Women since 1992, Balika Samridhi Yojana, Rural Women Development Project 1998, Indira Mahila Yojana as part of ICDS, Provision of Short Stay Homes for Women and Girls, Crèches for Working and Ailing Mothers, Support to Training and Employment Programme for Women, Rashtriya Mahila Kosh, Women's Training Centres/Institutions for Rehabilitation of Women in Distress. The National Charter for Children, 2003 stated the following strategies for the Protection of the Girl Child:

4.1(a) The State and community shall ensure that crimes and atrocities committed against the girl child, including child marriage, discriminatory practices, forcing girls into prostitution and immoral trafficking are speedily eradicated.

(b) The State shall in partnership with the community undertake measures, including social, educational and legal, to ensure that there is greater respect for the girl child in the family and society.

(c) The State shall take serious measures to ensure that the practice of child marriage is speedily abolished.

The National Policy on Education (1968) gave stress on education of girls. "The education of girls should receive emphasis, not only on grounds of social-justice, but also to accelerate social transformation." The NPE 1986 stated that: 4.2. "Education will be used as an agent of basic change in the status of woman. In order to neutralise the accumulated distortions of the past, there will be a well conceived edge in favour of women. The National System will play a positive, interventionist role in the empowerment of women. It will foster the development of new values through redesigned curricula, textbooks, the training and orientation of teachers, decision-makers and administrators, and the active involvement of educational institutions. This will be an act of faith and social engineering. Women's studies will be promoted as a part of various courses and educational institutions encouraged to taking up active programmes to further women's development."

4.3 The removal of women's illiteracy and obstacles inhibiting their access to, and retention in, elementary education will receive overriding priority, through provision of special support services, setting of time targets, and effective monitoring.

Various facilities that promote education of girls include: dress and reading and writing materials; reservation of one third seats for girls in Navodaya Vidyalayas, preferential treatment for opening of girls' schools, women's colleges and women universities; relaxation in age limit for women for taking admission in institutions and for getting into job; scheme of strengthening boarding/hostel facilities for girl students of secondary/higher secondary schools. Provision for condensed courses for educational and vocational training programmes, for higher education courses on women is made these days such as—Master of Women Studies, M.A. in Women Studies, Diploma in Women Studies; Women Studies as a subject at Degree stage, establishment of centres and cells for Women Studies by UGC in colleges and in university departments, women universities. Such centres arrange special lectures, seminars, conferences and workshops on the rights, opportunities, privileges, position and status of women, and also conduct certificate courses on women studies, nutrition and Health Education Scheme under ICDs for girls and women in the age group of 15 to 45 years, adolescent girls scheme under ICDS that focuses on school dropout girls in the age group of 11-18 years to meet their need for self-development, nutrition, health, education, literacy and skill formation and also mobilization and enhancement of their potential and to act as social animators through Mahila Samaksha (Education for Women's Equality).

TRAINING OF TEACHERS FOR EDUCATION ON GOVERNMENT POLICIES

Education is considered an essential function of the Government of every civilised nation. The Indian Constitution mentions about various functions of the Central Government and State Governments in relation to education. In fact, the Constitution makes provision for the education as a Right and discusses separately States' power and that of the Center in the field of education. The teacher trainees need to be aware of various constitutional provisions as regards the special roles of the Central government and the State governments and the Joint roles to be played by the Central and the State Governments. There are Constitutional amendments from time to time that concern education. 86th amendments of education has made elementary education for children from 6 to 14 years of age as a Fundamental Right (Article 21A of Part III) and ECCE has become part of Article 45 of the Directive principles replacing free and compulsory education. The teacher trainees are to be made aware of these. The awareness on various aspects of constitutional provision related to education may be developed through debates, seminars, conferences and discussion groups and guest lectures organised for the purpose.

The teacher trainees need to be aware of various Acts and provisions made by the Government (both State and the Centre) to take care of sexual harassment and for the promotion of education of girls. They should learn to acquire skills to take care of the special needs of girls. In case of many poor families, girls take care of their younger siblings and do also the house-hold work. Teachers should allow such types of girls to bring their younger brothers and sisters to their classrooms. The extra disturbance in the classroom has to be tolerated for facilitating education of girls from poor communities. The strict school timings have to be relaxed for such girls. There may be co-curricular activities that can take care of the training in cooking and in other household activities with the help of the volunteers from the community. There may be sex education exclusively for girls of secondary school classes so that they do not fall victims to HIV and AIDS. The teacher may take the help of the health officials or doctors available for the purpose. The teachers need to be trained as agents of women empowerment for the community. Girls, in co-educational schools, if in minority, sit idle when the boys are playing games. The teachers should be especially conscious about this and should take steps for games and physical education for girls, if possible, with the volunteers from the community. Gender equality and women's empowerment are at the heart of the constituent principles of knowledge societies. Teacher trainees need to develop skills of carrying out the activities that can help students remove gender disparities from their minds.

To our eternal shame we continue to get our national dailies, reporting every day about child marriages, rapes, dowry deaths, wife burning, etc.

for example, there is a headline *Tradition Mocks at Law in Rajasthan* (HT, May 8, 2008) wherein news relating to child marriage, sati and other bad social practices are reported in detail.

This paper was written with the intention to find out whether western exposure and British rule made us ' modern' in the western sense. Sadly enough we must conclude that we are nowhere near the goal of modernity. Not that all traditions are bad but the truth remains that most of them are more than obnoxious.

LET US DRAW SOME INSPIRATION FROM THE FOLLOWING CITATIONS:

"Let our mother (Teacher) equipped with divine qualities after acquiring extensive knowledge of sciences and related activities teach us children and inspire our intellect and actions." Rig-Veda/6/61/4

"O desiring, extensively knowledgeable and scholarly Teachers! Kindly equip us fully with your discriminating intellect the same way this lovingly rearing earth satisfies us with food grains" Rig-Veda/6/61/6

"Even as the dawn drives away the dark, similarly, equipped with proper attributes and good education destroying mutual jealousies the lady teacher advances knowledge being the protector of Truth and Knowledge. Such a teacher adopting the policies of great scholars and being the upholder of the truths contained in the Vedas removes the doubts of her girl students". Rig-Veda 1/113/12

5

Quality Assurance in Educational Research: A Quest for Possibility

"*We wish our Guru to possess highly specialized knowledge that is as dear to us as life itself and which could be acquired through harmless activities. We want him to have knowledge of sciences, speak cultivated tongue, know the meaning of the Sastras (Researches), reflect deeply on the richas (hymns) of the Vedas and thereby be a highly competent and knowledgeable teacher.*" —*Yajurveda* 36/16

WHAT IS THE NEED FOR THIS ESSAY?

The main reason why we have to talk about 'quality assurance' in educational research is that both the universities and the UGC have been indifferent to the reality that teaching abilities and undertaking research are different kinds of realities. A 'good' researcher need not be a good or effective teacher even as a good teacher may not prove to be a competent or a good researcher. It is a rare combination where a 'good' teacher is also a 'good' researcher. In most cases it has been found that these abilities are not positively co-related. It would be advisable and in the interest of maintaining high standards in both that the first step to improve the situation is to abolish the compulsory requirement of having a doctoral degree before getting a job. There is no need to maintain a farce like this requirement, which in any case is neither a healthy practice nor does it contribute to maintaining a high standard in higher education. The authorities should come out of their stupor and openly face a reality i.e. writing a Ph.D. dissertation has become a lucrative occupation and Ph.D. writing shops have sprung all over the country, wherein all types of corrupt practices are being followed. It is a rare scholar who undertakes a research. The manner in which the examiners are fixed leaves very little room for improvement. This in my opinion is the first step to improving the quality of research and assuring quality.

It is much better that NET is strengthened and its frequency reconsidered. At least we know that because of NET the insufficiency of scholarship is exposed. A Ph.D. degree does neither. Everything at this stage can be and in fact is being rigged. Then what is the need for this farce? It is now common knowledge that writing a Ph.D. dissertation is being undertaken on a contract basis and a few universities have specialized in this trade. Ph.D. examinership is perhaps the greatest racket in networking known in the field of higher education in India. It is because of these reasons and many more that need not be described that it is being pleaded that the UGC should revise its earlier decision and replace the same with some other mechanism which in fact does try to make higher education more respectable than a research degree in reality does.

Even before the floodgates of granting Ph.D. in education were opened, the quality of these researches was not very high. There were two reasons for it. Firstly, normally a Ph.D. degree was obtained from outside India. It did not mean that all those who obtained degrees from the West were very scholarly. Secondly, the themes selected for this degree did not always relate to the ground realities of India. These researches almost hung in the air because conducting research on some Indian topic abroad made these researches look somewhat superficial and the fruits of the labour remained inaccessible to the audiences for whom they were intended. Thirdly, official infrastructure was unwilling to accept any of the suggestions made in the research dissertation. After all a research ought to have an audience—someone who cares for the findings. In the absence of this principal concern and the receptive audience researches undertaken in the foreign countries could never hope to leave any imprint on the relevant audiences.

THE NATURE OF RESEARCH AND ITS DIMENSIONS

One of the striking achievements in education in Independent India has been the number of researches being undertaken in the field of education. If seen as part of the growth of education per se then it should surprise no one that researchers must grow with the growth of the system. If the number of scholars has multiplied in the field of education, so has the number of researches. Unfortunately, there is a general feeling that in the process of increasing the number, it is the quality of research that has been seriously compromised. Since no objective studies have been made in this regard and also no standard definition on the 'quality' of researches exists, any remark on the quality of research in education would remain an 'opinion'.

However, we do need to define several terms and try to understand the meaning and functions of researches also. For instance, our first concern should be to understand: why has one to conduct research at all and that too in the field of education? The simple answer to this query is: we want to distinguish our academic achievement from those of others. After all, education and its level define the quality of a nation's life. In a competitive market one must try to reach the pyramid to show one's idea of excellence. Although a research qualification is not a necessary requirement for a teaching job but additions in one's portfolio are always welcome. Researches help us to innovate. They offer insights into the mass of assorted materials. Being multi-dimensional, researches and their applications usually tend to give one an edge over others.

At times, however, it appears that the person who possesses a research degree is indistinguishable from the one who has no such mark of distinction. This brings us to the logical question: what do we expect from a research degree holder so that he or she is markedly different from the one who does not possess this particular qualification? If we talk of additional qualification then we should also be able to establish that the research degree holder has certain competencies or an insight into a particular academic area that a non-research degree holder cannot acquire on his own. In other words we are trying to talk of quality both of the possessor of the degree and also of the intrinsic quality in the degree itself which could help one hold one's distinct position, in an otherwise equally competent and crowded knowledgeable populace.

We should try to answer two questions here. One, what does the research degree signify? Or, why one must possess this degree? And, secondly, what ought to be the distinguishing features of a research degree holder? We know already that for certain types of jobs a research qualification is not only helpful but essential. Research trains an individual in innovating, learning techniques for acquiring new knowledge, experimenting, hypothesizing and, in the ultimate analysis, developing analytical tools for facing challenges and evolving long term goals. Researchers learn ways to deal with new problems and come out with 'made to order' solutions. After all, all civilizations and cultures are the cumulative result of researches. The degree of a civilization's advancement depends on the quantity and quality of its research outputs. At a given point of time India, Greece, Egypt and China were highly advanced nations. The proofs of their greatness are available for all of us to see. If the Vedas are an eminent proof of India's researches and development, the monuments and the literature of the ancient Greece, the Great Wall of China and the

Pyramids of Egypt showcase the advancements of those countries. The reason why the US today is ahead of all other nations is the money and time the nation spends on conducting research. The number of patents earned by the researchers in the United States is both numerically and quality-wise much more than any other single country in the world.

Interestingly, while the growth and development of nations vary individually and collectively at different points in time, the research methods per se remain the same. If they vary at all, the variation is restricted to theme and the nature of the study proposed. For instance, the steps and description of researches in philosophy or logic would differ from historical and scientific researches. Basically, the steps remain the same in most researches. I have with me a definition or two from the ancient literature and when the same is compared with the steps proposed by the advanced researchers, it can be proved that within them there is not much that is very different. This only goes to prove that a researcher needs to worry more about following the steps and understanding the techniques to adopt than to extraneous matters, simply because when a research theme is selected to be taken up by one or more scholars it should invariably yield identical results. If the results vary and at times they do, continuous researches need to be taken until we know which finding is finally acceptable. This will go to prove the scientificity of the research design.

I now cite a definition given by Kumaril Bhatt of 7th century A.D. which as the reader will notice applies to all types of researches—.be they—scientific, theoretical or philosophical. Even otherwise research is undertaken either to discover an unknown fact or conclusion; invent a new mechanism to help ease life, understand afresh an idea or to appreciate an unknown angle. In our mundane lives we either agree with an argument and therefore discover its positive aspects or disagree and find arguments to refute the same. Whether we like it or not we must admit that we are continuously engaged in dialectics either to support a viewpoint or refute it. This is typical human behaviour and this is what precisely Kumaril Bhatt has tried to indicate. Now read the quote;

Vishayo Vishayaschaiv Purvapaksha sthatotaram,
Niranyashchaiti panchang sashtradhikaran smritam

A research work ought to follow five steps, which, according to Kumaril Bhatt, are as follows:

1. Doubt in a conclusion already made or identify a problem that needs a solution,
2. Listing all the variables that relate to the problem and citing the

names of the preceding researchers i.e. prepare a list of those who have already worked in this area/or, write down about the related literature.

3. Listing the negative aspects—i.e. presenting the arguments where one disagrees or the negative data already in existence.
4. Finding answers to the arguments where one had a doubt or citing the grounds where one had disagreed in the light of fresh evidence.
5. The judgment or the conclusion and the solution to the problem with which one started.

As we study the sastras (a sashtra is a scientific, research work such as Vaastusastra or Kamasastra) or the ancient research works we find that a sashtra follows all the steps that we are supposed to follow today in our research study. It is important to remember that the major step in the ancient and modern researches is to detail all the known facts in the beginning itself so that before we refute the existing or known arguments, we are sure that we are taking into confidence our reader/listener also. A strict adherence to these steps alone can lead us to our achieving the goal that we have set out to achieve.

Now after so many centuries and continents apart the Western scholars are also advancing similar steps for their research studies. For instance we have here steps proposed by two scholars—one, Carlo Lastrucchi and, two, Theodore Caplow.

The first scholar i.e. Carlo Lastrucchi suggests the following steps:

1. Problem formulation
2. Related Literature
3. Research design
4. Fixing the size of the sample
5. DATA Collection
6. Interpretation of the data
7. Verification of the data interpretation
8. Writing the report or the thesis/dissertation

The second scholar has this to say on undertaking scientific research

1. Planning the project
2. Designing the procedure or electing to programme the work schedule
3. Gathering data
4. Analyzing the data
5. Writing the report

In the second description what is missing is the step that relates to 'relevant literature' while all other steps remain the same. We need not go into details of the problem here because we are right now discussing only the steps. Researches can be and are conducted in all areas of human knowledge. Remember all researches need not follow identical methods or take similar steps. They would vary according to the nature of knowledge one is dealing with. For instance, we are aware that all human knowledge is divisible into following areas:

1. Humanistic—folklore, literary
2. Scientific
3. Philosophical
4. Mathematical
5. Theological
6. While all the above types of researches could help one in making a Policy, policy researches are specially carried out for the purpose of making policies. For example, collecting data on universal literacy is different from the data which one will require to make a policy about the way it is working on the ground.

While all types of knowledge pursue identical goals and are learnt with equal vigor for satisfying human curiosity, inquiring into areas like logic or mathematics, demands the most rigorous course. Herein stands everything well-defined and well-designed. One cannot take liberties in these areas with either the methods selected or the conclusions arrived at.

We must not overlook the following facts:

1. All research is not scientific
2. Scientific research has to deal with abstraction of reality
3. All research produces knowledge that has generalization beyond spatio-temporal context
4. Science alone does not produce valid knowledge. Scientific research is tempered with the logic of inquiry.

The quality of Research is entirely dependent on the quality and the types of tools employed. Generally the tools are selected according to the theme of the research and the time one has at one's disposal. The tools keep on varying in consonance with the choice of subject. For instance, the tools employed for dealing with literary or historical themes cannot be the same as those that are selected for experimental or empirical research. One must be very careful in selecting tools and methods for one's research. Generally, methodology covers tools like preparing questionnaire, schedules, etc. These tools are meant for collecting data. Research also uses analytical tools like statistics and classification theories. In areas like philosophy or logic one has to depend entirely on one's maturity of understanding and a sense of discrimination besides the existing arguments whose validity has to be checked against the backdrop of one's own knowledge. In essence, one has to be extremely careful in the selection of tools, because without a proper tool one cannot expect proper results.

In a book titled *Making Sense of Research* (2003) (Elaine K& Patrick J. McEwan), Corwin Press; it is suggested that one ought to put a few searching questions while making a judgment regarding policy research. It is expected that the reader is aware of the distinction between ordinary scholarly research and policy research. While the earlier ones are either to obtain a degree or diploma but the policy research is primarily to formulate policy on the basis of the data collected. Therefore in this research the data collected is on a massive scale and the number of variables examined are equally multiple. It is because of the budgetary provision involved and the staff employed for collecting data. This kind of research is usually outside the purview of the university system. Therefore, the points raised here by the twin authors are both valid and relevant. These questions are:

1. First, the causal question: Does it work?
2. Next, The process question: How does it work?
3. The cost question: Is it worthwhile in terms of money needed, and the time to be consumed?
4. And lastly; the evaluative question: Does it work for me/us? If yes: adopt it and if No: drop it.

Normally, governments or multinational companies undertake these policy researches for making long term decisions. Therefore, they have to be very careful at the time when research findings suggest ways to resolving problems. They dare not take decisions wherein a doubt crops up about the future prospects from a policy adoption.

In majority of researches in the area of social sciences one follows the survey method—collecting data through interviews, personal intercourse or observation. Let me take an example. One chooses an area for one's study such as tribal culture, tribe's life and interests, levels of advancement in terms of modernity, while comparing or judging them all the while with the non-tribal populace. This data has to be either qualitative or quantitative. In either case one has to have a mental image of what one is actually doing. The research and its reporting would differ according to the purpose of one's undertaking. If the research was undertaken to investigate some aspect of tribe's life and report it for mere dissemination of information then the report would be markedly different in focus from the one wherein the intention is to introduce measures to improve the quality of its life. While in the former reporting one is indifferent to the problem aspects and the eventual measures to be adopted, in the latter the focus is on these aspects alone. One has to be very careful about the purpose of the undertaking. All researches could be divided into two major categories. These two categories are: 1. Qualitative and, 2. Quantitative. But then there is a possibility of having other categories also. These include experimental/empirical, reflective, model building or analytical, etc. Each of these additional categories has a definitive purpose and design. For instance, an experimental research is taken up to improve the quality of a practice. Experiments by their very nature are possible in all areas both major and minor—be that business or pleasure. The nature of reflective research suits philosophical themes even as it suits the area of logic. There could be considerable library work, involved in such researches but the best method is to have dialogues or discourses with some knowledgeable persons. These researches also require lots of meditation and self-reflection. The problem with these researches is that no one can cover all the aspects of a problem. A few aspects of the problem would remain uncovered, no matter how one tried. Reflective research can have its anchorage in one or more paradigms. For instance, it could emanate and end with Marxism, liberal democracy, or with the philosophy of Congress/BJP.

Quantitative researches are basically rooted in numbers. They have their philosophical bases in the thinking of Auguste Comte (1830). The Positivists as the followers of Comte are called, regard social science as social physics. This philosophy is quite critical of democratic procedures. They envision a stable society, governed by scientific elite. They would resolve all human problems by using scientific methods. It is because of this reason that Herbert Spencer modeled Sociology on the Natural Sciences. The most popular method of presenting any quantitative research is to use statistical method. Quantitative research has logically to be presented in statistical format. The main tenet of Positivism is that, it believes in the unity of scientific method because this method is equally applicable to both sciences and social sciences. After World War 1 the prevailing Positivist school of thought became Logical Positivists.

Then appeared on the scene Sir Karl Popper, who proposed a theory called critical relativism. He observed that while trying to discover the true value of truth simple verification of the truth was not enough. This verification ought to be resilient against falsification of truth. He held that scientific truth could only be corroborated and not verified. Secondly, scientific truth is a myth. The falsity of a theory can be inferred from empirical evidence. Thirdly, Popper also upheld the unity of scientific method—not of subject matter. While the relationship of cause and effect is true for science but this principle fails to apply to social sciences. It is interesting to note that social science refuses to accept the hegemony of Positivists. In its place it has its own methods of verifying truth.

The most important step in any research is the proposition of a hypothesis. It is the assumption behind a hypothesis that plays a major role in the importance of a research study. It is to be remembered that even the best and the most mature people commit errors at this stage. Even before a research is taken up we have a vague idea that we study this subject properly, the likely results will conform to an idea we already have. A good example of this error is a book titled *A History of Indian Education*, written by J. P. Nayak. In the introduction of the book he writes that the British came to India to educate it and improve its scientific information. This assumption is basically in disharmony with the reality. Firstly, they had no design to govern India. Secondly, all the evidence at our disposal points out that they had come for trade and that they accidentally came to govern it. Nehru famously recorded a reality of which Nayak had apparently not been aware. Therefore his entire book is marred by inaccurate and false interpretations.(Pt. Nehru's had observed "that the British succeeded in dominating India by a succession of fortuitous circumstances and lucky flukes"). Secondly, Macaulay's main aim of offering Indians was not to offer them English education because he was interested in educating Indians to become modern but to convert them to Christianity. Read, for instance, this observation of Macaulay to come to any proper conclusion. Apparently, no Indian Historian of education ever cites this quote. ["No Hindu, who has received an English education, ever remains sincerely attached to his own religion..... It is my firm belief that if our plans of education are followed up, there will not be a single idolater among the respectable classes in Bengal thirty years hence." T. B. Macaulay, (1836)] It is this lacuna in their information and knowledge that makes both Nayak and his followers go astray and come to inaccurate conclusions. I believe this inaccuracy in Nayak's principal assumption is responsible for the entire Indian nation and subsequent historians of education to mislead in writing and teaching about Macaulay and his real intent. A single mistake on the part of a writer could result in such a monumental error which it has been difficult to remove thus far and it is likely to remain etched in the minds of all Indians forever.

It is, therefore, important that before hypothesizing in a research study one is extremely careful. Remember that research hypothesis is derived from a theory and it is because of this reason that all researches tend to test theories. Researches normally strengthen theories. It is important to remember that all theories have a few characteristics. Theories are based on concepts. A few concepts are merely descriptive and others are operative. The concepts are variables. These in turn are of two types—dependent and independent. The dependent variables are those that are dependent on some other factor. For instance, one's academic achievements are dependent on the number of hours one reads or on how much one concentrates on one's studies. The independent variables are not so dependent on other factors. These variables in fact influence other factors and bring about results. For instance, the looks of a person have nothing to do with his/her academic achievement but the reality is that at times looks matter more than one's competence. A theory makes it explicit that some of the propositions are tested and their validity tested/determined.

This discussion has helped us to conclude that assumptions can be the basis of research but the hypotheses—based on assumptions are formulated only at the second stage for research. This means that there is a very fine distinction between an assumption and hypothesis in terms of which the former comes first. One can not hypothesize without an assumption.

Secondly, assumptions distort facts if not restrained or clarified. We have already seen above how the assumption of J. P. Nayak about the real reason behind the British rule led him to make several observations, which eventually resulted in writing an inaccurate History of Indian Education. This makes it obligatory on the part of the researcher to be well read. Research does not impact any assumption because of the reason that assumptions come first, hypothesis emanates from assumptions and research comes in the end.

There is difference between the assumptions in social, natural and or physical sciences.

(a) In science there is a definite order or sequence in occurrences,
(b) Here knowledge is superior to ignorance

(c) Communication is based on empirical assumption.
(d) There is causal relationship between the physical and social order.

Assumptions can be based on observation. These are called observer assumptions For instance, one can easily assume that knowledge is meant for public good; while it is quite possible that knowledge in reality is rooted in political intents. Recent discussion on History books written and produced by the NCERT has shown that knowledge of history can easily be distorted and made to suit particular party interests. In Communist regimes knowledge is definitely made to suit political interests. Secondly, it is commonly assumed that the observer has the capacity to conceptually relate observations in the pursuit of knowledge. Lastly, it is assumed that society will sustain the observer in the pursuit of Knowledge.

Assumptions continue to vary in qualitative research. It depends on the honesty and impartiality of the researchers how they would ensure whether or not their assumptions stand the test of rationality. For instance, when trying to find whether or not Muslims in India are educationally backward as compared to the Hindus it depends largely on the researcher what tools he applies and what hypothesis he advances. A report by Sachchar on the educational backwardness of Muslims suffers from major flaws of rationality. There were several ways of looking at the problem. He could have compared the rates of literacy in the entire sub-continent, including Bangladesh and Pakistan and then prepared a comparative chart. He could have easily seen that the reality is very different from the allegations made. If Muslims are educationally backward even in the Islamic nations like Pakistan and Bangladesh, it means there is something inherent in the Muslim community which prevents them from acquiring the knowledge of alphabets. It was also possible to make class comparisons. For instance, one could have made comparisons between the upper and middle classes in all these three nations and then declared the results. One must remember that education and class are inter-related. It is not possible to find a middle class person illiterate. The size of the middle class determines the rates of literacy in a nation.

OBSERVATION IN RESEARCH

It is interesting to see that observation itself suffers from some limitations. Several scholars have examined the nature of these limitations. For instance, a few of these limitations have been identified and even detailed. For instance, observations are marred by several effects:

1. *Heisenberg effect*—Immediately after an inquiry into the health of a patient and having been told that patient is doing well, the patient dies. There is time gap which makes both realities correct—the reported improvement or the wellness and the reality of death. This observation is known as Heisenberg effect.
2. *Hawthorne effect*—When performance improves during observation but otherwise it remains slack or totally absent. This is the most common effect in government offices when under observation of a superior things improve but in reality they remain as slack as ever.
3. *Message image*—The best example is seeing an object with or without telescope wherein the real size of the object varies between the two observations. In fact, in one case the message is audited and in the other it is not.
4. *Communication of an interpretation*—Wherein an observation is being communicated differently by different people such as a mountain top or a scenic beauty is possible to be communicated differently by different individuals. Herein the object remains the same but it is the interpretation of an object that varies. It happens because the communicators suffer from inadequacy of either command on language or of eyesight.

Qualitative research sticks to a theory. Also its paradigms are fixed. Quality research could be related to a perspective which means a study could be undertaken of events, actions, norms and even values. A faithful description in a naturalistic setting is called for. Such studies follow inductive logic and adopt flexible approach.

METHODS OF STUDY

They constitute ethnography, participant observation, unstructured open-ended interviews, life history, case study, group discussion, analysis, etc. Grounded theory is where statistics is banned and data are gathered through tapes, documents, census data, etc.

Grounded theory is a scientific method (which is normally associated with Positivism) that has an elaborate and rigorous procedure for coding, theoretical sampling, conceptualizing, identifying properties and their dimensions—all aimed at building a theory which is grounded in reality.

Interpretation of the Data and Writing of the Report

The interpretation of data is nearly as important as the research itself. In social sciences it is the interpretation of the data that is most important because it is here that researchers keep committing errors and mislead the users or readers of research. It is easy to misinterpret because being humans, researchers can also be prejudiced. For instance, there are two points where one has to be cautious before interpreting data. If in a given situation people of a locality do not participate in a programme there could be several interpretations of the same data. (1) They are not aware of the programme; (2) They imagine the programme would be uninteresting or hurt their feelings; (3) There is rumour that the organizers of the programme are not good people, although per se the programme is good; 4. While the elders know the programme would be interesting and wish to attend it; the younger generation imagines the programme to be boring, therefore they mobilize public opinion against it; etc. If the research is related to religion or social norms, the possibilities of misinterpretation of the data get heightened. Even in physical sciences the possibilities of misinterpretation are enormous. Therefore, one has to be very careful about the interpretation and the limitations of the data.

The next stage is writing of the Report. Here it is possible to write a very boring report. Considering that the Report writing is the most important part of any research it has to be made readable and the conclusions arrived at have to be made very specific. The latest trend is to include some statistics in the final chapter. It is advisable that the final chapter is as readable as it is possible. After all, one undertakes research to inform the readers or help policy makers. Any misrepresentation or misinterpretation of data can mar the value of a research.

How is this Discussion Related to Quality Assurance?

There are several ways of looking at this discussion.

Firstly, one should try to compare the European system with the Indian system. We notice that there is vast difference between the two. For instance, in most cases the Indian scholar undertakes research work immediately after his post-graduate degree. In a way he/she does not have the feel of the working of education system. Therefore, he/she is not even aware of the *real* problems. In most cases the problem a student chooses is related with the problem his or her supervisor had taken for his work. It is also a fact that the supervisor too may not be very well read or concerned about the problem. In any case, the scholar fails to realize that for working in the system one has to relate one's life's work with his research. After all, a researcher too is a cog in the huge machine of the educational system. All teachers have to teach. They have therefore to be knowledgeable. Researchers must realize that they must relate their entire studies with the classroom instruction. A good teacher is both knowledgeable and effective. One cannot become an effective teacher unless he feels concerned about the work he does It is therefore imperative that a research scholar must take up a research project which he has himself selected and not take up a study which his or her supervisor is familiar with. I know of a case wherein a supervisor applied for approval of topics that were modified versions of his own Ph.D. dissertation. The lack of scholarship on the part of the supervisor and the helplessness of the student was reflected in this case. But then had the research committee not been careful, all the variations of a single study would have got duly approved. Now all that I am saying is that unless the research scholar himself feels and knows that his interest lies in a particular area he should not take up a study and that too on the basis of the advice of his selected supervisor. The supervisor could be selected according to one's choice of the subject area. This is the common practice in the West. It is the scholar who brings the theme for his study to the university and this procedure is strictly followed. This implies the maturity of the scholar and the degree of independence he is expected to show while selecting/sampling/determining the size of the data, and the proper scheduling of the entire research period. This also implies that research work is done by the scholar himself and the supervisor has been instrumental in merely guiding on the sidelines to see that the scholar does not go astray from the course the research scholar must normally follow..

Briefly, the research scholar should be mature and well read. The selection of the topic should be his. He must know how to consult the library and must learn to take help of the internet to prepare the chapter on relevant literature. The supervisor is there to guide only when there is some problem to discuss or when one has to be restrained from going astray and at the stage when the data are being interpreted or for some other important, specific guidance. In the writing of the dissertation the scholar is fully responsible and the guide plays very little role. Now compare this scenario with the one that prevails in India because I have described what happens in the West. This also explains why researches in the West are far superior to the ones that we submit here.

Secondly, I am proposing that in India we should introduce a short test to see whether or not a research scholar is ready for research work. The items for examination may include the following:

1. Does the prospective researcher know the steps necessary for undertaking research?
2. Test whether the researcher knows how his/her research is related to improving some aspect of classroom instructions.
3. Is the researcher capable of undertaking research without much guidance.
4. Invite suggestions for breaking the Ph.D. examination network and see that the examiners are nationally approved?
5. Those that submit brilliant piece of research its findings should be nationally broadcast—a practice common in countries like China/Japan.
6. The NCTE should enter this area for the promotion, dissemination and logistical support of research. It should at least oversee the mechanism of approving and guiding research so that Indian work could also become internationally competitive. In the process this will add to the value of work NCTE does or at least claims to do.
7. It should be the primary obligation of the NCTE to open a register for the nationally recognized researchers and publication of their researches for the benefit of all.
8. All important research findings that relate to classroom instruction or management are to be highlighted and circulated. This single act alone could transform the image of the NCTE.
9. The prospective researcher may be examined in preparing an outline of a research proposal. Since the format of a research is more or less similar, the themes for research may be given along with their subject classification. For example, a candidate could be asked to prepare either an experimental or historical or sociological proposal for research.
10. Questions in the examination may relate to the description and analysis of the chapter schemes of research in various subject areas. For instance, a candidate could be asked: How would the chapter scheme differ in a historical research and experimental research?

The idea behind this kind of testing is to enable the supervisor to judge whether or not a prospective researcher is fit to undertake his/her work independently or needs some kind of spoon-feeding.

We only assume that some one who has done M.Ed./M.A. Education is ready for research. Perhaps we need to take a re-look on the situation. We should know for sure that a research scholar knows all the steps necessary for a piece of good research. Therefore, a preliminary test for knowing about the maturity of the research scholar is to be made a necessary condition. This will ensure the quality of research. I have already described the distinction between a hypothesis and an assumption. Similarly, I have tried to point out the pitfalls in writing report. This knowledge is very essential, because, a scholar can easily slip here and commit unforgivable errors.. The system has to be careful about it all, which unfortunately it is not. This is one responsibility that the NCTE can be asked to shoulder.

Thirdly, we must also realize that researches are made to improve the quality of information and bring about greater rationality in the system, besides adding to the quality of research work. A good research is supposed to improve classroom instruction and the level of teaching. The main question is; Do departments of education feel really concerned about their major obligation? A professor of education has to be responsible in improving the quality of classroom instruction. He is not supposed to be living in some kind of ivory tower—totally unrelated to school. In fact, one of the reasons why Education is not part of the higher education stage is because of the responsibility it has toward school education. Whatever be theme of research the major function of research in education is either to improve the quality of school instruction or the examination of the school content. All the functions of school education are the major responsibility of educational research. The entire gamut of teaching at school level has to be the departments of education. Somehow this fact seems to remain out of sight of education researchers. Remember that teaching is meant to inform (wherein information has to be accurate, relevant, and of the mental level of school going child), educate (wherein education means making a child worthy of living in a society he or she comes from in terms of acceptable mores and occupation) and feel responsible as a rational being.

6

Tech-Savvy Teachers: Enter 21st Century

VIRTUAL TEACHER GOES ONLINE

"You can now get in touch with teachers and students across the country to seek help in studies, compare notes and give pre-board exam like test several times at leisure with a click of the mouse during preparation for the crucial Xth and XIIth CBSE examination starting from March 1, 2008..

"Last week a team of entrepreneurs in Delhi launched a web-site service that is a cross between social service website and a handy tutorial for CBSE students and teachers. Named **cbsetutor.com** this website contains the entire NCERT curriculum in toto, the extensive CBSE prescribed reference material, specially designed notes, and loads of tests on each chapter covered by the syllabus.

"'In the next three months, thousands of students will need value-added study material to prepare for the boards. They will need to know where they stand on an all India basis. And they need to distress themselves under pressure of examination. The website tries to cater to these needs'

"To begin with, the company has a panel of experts who are professional tutors, former educationists etc who have designed the tests and the content. In the UK virtual leaning is mandatory but not so in India because here we have not been able to provide intrinsic value to students and teachers. The best part of the facility is that it is absolutely free."

***The Hindustan Times* (Dec. 31, 2007)**

Seen against the above backdrop is the remarkable fact of continuously reducing the eligibility qualifications for teaching B.Eds in the institutional-mushrooming scenario the NCTE has created; and now in its reformist zeal it has further brought down the marks percentages of future teacher-trainers from earlier 48 to 45 per cent. In the past one year or slightly more we have learnt the reactions of both the Government and also of the corporate sector that even the present day products are totally unacceptable (when being taught by M. Ed.s & Ph.Ds), then where does the NCTE think it would make these 'unemployables' acceptable? Is NCTE playing tricks with the gullible lot? Also, it remains to be seen what impact it would have on the university departments of education that produce 'meaningless' M.A/M.Ed. s and the Ph.D.s.

There is a lot that has been happening in the field of education, especially in the classrooms but thus far I have not come across any serious academic paper on the direction in which we are moving. Despite the NCTE (or, maybe because of it) we are nowhere near preparing 'effective' teachers who are knowledgeable as well as 'reasonably good' communicators. After all, the main function of a teachers' college is to produce teachers who know how to communicate and present the updated subject matter in a manner that is easy to understand. But are we preparing teachers with these twin ends in view? I doubt it.

In fact, all the indications are that we have miserably failed on both counts. Communication is a skill and skills can be developed only with practice. One has to see the functioning of a present day teachers' college (even among the so-called best ones) and realize that there is nothing in the teacher education programme that ensures this type of training. Apart from a meaningless debate on the theme whether or not practice teaching should be based on 'block' basis, there is no model available for us to fall back upon. We have yet to come across a single university department of education in India where this question has been taken up seriously and some empirical research finding is made available for guidance. This obviously implies that generally teachers' colleges are not serious about imparting this 'skill'. If they were serious the reality should not have belied the truth. The perfunctory and mechanical way teaching practice is conducted makes a mockery of the 'communication' skill. Remember we do not bother about this skill. At the time of selecting a candidate for teacher training marks in an academic examination are considered and they are based on testing one's memory. And with the so-called management quota in self-financed colleges all academic and professional considerations are thrown to the wind. Who will or who will not become a teacher is dependent on the fees one can afford.

There are essentially two problems with this ongoing callousness about the neglect of this basic skill. Those that know nothing about how to speak or communicate are not merely under-rating the value of this skill and additionally they are corrupting the youth from the homes where purity of language is still considered a value and that which needs to be taken care of and for all others the choice of words, the syntax and the correct pronunciation have lost meaning. We seem to have forgotten that in the oral tradition one does not have to remember only the text but also the proper pronunciation as well. In such a scenario the importance of this skill is not lost importance by any chance. A whole lot is dependent on the quality of spoken language. A single mispronunciation can spoil the meaning in a poem or impact adversely the good taste. A bad communicator is unlikely to be good teacher.

The other point that needs to be paid special attention is that developments in technology have brought us to a stage where it looks as though we do not need to train teachers at all. Even otherwise teacher education is no more than two hundred years old. It has no philosophy or psychology of its own. Indeed all that we teach at this stage is merely derivatives from the basic disciplines. Everything that we teach at the teachers' college is borrowed—the entire content and all the methods. Therefore to claim that teachers colleges teach something that they have themselves created or evolved would be unreal. Those who survive on borrowed knowledge can not be called scholars or innovators. After all only very few teachers are either creative and teach what they have evolved themselves.

To recall Kendal "things outside classrooms matter more than within the four walls of the classrooms" has acquired new context and meaning. For example, teachers' colleges are supposed to be teaching values but surprisingly they have not been able to evolve any tool to assess whether or not the training has been demonstrably successful. Linked with this failure are its other failures also. Read any national daily and find out how many teachers are found morally deficient and criminally inclined. I wonder whether any university department has ever tried to unravel the phenomenon and suggested corrective measures. These lacunae speak volumes for the failure of the system and suggest that the ones who should be responsible for guiding others are in fact basically unthinking and lack the 'Will' to resolve some of the basic problems this sort of training curricula face. It is possible to argue that all management courses do not equip or ensure every manager of either success or honesty. Yet the fact is that the majority of the products do succeed and management skills can be easily showcased.

Teachers' colleges can be accused of being both unimaginative for the way they select prospective teachers for initial training and being totally irrelevant for the courses they offer. Regarding the first allegation one could easily state that no one has thus far done any empirical research to suggest that the method evolved for selecting candidates for initial training are either predictable or demonstrable. There is also no proof to show that the cut-offs adopted in one university match with the norms followed in the other; or, for that matter the quality is or can be homogenized. In fact, talking about the quality of the products this is one area where the quality of the products is so uncertain that nothing could be ensured. 'Quality assurance' is an unheard of requirement and few, if at all, could guarantee that their products have matured to some level of quality. One rarely comes across a teachers' college which enjoys the reputation of producing consistently good teachers. In fact, both the corporate sector and the Government of India recently admitted that these products are not even employable.

After the arrival of the self-financed colleges on the scene the overpowering greed among both the managers and the Inspectors drawn from the universities and from amongst the teachers' colleges has established that teaching is no more corruption-free than the other government departments, and the claim that teachers are above material considerations because of their high-ended values fails to describe the reality. Teacher trainers can be shown to be as susceptible to common weaknesses as anyone else. The fact of the matter is that even the universities are found to be guilty of money making via teacher training. It is now public knowledge. The twin universities of Annamalai and Rohtak for the past several decades have gone on scandalously minting money from teacher education courses and financing their other faculties. It is equally known to both public and the regulatory body called the University Grants Commission. The NCTE, an apex body for teacher education, is equally guilty of not adhering even to its own declared norms anywhere in the country and for creating confusion by leaving several important areas and terms undefined. It has failed miserably in assuring quality control and preventing the unscrupulous elements from entering this area.

The meaninglessness of the teachers' courses can be shown by pointing out that even the NCTE finds it hard to explain why tailors and *panwallahs* (also, non-existent colleges) have come to offer teachers' degrees or prevent the *absentee* candidates from getting university degrees. This is one single cause that devalues teachers' degree or diploma that qualifies one to teach. It would be interesting to collect data after undertaking a proper comprehensive survey of teachers' colleges, to learn about the real face of the owners of these teaching 'shops', and if a test was conducted on the staffs of the these teachers' colleges and the university departments of education about the subjects they teach and the quantum of new knowledge they have acquired in the field, surely the appalling lacuna in their knowledge would be more than apparent. The most miserable part of the finding would be that we would know for once that the content they teach became obsolete ages ago. The 'airy nothings' they produce in the name of educational research are mostly woefully short of real relevance and utility. Because of the lack of seriousness attached to the areas of research and the way areas of research are identified make it much easier to obtain a Ph.D. in education than to pass a high school examination. Thus far there is no proof whatsoever to show that any doctoral research in the area has led to any policy change or the creation of new knowledge. One is yet to hear of a finding or the name of a professor of education in the country whose work has evoked public admiration or received widespread applause.

One of the major functions of universities is to be repositories of wisdom and the centers for the creation of new ideas. The great universities of the world function as the vanguards of change through innovations and creations of 'new' knowledge. If nothing else, they at least give us new interpretations to age-old ideas. One would like to inquire and collect data on these scores from Indian departments of education, where its present day functionaries are generally known only for their net-working and mutual back scratching—in brief, for everything except for their academic excellence. One wonders whether *anyone* functioning in this field has ever produced an original piece of research and can stand up to a comparable scholar in any other university discipline within this country or abroad. I am not sure whether it would be possible for this professorial class to find out the relevant or the irrelevant course of study and offer guidance for the posterity to save on time and energy.

These departments of education are not even thinking of the days ahead wherein the whole variety of knowledge will become a marketable product. The day is already very near when 'packaged' knowledge would be made available on the supermarkets. Already numerous agencies have entered this area and their products are available in select areas. This belief holds out a challenge for the survival of teachers' colleges. The 'old' horses will have to learn 'new' tricks to remain in business/competition. Let some one show concern about the challenges that modern technology is posing for teachers in the area of classroom instruction. Way back in the late 80's I had talked of *Future Classrooms in India*—a book brought out by a Delhi publisher. At that time no one had thought of a day when most of the tutorial functions of a classroom teacher could be transferred to a machine and it would be possible to teach inexpensively across the nation without much ado. That these machines/products would one day make revision of a lesson easy and at one's own pace was absolutely unimaginable.

One needs to think seriously about the future course of action vis-à-vis modern technology in terms of what we are currently teaching and what could be taught inexpensively with the aid of internet, virtual classrooms and with multi-media techniques.

This thinking will have several dimensions. For instance, the first dimension of the problem raises the question of relevance of the theory papers that we are teaching. Additionally, the items under each course of study have to be seen against the backdrop of examination that we wish to conduct. We have to identify not merely the subject matter but also the tools of testing for ensuring that the same have been learnt. And this could be done only after we have devised methods and tools to examine the candidate against the backdrop of the aims that we had originally thought of and devise ways to teach the same properly and scientifically. The main question is that teaching has a purpose. And the function of examination is to ensure that the efforts have yielded results. There is thus a direct linkage among the goals identified, subject or the content fixed according to the laws of the possible, and eventually the examination to ascertain that the goal has been achieved. This triad in teaching is well-known. This has to be specified for each course of study. Supposing we had aimed to teach a given candidate to be able to communicate or acquire some values or learn techniques and canons of logic, then the examination should be able to demonstrate one's success or failure. Where do we stand in this regard?

Look at the syllabus of a teachers' degree. What do we teach here? We teach Philosophy of education, Psychology of Education, History of Indian Education, Sociology of Education and Teaching methods. Besides, there are numerous optional papers offered to specialize. The names of the papers or their content may be different in individual cases but by and large this is the common pattern. As an example we have a few details for discussion.

Here is an *alternative* to the courses already on offer.

B.ED. SYLLABUS

PAPER I
Philosophical and Sociological Bases of Education

Unit-I

Meaning, functions and nature of the following academic areas vis-à-vis classroom teaching: by discussing the relevance of the following to a schoolteacher:

- Philosophy
- Sociology
- Economics
- Political Science (15 lectures)

Unit-II

Defining Indian contribution to educational thought and its relevance today Here one should also talk about Takshila and Nalanda as centers for learning.

- M. K. Gandhi (Basic education).
- Swami Vivekanand (Ramakrishna Mission).
- Sri Aurobindo (Spirituality).
- Gurudev Rabindra Nath Tagore (Bolpur Experiment) (10 lectures).

Unit-III

Selected Western Thinkers on education and their relevance for an Indian teacher:

- Plato
- Aristotle
- Rousseau
- Pestalozzi
- Maria Montessori
- Karl Marx & Karl Popper (The nature of society and the concern for freedom) (15 lectures)

Unit-IV

Education in a Globalized World (offering a competitive edge):

- Nationalism (versus patriotism) in the modern context (the question of identity).

- International Understanding and brotherhood (competition versus co-operation)
- Pluralistic Societies and the culture of tolerance (religious exclusivist versus accommodation with understanding) (8 lectures)

Unit-V

Knowledge Society—the questions of Power and Class conflicts in a Pluralist society

- Education for social change
- Education and Human Resource Development. (12 lectures)

In all not more than 50 lectures

PAPER II

Development of Learner and Teaching—Understanding the Learning Process

(Also include the models of present educational international experts like Bloom and Gagne).

Unit-I

Nature of Psychology and understanding the learners:

- Educational Psychology: Its meaning, nature, methods and scope; functions of educational psychology for a teacher
- Stages of human development; stage specific characteristics and development tasks.
- Adolescence in the Indian context—characteristics and problems of adolescents; their needs and aspirations.
- Guiding and counseling adolescents. (15 lectures)

Unit-II

Learning and Motivation:

- Nature of learning; learning theories—Behaviorists (Skinner's), Pavlov's classical conditioning, Thorndike's connectionism and Kohler's insight learning theory.
- Factors influencing learning and teaching process; learner related; teacher related; process related and content related.

- Motivation—Nature, types; techniques of enhancing learner's motivation. (15 lectures)

Unit-III

Intelligence:

- Nature and characteristics of intelligence and its development.
- Theories of intelligence, two factor theory—Multifactor Theory (PMA) and SI Model.
- Measuring Intelligence—Verbal, non-verbal and Performance tests (one representative of group test and individual test of each). (10 lectures)

Unit-IV

Exceptional/Challenged Children:

- Understanding Inclusive Education
- Exceptional children—types and characteristics of each type including children with learning disabilities.
- Individual differences—nature, accommodating individual differences in classroom.
- Learner centered techniques for teaching exceptional children. (15 lectures)

Unit-V

Personality and Mental Health:

- *Personality*—Definition, meaning and nature; development of personality; type and trait theories of personality.
- *Mental Health*—meaning, definition of mental health; factors affecting mental health. (10 lectures)

Unit-VI

Educational Statistics for a schoolteacher—defining and explaining its need:

- Data, frequency distribution and tabulations
- Calculation and uses—central tendencies (mean, median and mode) and variability with special reference to standard deviation.
- Correlation (Rank difference): Meaning, definition, calculation, interpretation and users. (10 lectures)

PAPER III

Essentials of Information and Communication Technology and Management

Virtual teacher goes online This paper should also include the use of latest educational technological tools like digital boards, digital pen and pencil, their use in the typical classroom situation including close circuit monitoring system where a large class of 40 students could get all aspects near their sitting arrangements as well as interactive modes.

Unit-I

- Definition of information and communication technology, distinction between hardware and software technologies. Their role in modern classroom practices.
- Hardware technologies: Important accessories and their application OHP, Still and Movie Projectors (LCD, DLD) Audio-Video recording instruments; T. V., Computer, New technologies like e-mail; internet; etc.
- Use of strategies like teleconferencing, CAI, language laboratory. (20 lectures)

Unit-II

- Psychological uses for use of modern technologies—Core of experience (Edge Dale, Multi-sensory Instruction—advantages).
- Developing programmed instructional material—linear, branching programmes, tryouts and validation, etc. (15 lectures)
- *Footnote*: Communication skill is also essential for making classroom instruction effective. Here one needs to elaborate how the given lecture with the help of latest technologies and multimedia uses has been educationally effective and also more interesting.

Unit-III

- Teaching and teacher's behaviour modification strategies—with special reference to classroom lectures, question answer, demonstration, discovery, heurism, projects, assignments, tutorial group, brain storming and role playing, minority, SC/ ST. (10 lectures)

Unit-IV

- Modern Administration and Managerial Skills and leadership traits

(a) Organizing a system (Schools and academic ambience)
(b) Leading (purposive behavior)
(c) Controlling (with consent for designed end-results) (10 lectures)

Unit-V

Quality management in Education:

- ❖ Evaluating institutional performance—Methods used—pupil evaluation, teacher evaluation. Evaluating Institutional performance.
- ❖ Methods of teacher evaluation—pupil rating, peer rating, supervisor rating, community rating—ratings used for institutional improvement and individual promotion
- ❖ Accountability in school education—methods used for assessing accountability.
- ❖ Use of Professional norm and ethics (10 lectures)

PAPER IV

Development of Educational System in India

Unit-I

- ❖ Education in India during ancient and medieval periods, only the salient features (5 lectures)

Unit-II

- ❖ Colonial rule and the educational systems in India (Portuguese, French and the British) and the seeds of modernity
- ❖ Language policies in the Indian colonies with special reference to the East India Company.
- ❖ Wood's Dispatch—1854.
- ❖ Lord Curzon's educational policy, Growth of national consciousness, National education movement. (20 lectures)

Unit-III

- ❖ Educational Policies during pre-Independence phase
- ❖ Indian experiments and policies after 1947 till date. (10 lectures)

Education Commissions and the Government Policies in Free India

- ❖ University Education Commission (1948-49).

- Secondary Education Commission (1952-53)
- Indian Education Commission (The Report) (1964-66)
- National Policy of Education (1986)
- Revised National Policy 1986 with modification made in 1992. (15 lectures)

Unit-IV

Development of Teacher Education in India:

- Objectives
- Problems of teacher education in India
- Role and functions of the N.C.T.E. (5 lectures)

Unit-V

Problems of Education in India at different levels:

- Primary education and its major problems (Universalization, wastage and stagnation).
- Secondary education and its major problems (Expansion and vocationalization)
- Higher education and its major problems (Autonomy and Privatization). (10 lectures)

PAPER V

Communication skills

1. written and oral
2. learning to write
3. learning to speak—coherently and logically
4. using quotes
5. highlighting positive ideas
6. application of logic in speech

(Remember that instructional strategies have to be thought of anew because already we have in the market several agencies that are offering ‘ready to use’ instructional material. For instance, SANSKAR the co. educational school is one of the few in Ghaziabad which is using audiovisual aid for teaching purposes. A number of school related programmes are on offer from JIL, NIIT, and EUREKA etc. This school has chosen EUREKA which has science and mathes, lessons based on N.C.E.R.T syllabus as prescribed by CBSE from classes 1st—10th The programme is excellent visually and is also self explanatory. In the absence of a teacher a student can see it and understand himself/herself also.)

The B.Ed programme should cover comprehensive, systematic, scientific approaches of Health Education and Health care and include points usually considered necessary the world over in the light of the work done by the WHO and the UNICEF.

The new curriculum should reflect disability component keeping in view the Human Rights perspective. The needs of Special Children as covered in the Comprehensive National Action Plan may be included at the appropriate place.

The problems and the issues concerning the Education of the minorities as recounted in the Sachchar Committee Report have to be included in the Indian Education paper.

All discussions on institutional life have to be based on values and ideals enshrined in the Indian Constitution among all stakeholders.

Reconsider issues related to promoting ICT as an integral part of teacher education and improve the quality of teacher education by giving more time to practice teaching than currently being given.

Consider upgrading teacher education programme suited for a Knowledge Society.

A plan of action involving CTEs, IASEs and DIETs in in-service education of the school teachers and the teacher educators is proposed. Environment education is part of school-teachers' curriculum. Specialization in this area is proposed at the M.Ed level. While theory is compulsory, *the duration of practice teaching has to be prolonged so that a regular internship programme could be developed and practised.*

Gender Issues: There are special teacher education institutions for women teacher trainees. Comparative study of effectiveness of training of these trainees in separate women institutions and in co-education institutions might be of help. Comparative studies on the effectiveness of female and male teacher educators are recommended. Comparison of facilities available in the co-ed and non-co-ed is also advised for policy making.

Liberal use of technology (ICT) is advised and all teacher trainees should know how to use Internet and all the associated activities and functions of a computer.

NATIONAL RESOURCE CENTRE FOR TEACHER EDUCATION

There is an urgent need for starting a National Resource Centre for Teacher Education, which should function as a lighthouse in the field. It is expected that this organization will inspire, guide and lead the entire system through funded research, developing quality assurance tools and drawing blueprints for future as the Americans and the British do.

In the alternative classroom instruction and packaged knowledge it is essential to see that the teachers are given training before being brought into this skilled job.

Lastly all the schools should be instructed to essentially include training as a basic norm to promote the good teachers which include their participation in various international and national seminars, conferences and should have at least minimum one basic research input for better skill development.

ALTERNATIVE CLASSROOM INSTRUCTION AND 'PACKAGED KNOWLEDGE'

India is already a leader in information communication technology. While its application part is well known in numerous areas like banking, industry, business, etc. very little is discussed when it comes to the revolution it has already brought about in classroom instruction. Of course what is happening in the metropolitan classrooms is not nationally possible. But we must not forget the goal has to be simply that.

We have the technology to create virtual classrooms and also simultaneously take classes across the nation. We have learnt to store knowledge and package it for its possible use according to our convenience. Once this packaged knowledge starts getting into mass circulation it would not be possible for the mediocre to survive. Bereft of the knowledge to use modern day technology, the present mass produced B.Eds will find it hard to survive as teachers. No good school will ever hire a newly taught teacher whose language and other skills are markedly poor.

For instance, look at the title of a news item which says *'Digital classrooms make learning fun'*. This news item goes into detail as to what is going to happen within two years or even less in India. 'Circa' 2010 You enter a classroom and have a teacher explaining on a plasma screen in an audio-visual format. As and when she asks a question, you do not rush for your pen and the class work book. Instead you log in to your palm top computer and press the answer option. No baggage of homework books, as the assessment is derived on the basis of your homework, has been replaced by what skills you have. All this may sound futuristic but companies are already working towards changing school learning in India in this direction. Educomp Solutions, a technology driven company that has also made forays in "education process outsourcing", has launched its Millennium Learning System (MLS)—a combination of technology, training and new learning methods for schools.

The system includes a whole new set of pictorial books, digital content, plasma TVs for classrooms and 3D multimedia content, to be followed by classroom PCs which are on the way. The content is based on NCERT syllabus, which opens up the possibilities of addressing schools across the country that follow NCERT agenda on educational content. Educomp will enter into a revenue sharing arrangement with the schools involving aspects like designing the classrooms, furniture and teacher training in building a tech-centered learning program.

Now a PC is available with education software at nominal cost using LINUS system. This kind of system is available for both the normal and the challenged children. For them very soon the Microsoft and DAIS (Digital Accessible Information System) are jointly going to come out with plug-in software which will help the visually challenged to read digitally prepared books that they could never had access to. And to think of the software being free is beyond belief. The National Association of the Blind which is a member of the DAISY has called it "giant step towards creating equal access to information" Things, companics, software and costs are all changing and changing fast. Under the circumstances the NCTE approved B.Ed.s with 40 per cent marks would not fit into the system.

7

Education as an Institutionalized Network

God has established among mortals, knowledge, which is acceptable, purifier, knowable, wise and immortal. The same knowledge, with its active brilliance, pervading the universe, and sustaining the world, dispels darkness devoid of light. —*Yajurveda*, XII. 24.

INTRODUCTION

In this unit you will be introduced to the purposes and functions of organizing education institutionally. It will be made clear why education must exist as a distinct entity/institution. You will also be explained the distinction between acceptable and unacceptable forms and content of knowledge/vidya. Education does not always mean either information or skill. It is much more than that. An institutional organization is generally needed for offering acceptable knowledge and skills. Since education is a social requirement, societies therefore invariably support it. These institutions are only a formal arrangement. Some undefined, informal systems also exist. A few of them can be serious contenders in the field of education. Religions are one such example. They are not always financially supported by the State. Religious institutions are seldom clearly defined or get universal acceptability. But they play an important role in all societies. Similarly, the peer groups, the mother-child relations are not institutionalized. But they exercise tremendous influence on the growth and development of a child. They play important roles in offering social intelligence, especially about prospective societal expectations and requirements. Also, there are areas of knowledge that are extremely difficult to organize. For instance, it is not known how to make one a philosopher. While it is possible to improve one's logical abilities and teach ethics institutionally, one would be hard put to organizing distinct institutions for preparing philosophers. Institutions are funded either because they help improve one's skills or help generate quality information.

CONCEPTS AND DEFINITIONS

It will be appropriate to consider here the birth and growth of education as a distinct institution in human history. This understanding will enable the reader to appreciate that education does not deal merely with social conduct or imparting of skills and approved knowledge. It also creates conditions for the perpetuation and refinement of the means of earning one's livelihood and acquiring a decent life style in an ascending order commensurate with one's native intelligence, industry and luck.

We have in this world only a few *living* ancient civilizations. The Chinese and Indians very legitimately boast of their antiquity, but we must not forget that Europe too draws its inspiration from an ancient civilization—that of the Greeks. In the ancient literature available with us today we have discussions about the growth and development of education as a distinct institution created for a specific purpose. These references are very relevant for our purpose. The Vedas in India, Confucius in China, and Socrates, Plato and Aristotle from amongst the Greeks provide an insight into the nature and origins of education as an institution. Additionally, the great Indian epics viz. the Ramayana and the Mahabharata and the Jatakas i.e. Lord Buddha's birth stories—all of them discuss and relate stories of the origins, purposes and importance of education. All of these put together give a worldview of the meaning of education.

Let us now look into some of the material available with us today:

Rigveda 8/48.14

O the Protectors, O the scholars! Join hands to educate us—the uneducated, properly, so that such weaknesses like sleep and carelessness, etc. do not afflict us and the backbiters do not dominate us. Let us remain forever the favourites of the pleasure-giving God and by becoming the bravest propagate knowledge everywhere!

Mahabharata 40/5/6

Students must overcome these seven weaknesses: lethargy, ego, restlessness, reading without concentration, demonstrating pride, and not telling others what they understand or know.

Rigveda 1/164/41

The girl who wishes to practice a single Veda, the two Vedas or the four Vedas and the four Up-Vedas besides acquiring expertise in Grammar can become herself a scholarly teacher for other comely girls. By becoming a learned scholar she can experience sky-pervading Supreme Being and for educating other girls, she can select clear statements like sparkling water and remove their dirt like ignorance.

A Chinese proverb perhaps explains the best the mode of ensuring the perpetuation and spread of education in which the greatest importance is accorded to girls' education. If one is planning for the perpetual happiness of society, educate the girl.

I now cite from Plato and Aristotle. Both philosophers from ancient Greece talk of education in their classical works on Politics. In his *Republic* Plato feels concerned about the education of the guardians. He obviously believes that any and every type of education will not do. Instead while educating them, both girls and boys should be given similar education. The curriculum offered to them should suit their future assignments. Therefore, he goes into details of what and how to teach them. Plato's *Republic* is singularly well-thought out work. Aristotle's *Politics* is a research work on Constitutions for running and regulating State. For writing this book he is believed to have consulted about one hundred and fifty-three written works on city-states. While both these works deal essentially with politics and the rulers, the discussion on organizing education in such write-ups throws light on the relationship of education with politics and the governments. In other words, *education is basically a state-approved organization* and even if some other arrangements can be considered they can never be allowed to remain outside the purview of social approval.

It is against this background let us see what Plato and Aristotle have to say on education and examine the relevance of the quotes.

'Well, Glaucon,' I said,' what should men study if their minds are to be drawn from the world of change to reality? Now it occurs to me that we said our rulers must be trained for war when they were young.'

'We did.'

'Then what about the literary education which we described earlier on?'

'That' he reminded me, 'was the complement of their physical education. It gave them a moral training, and used music and rhythm to produce a certain harmony and balance of character rather than knowledge; and its literature, whether fabulous or factual, had a similar ethical content. There was nothing in it to produce the effect you are seeing.'(Education of the Philosopher, Part eight; book seven, Plato)

In the context of a discussion on *Imperfect Societies* Plato reproduces the words of Socrates,' Well! that's that. What we have agreed, Glaucon, is that in the perfect state women and children should be held in common, *that men and women should share the same education and the same occupations both in peace and war*, and that they should be governed by those of their number who are best at philosophy and war.' (Part nine)

The reader is advised to go through these citations carefully to realize that Plato is advocating a total control on education and its organization besides overseeing its provision for both boys and girls alike.

Now we should see what Aristotle has to say on the subject. The following discussion and quotes are from T. A. Sinclair's translation of the work but presented and commented upon by T. J. Saunders. As against what Plato has said about providing education, here is what Saunders' comment is while he distinguishes Aristotle 's views with those of Plato's." Aristotle in this chapter (VII xxii)," remarks Newman (III, 478), "*Education up to 5 years of age needs no formal teaching; from 5 to 7 visual methods may be used. The main periods are the next 2, 7 to 14 to 21.* " While Plato wishes to preserve the same educational programme in perpetuity, even down to small details like the children's games, on the ground that novelty makes for social instability. To that extent Aristotle is less Utopian. He does not wish to freeze society in time.

It is here Aristotle is very clear. He says, " the rearing and education of the children of citizens should indeed be a matter of public concern, since they are the future citizens, the future rulers of the state and one learns to be citizen, just as craftsman needs to be trained in his particular skill. Moreover, the education of the potential citizen will depend largely upon the type of the State and on the kind of life, which it is desired to lead. Aristotle himself has in mind especially the intellectual, artistic, cultivated life, which the Greeks called scole, usually translated 'leisure'. *No citizen, therefore, 'belongs to oneself': he is part of the State, and is not entitled to be educated privately in private tastes and standards.*" (VII. 1; p. 451)

It should be clear by now that the Greeks believed in institutionalizing educational provision. They in their own ways also defined who should learn what and at which stage. They were against the provision of private schooling. Also, they knew that education is a purposive activity/process. It is very interesting to note that while the Chinese evolved an excellent Mandarin system, the Greeks also did not hesitate to prescribe courses of study and laid down clearly goals of education. We have Indian parallel to these two systems in their contemporary period of time. This is not the place to go into the details of what Indians in different period of time wished to offer. Suffice it to say that institutionalization of education is an old hat.

We have seen that in both ancient Greece and India the courses of study were invariably fixed and the period of studentship laid down.

Education of girls in India and Greece were differently conceived but there was never any disagreement about the need for offering them education. They must also be educated along with boys. The State was responsible for the provision of girls' education. The length of their studentship was rarely disputed. In fact, some of the well-known names of women rsikas who composed the Vedic hymns have been duly recoded in the Vedas.

ORGANIZATIONS AND INSTITUTIONS: (NEEDS, INSTRUMENTALITY AND FUNCTIONS)

Needs

No society can survive without organizing itself into a variety of institutions. Institutions perform numerous functions. They carry on functions that are assigned to them by their organizers. These organizers belong either to various government departments or to private Trusts, voluntary organizations, associations or philanthropic bodies. It would be proper to remember that to organize means to arrange. Therefore, an organization is a built-up arrangement for performing a specified function. At times these institutions become indices of societal functions. At times they can also reflect the practice of a political ideology or a kind of philosophy in action. The existence of Panchayat, for example, in an Indian village is an indicator that people take their own decisions and are not dependent on any external agency to regulate their life-functions. No autocratic system ever permits the setting up or allows the functioning of a Panchayat. T. Parsons in his books *The Structure of Social Action* (1937), New York, McGraw-Hill and *The Social System* (1951), New York, Free Press describes society in terms of general value consensus. " Modern societies, though complex and fractured, are capable of expressing common goals. They operate according to established norms that positively express the shared common goals of society. Social equilibrium is an ideal state of balance. It will be more or less realized in social structures. *The family and the school are* the positive and necessary institutions through which social values and cohesion are maintained." A few scholars have been critical of Parsons for taking a thoroughly systemic view of social structure which he accounts for in terms of four principles: *adaptation, goal attainment, integration and pattern maintenance.* His theory envisages change, taking place only gradually and not radically.

It is important to remember that contemporary West by and large rarely approves of totalitarianism or autocracy. It lays great store by democratic norms and practices. Parsons' views are therefore in consonance with the generally endorsed and sanctioned Western philosophy. I should like to stress on the need to take a note of the Indian philosophies in this regard. Indians ever since the days of the Vedas have practiced democracy. With occasional bouts of non-democratic rules apart, in both social and political life Indians have rarely deviated from their cherished life style—freedom, democracy and public discourse. As far as we are concerned, rigid bureaucracy and centralization of administration are the western gifts to India. Even the Muslim India hardly, if ever, succeeded in centralizing power—the way Germany, Italy or the USSR once did. Indian institutions seldom overcome strains of anarchy in their systems.

We need not go into the details as to why the above-described viewpoint of Talcott Parsons is only partially true. Because there are other theories too, which hold the view that social institutions may have 'contingency' plans, wherein one might trace some kind of arbitrary roots. For instance, Marxism provides a radically different alternative route to organizing society and its institutions. Parsons overlooks the conflict inherent in the nature of society and adopts a myopic view of conflict resolution.

We have thus far indicated that organization of institutions has its roots in the basic nature of society. Nomadic societies must, therefore, organize themselves very differently from the aborigines. Societies get their indicators for organization from their specific functional requirements. For instance, any group of human beings must procure food to live, organize itself to defend from the vagaries of Nature, protect itself from another similarly organized hostile group, etc. Civilizationally, when they become more mature societies organize themselves even better. For each function and need they help develop framework, sustain and supervise institutions within that framework. That is how societies ensure institutional accountability. No institution is permitted to go against the society that sets it up. With every stage of social and technological development and growth, the number of institutions also increases correspondingly. It is at this time these institutions acquire their separate identities. Societies keep their control on them by creating intra- institutional and inter-institutional ambience and relationships.

In their book *Introduction to Educational Studies* Steve Bartlett, Diana Burton, and Nick Peim (P.C.P. London, 2001) discuss problems related to the topic in hand. They say, "All sectors of education are made up of organizations of various sizes: *schools, colleges, universities, local educational authorities*. Organization theory and the study of behaviour in organizations constitute important elements in education studies courses. As many postgraduate students of education work in the field, there is a particular interest in theories of management and their application as part of professional and academic study. By considering organizations which are primarily people-centered, an emphasis is placed on theories related to performance management or management by objectives, human relations management."

Other aspects of organizational theories treat the nature and purposes of educational organizations. Here the important components of organizational theories revolve round the pupils and teachers—*learning, classroom practices, homework, teacher –pupil relations, examinations and the like.* Each of these aspects of an educational organization lead, to learning either more knowledge or skill. It is then that they too fall under microscopic scrutiny and further examination.

We have come to the point where it is possible to say that organizations have clear-cut goals defined for them by societies within which they have to function. It is within a given framework that they can function. They can outgrow these functions too but only when society so desires. This is one reason why education is called a subsystem of society. The organizations/institutions have their goals clearly laid out for them. In the educational institutions their functions are limited to developing and sharpening an individual's cognitive abilities. In fact this is what *Education* is all about. The levels of institutional arrangements are, therefore, fixed according to the difficulty levels in cognizing information, knowledge or skill. For instance, the prescribed age of the pupil attending an educational institution is determined by the formula which fixes age when a child/ person of a given age can learn and that too, the exact quantum of knowledge/skill. The basics of the formula derive their inspiration from the exact requirement of information/skill calculated on the basis of a child's immediate needs, and those too in keeping with one's basic/innate abilities. If at the primary school level a child learns to read and write, the society takes care that the time is not wasted on teaching unwanted bits of information. In other words, what I am trying to communicate is that no society leaves anything to chance. The support systems it creates besides the supervisory roles, it delineates to differentiate among bodies, and levels of functionaries that are obliged to keep track of everything are important to take a note of. A specific designated support system is obliged to keep track of various functions being carried out within the framework prepared for an organization under its charge. For instance, Departments of Education under a Director of Education oversee only the work concerning their own territory. Here too, depending on the political ideology of the government, a country runs its institutions. Each major political change gets reflected in the school curricula or the examination system. This has inevitably to happen. Therefore, certain clauses or special provisions within the law are provided initially to see that the organization comes to no harm when governments change. These arrangements have of necessity to be anticipated with clauses for flexibility. Once one comes to institutions of higher learning where the development of an individual is gauged in terms of one's reflective abilities, the organizational climate becomes suddenly individual-friendly.

Instrumentality and Functions

Before we define functions of various levels and types of educational institutions, we should understand that each institution is answerable to the society in general and to its designated functionaries in particular. Had this not been true, it would have not been possible to prevent opening of such schools like *The School of Pickpockets* that Charles Dickens refers to in one of his novels. Secondly, each educational institution has to serve as an instrument to fulfill certain well-defined functions. The act of performing or the process of institutional performance is its instrumentality. It merely means that if an institution is performing well and to the satisfaction of the concerned people or the relevant powers that be, the instrumentality of the institution is beyond any doubt. This word *instrument* is derived from the Latin word *instrumentum*. The meaning of this Latin word is *to instruct*. The Latin word for function is *functus/function- em1-fungi* and they stand for the verb *to perform*. In other words both terms i.e. *instrument* and *function* when put together mean *performing the act of instruction*. The other meaning of instrument is to be *a tool*. In the present context the instrumentality of an educational institution is to work as a tool in the hands of society to meet its imagined or actual requirement.

In this context it is perhaps necessary to remember that education, as a human right, is historically of very recent origin. In India it is hardly two-year-old recognition. One should distinguish between the existence and running of schools and universities, and acknowledge that it is an individual's fundamental right to be educated. The concept of education is here related and contextualized with empowerment. There was a time when education was defined as making an individual a gentleman or a culturally refined person. These days education is meant to improve one's individual skills so that economically one is independent. Education for a vocation or employment is hardly a century old concept. Currently, education is also supposed to empower an individual.

China, India and Greece have been ancient seats of learning. They have had institutions in the past that are even now referred to with respect. But the way education is currently being defined was never the primary function in these old civilizations. It is good to cite their examples in historical context only. But to emulate them today would be out of context and ridiculous. Also, education ladders like primary, secondary or higher are twentieth century inventions. Similarly, professional and vocational schools of today may appear to have their parallels in the past but in reality these arrangements were made through their respective guilds the parallels of which are hard to come by. There were no open or distance systems and neither those societies had a competition like the one that we have today. If there is no need, the society is not likely to be motivated to respond to a vacuum. Therefore, a progressive diagram will look like the following:

Need → Response

Planning → Designing → Assigning → Supervisory/Support System → Institutional Functioning → Social Recognition = Social Approval

In a way Education, its support systems and supervision and control, etc. are a cyclic affair. Steve Bartlett says the development of modern education, can be traced through the rise of nation states in the 18th and the 19th centuries. Legislation appeared through the 19th century to control the employment of children, to protect children from sexual abuse and from exploitation as cheap labor. This whole process has been called the invention of the childhood." In India we still need to do a lot more before we come at par with the achievements of the West/advanced nations. There is little that has thus far been done in India, particularly in this direction beyond words and airy nothings. Even the Sarva Shiksha Abhiyan supported by the Constitutional Amendment is unlikely to achieve the target. It is an expression of a wish totally unrelated to reality that exists.

The question is why India has lagged behind in providing education for all despite its glorious past and not very unenlightened medieval period. The reason is simple. We have seldom regarded that education for all is our cherished goal. In ancient India education remained a monopoly of the elites and a designated caste group. The medieval India created a new elite group and introduced a new language of culture, but in societal terms it was no different from the ancients. What was open for the upper castes among the Hindus during the ancient period became the norm for Muslims during medieval times. Therefore, the education that we are talking of now has little in common with either the ancient or the medieval periods in Indian history. Also, similar changes in outlook have more or less become dominant universally.

The other point that needs to be underlined pertains to financing of education and the reasons why private parties are so eager for providing educational facilities. After India became free, the government of Free India wanted to spread literacy among the masses. Since poverty prevented Indian masses from taking benefit of education, the Government financing started playing a significant role. If the British rulers were indifferent to providing education for the masses and therefore they created a grants-in-aid system to support education given by private bodies, the present-day government is finding it difficult to support the system single-handed. They are interested in taking help from the people—the ones who regard education to be a big business. *The education scenario has thus become both highly contentious and confusing.* A caste –ridden country is now getting further subdivided into two groups, one who have access to quality education and the other who have access to only partial benefits being doled out either by the governments of both the states and the center, or by the voluntary bodies—majority of which has their own axes to grind. It is the digital divide that Indian masses are facing; they are confronted with other types of monopolistic onslaughts. For instance, the locally educated youths are facing foreign educated Indians. Foreign universities are challenging the system, run and supervised by the UGC since they have opened their campuses in India. In brief, we are faced with several networks—both Indian and foreign, the government and the non-government, the private businesses and the philanthropists, etc. If the end product was the basis of adjudging one's quality of educational competence, we would be surprised by the findings of any research undertaken in the field. The variety and the gradations are as endless as they are baffling.

Stages and Levels

Education the world over is organized in various stages and levels. The reasons are not far to seek. The first reason is the chronological age of the individual who is likely to be offered education. The second one pertains to the mental age or the intelligence one has to have to grasp the meaning of what one is told to learn. The third reason lies in the socio-economic level of the person trying to learn. And lastly, the difficulty level of the subject matter also matters in these considerations. We shall go both by the way these stages have come to be evolved and the way levels define the quality and quantum of information and skills.

As mentioned above, modern Indian education has taken about three centuries to take its contemporary shape. At the time when the East India Company started making inroads in this country, they supported the idea of implanting of their own system of education here. The reasons were both political and economic. The political reason was that they wanted to create a whole cadre of Indian intellectuals who would with time develop stakes in the Company's perpetual, continued presence. This is what Macaulay said would be a class of Indians in color but English in tastes and habits. The second reason was economic. To look after Company's business interests they wished individuals who would work for them in lower jobs and on subsistence allowances. If they imported English accountants and clerks, that would cost them a fortune. Local employees were less of a bother and could be hired for the minimum wages. It is these two major reasons that forced them to introduce in this country a system of education, which was good for them. It mattered little whether or not it was good for the Indian masses.

It is during these initial stages that Company started expanding its vast business interests here in India. Therefore, it desired to study the indigenous system of education. The initial surveys of Adam in Bengal established beyond doubt that India did have an effective indigenous system of education. But this system lacked clear-cut gradation and neatly divided levels of education. At times the same teacher taught all classes, mostly simultaneously. These schools had no interconnectivity and neither did they have any supervisory system. They were locally financed. The salaries to teachers in these schools were neither fixed nor structured or regular. There were no textbooks. Therefore, standards of education were difficult to assess. Of course, in exceptional cases, the Madarsahs and Sanskrit Pathshalas appeared to be fairly close to the modern system in organizational terms and also in being acknowledged as centers of learning and excellence.

In fact, what the indigenous system lacked, the new system had it in abundance. The modern system of education took considerable time to grow and develop into a well-knit institutionalized shape. The educational system both in India and elsewhere does not seem to have grown and developed very differently. If the priests wished to remain educated and organized they had to have some system to perpetuate themselves.

Education for the rituals motivated them to develop an institution of priesthood. In Europe it was the Church and in India the Yagnas for the Vedic rituals were the single potent reason for the spread of institutional arrangement for literacy and education. All other religions too pursued an identical path to keep their identity distinct. Education had, in fact, within itself the seed to develop distinct identities. Likewise, literacy was essential to run business establishments. The third source of motivation for education, literacy, training and organized education came from the ruling elites. If seen in a perspective, education as an institutionalized identity had very valid reasons to grow the way it grew.

Let us now see how it grew into its present form and purpose in India. The Rgveda is the first to record this kind of growth.

There are friendly Brahmans who concur in the mental apprehension, conceived by the hearts (of the wise). And *yet they abandon that person who is ignorant to such sciences as are essential to knowledge.*

—*Rg. X. 71. VIII*

One of the priests (the hotra) becomes diligent in the repetition of the verses of the Rk.; another (the udgatr) chants the Gayatra Saman in the Sakvari meters; another the Brahma declares the entire existing knowledge; another (the adhvaryu measures out the details of the sacrifice.

—*Rg. X. 71.11*

May Bharati (Goddess of Enlightenment) and Ida (Divine Speech) come quickly to our place of worship, personified in features, and may Saraswati (Divine Knowledge) also—the three goddesses—sit down on their assigned seats. —*Rg. X. 110. VIII*

Here are the details of why and how one could obtain and retain knowledge:

For the attainment of full knowledge, noble deeds; for the attainment of happiness, religious life; for the attainment of definite object, activity, for the advancement of wisdom, the habit of reading and teaching; for retention of knowledge, truthful speech; for arithmetical measurement of the day, the science of arithmetic; checking the waste of time in infatuation, a word of wisdom; for the fool who revels in vice a word of caution...

—*Yajurveda* IX. 20

The idea for citing the Vedic text was to get support for the point that learning and acquisition of knowledge had their root in religious rituals and needs. In all societies we find similar motivations. Even such religions like Buddhism lay a great store by monastic education. Similarly, the Jain Munis never ceased to be the repositories of sacred knowledge. In Britain it has always been the Church (until of Rome; and, thereafter Henry VIII of England) that held sway over knowledge industry. For example, the Tracts written by a poet like P. B. Shelley at Oxford invited the wrath of the same religious coterie in England. During the medieval times Islamic knowledge was the monopoly of religious groups and we find considerable debate on the same issue even now. It is this small group of the clergy who opposed vehemently the suggestions made by Avecenna (Ibn Sinah) and Avecerros (Ibn Sirah) for making Islam more open to debate than it then was or is. That way the Hindu priestly class could never control wholly the knowledge industry, although they too were relentless in their efforts to do so. Irrespective of the religious variations the priestly class per se initially held a tight control on educational institutions and strictly regulated and supervised them.

But beyond the priestly domain the knowledge and learning had equal number of votaries from amongst the ruling and the business elites and their establishments. In different countries the development of education may have taken different routes but the basic control, provision and spread followed an identical path.

During the Renaissance in Europe and the advent of East India Company in India opened up vistas of knowledge beyond the narrow bounds of religious consideration. For the first time we find the emergence of a strong scientific lobby both in India and in Europe. This brought in objectivity and logic in the acquisition and spread of knowledge. Formal schools started appearing all over Europe and in India. The Company for its narrow and selfish reasons supported a school system that was intended to provide them with native recruits for lower jobs in their business establishment. In the secular sector industry was the first to provide patronage to education, especially to such branches of education that could be applicable to further growth and income. Once the Company developed a taste for acquiring political clout in India they needed lower rank judiciary staffs, teachers, clerks and administrators, etc. and those too on petty salaries and in large numbers in the same ratio as was necessary for territorial control and power. Thus the modern system of education with which we are so familiar had its roots in religio-political and business requirements. It did not matter much if this requirement covered other areas too beyond political, military or other requirements. The basic cause for introducing the modern system, however, lay in advancing business tentacles across the sub-continent. The gradation and level fixing of the school curricula, according to the type of education that served the requirements of the Company, is very interesting to analyze.

This is not the place to go into the conflict this modern system faced from two existing systems—the Sanskrit pathsalas and the madarsahs and maktabs. The latter were controlled and run by charitable people for promoting religious causes. The modern system, introduced by the alien intruders through their Company rule, came as a strong alternative to the indigenous schools and the indigenous priestly control. For the first time India faced a challenge from within the school boundaries. The knowledge that came to be offered was not religious; it had certain dimensions never experienced before. For instance, a new language was introduced. Textbooks started being written in place of what the teacher wrote or decided to teach in the indigenous system. A whole department of education came up to supervise the opening of schools, their teaching, providing textbooks and fixing what was to be taught at which level and when. Until now individual teacher was the best judge. The native teachers in their respective areas were virtual leaders in all social and moral spheres. The new system took away this power from them. They came to be seen as mere employees.

The new school and the new teacher had their assigned roles meticulously defined. They no longer occupied the high pedestal, which was once theirs just for the asking. There now was a department of education where the officers had tenure positions. There were written rules and regulations, a tentative budget and a specific geographic area to supervise. In brief, India was witnessing a system of education that it had never known before. For the first time ever, the amount of knowledge and its variety came to be fixed by a group of people who were supposed to know more than the classroom teacher. Subjects like health and hygiene, geography and history of Europe came to be introduced besides a brief introduction to civic duties and a smattering of science. All this needed fixing of the stage and the level of educating a child. It was natural therefore that grades got introduced into the system. Starting with the teaching of alphabets to the formation of sentence structures, a new kind of grammar became essential. The major difference between the promotion of a child under the two systems (the old and the new) from one class to another lay in downplaying the role of teachers' individual discretion. The system claimed to be more objective-and-learning-quantum based. Even an external examination by Company's nominee came to play a significant role.

It may be remembered that long before the Company introduced an official system of education, numerous Missionaries were already actively promoting European education and knowledge for the spread of Christianity in India. This was one single reason why the Indians opposed this knowledge then and even now in numerous areas of Free India. A section of Indians continues to be suspicious of missionaries and their activities. But it should be acknowledged gratefully the way the Christian Missionaries brought modern knowledge to India. There is record that in the beginning of the 19th century (*Samachar Chundrika,* dt. 16th June, 1845; Vol. VIII.) a school was teaching " through objects and pictures after the Pestalozzian system." The curriculum included English, Menstruation, History, Geography, Map drawing, Natural History and knowledge of plants. This may not have been common to all missionary schools but the ones that the Company opened or supported taught uniformly the same curricula all over its territory.

What is significant is to know the way levels and grades got fixed in the modern educational system. The Sanskrit Pathshalas and the Maktabs and Madrasahs did have their own gradations but they were found wanting in defining gray areas in their systems. It will require a separate paper to trace the history of fixing school and college grades in the modern system. It will suffice here to remember that it has taken almost two centuries to evolve grades in the educational system and to define the specific goals/ aims commensurate with their individual academic achievements. The concept of awarding degrees and diplomas too has its own history. In brief, today the system of education functions almost parallel to other such establishments as the judiciary, the police or the army. The only thing common between these institutionalized systems is that they are all committed to social upliftment and service.

Let us recall that the Indian or the indigenous system and its European counterpart—the so-called modern education—grew from religious or monastic traditions. Most of the designations that teachers get addressed by are religious in origins. For instance, the terms Pandit ji or Maulavi Saheb are as ecclesiastical in their origins as the designations like Lecturer, Reader or Professor are. Currently the defining terms employed for the levels of education like the Nursery, Kindergarten, Primary, Secondary, Higher Education etc. have their individual histories because each one of them has evolved over a period of time. However, they have nothing to do with religions. For instance, Professor R. H. Tawney was the first person in 1928 to define secondary education. Until then it may have existed but it was not regarded as the link between elementary and higher education.

Earlier, there were only two stages of education in the UK—the elementary and higher education, without a secondary stage. Those who wished to go for higher education could prepare either privately or through a system called the Sixth form, available with some Public Schools. It took considerable time before the link between the Elementary/primary and the higher (university) got streamlined in the UK. In India, interestingly, colleges got set up long before universities came into existence in 1858. For Kindergarten the birth of Froebel was necessary; and, for Montessori schools one had to wait for Maria Montessori to be born. If Sadler Commission in 1917 gave India its Intermediate colleges, Mudaliar Commission in1951 gave us higher secondary education of three years duration with 11-year multi-purpose higher secondary schools. The 10+2+3 was conceived by 1986 policy of education. All this recounting of the events must have helped the reader to realize that education; its system and content, continue to change for a variety of reasons—religious, social or political. There is nothing static in education. If it changes for political reasons, it may change with technological reasons also.

Similarly, for adult education programmes the consciousness about the meaningfulness of education was essential. The failure of formal system and the presence of a vast number of illiterates made it obligatory on the part of Government of India and the voluntary agencies to start a Non-Formal system. The parallel of the same at the higher education can be seen in the birth of distance and open learning systems. Additional inputs for the non-formal and the open/distance systems come from the development of technology like the invention of satellites and the computers. We also see a tremendous growth in the birth of numerous institutions with a wide variety of courses. Until a couple of decades back not many heard or felt the need for opening Business Management Institutes. In the recent years, global wars and Space-related engineering courses have helped major technological developments. All this goes to show that as the needs of the society increase, educational system must respond accordingly. Education as a system does not operate in a vacuum. It must remain sensitive to the social vibes and continue responding to them. It must also continuously adapt and adopt ever-newer technologies that are getting invented or developed. The interdependence of society and education as a system is a reality. But even greater reality is that education has a distinct identity. In other words, education is a distinct institutionalized system—identifiable in terms of its goals, levels and types. At times the technology it uses also makes it a definable institution.

PURPOSES—GENERAL/SPECIFIC REQUIREMENTS—SOCIAL/INDIVIDUAL

In this section of the chapter we shall define the specific and general purposes of education as an institution. Although in a way we have covered the outline of the area but here we shall go into details.

Education, as we all know, is a man–making process. Without education there is nothing to distinguish between a human being and an animal except that a human being lacks horns and a tail. The purpose of education the world over is to liberate human beings from the misery of needs—both material and spiritual. To think of either purpose in isolation is to deny education its depth and coverage. The opposite of knowledge is ignorance. Ignorance is equal to darkness. The Gayatri mantra therefore carries the import of giving the intellect more and more light. This light the brain receives is capable of giving salvation from all miseries. It is in this sense Education is a liberating agent. —Sa Vidya Ya Vimuktaye.

Indian education is witness to three phases of educational developments—the ancient, which lasted until the arrival and rule of Muslims around 1000 A.D., the medieval and the modern. What is most interesting about Indian education today is that all the three continue to flourish. The Sanskrit universities are getting a new lease of life, even as the Madrasahs and Maktabs have their firm votaries. The system that gets maximum financial support and clientele is the one that the British introduced in India during their rule. It would be unfair to talk of just one system as though other systems have not contributed to the economic growth and knowledge of this country.

We shall, therefore, go step by step in the historical sense and describe the goals, purposes and the curricula followed in all these three systems. The ancient system defined knowledge as para and apara. While the *para* is higher knowledge (Spiritual in content), it is the *apara*, which is pursued by the majority since it helps one to earn one's livelihood. Even the ancient Indian period should be divided into two parts—the Vedic and the Buddhist. The Vedic period lasted till 600 B.C. and the Buddhist until 100 B.C. Thereafter, we see the revival of Hindu learning until 1000 A.D. when the Muslims arrive with their distinct culture, system of education and curricula. About the ancient system there are so many myths—majority of which is located in ignorance. The relevance of studying the Vedas lies for tracing origins of our knowledge and learning. For instance, for the classical music (Samaveda), for Ayurvedic system (Atharvaveda), for oral mathematics

(Yajurveda), for agricultural sciences, geometry, logarithm, prosody, protection of environment, etc. the (Rgveda). They can be consulted even now with considerable benefit. The Rgveda. 10.71.4 says, "A few do not understand the secret of language even after reading it, and a few others do not realize its reality even after listening but there are some for whom the language presents its true meaning as a fully bedecked beautiful wife reveals herself before her spouse." The best recounting of the curricula at the highest level and the distinction between higher and lower knowledge in ancient India can be found in the following dialogue between Sanat Kumar and Narada. Narada tells Sanat Kumar what he has read thus far, but now he wishes to go beyond it. He says, "Sir, I know the Rigveda, the Yajurveda, the Samaveda, and the Atharvaveda as the fourth legend and ancient lore as the fifth, the Veda of the Vedas (grammar), biology, mathematics, augury, chronology, logic, polity, the science of snake charming, and the fine arts. "This, Sir, I know." The implied meaning is that he now wished to learn something beyond the knowledge books offer—that is *para* vidya. It should be clear to the reader that "Man does not live by bread alone" and therefore, when he is well-fed he wishes to go beyond the material goals in life. The spiritual knowledge is needed then.

Ancient India had all professions—like Medicine, Engineering, Architecture, Law, etc. They maintained a distinction between the learned professions and vocational studies and for each one of them they had evolved a system. (For details see: *Professional Education in Ancient & Medieval India*, by R. P. Singh). The Buddhists developed a monastic system for providing their type of spirituality. This system flourished for about 4-5 centuries and then died out in India.

Medieval education had its own curricula for each stage—the primary and the higher, which in its own sense maintained a distinction between professions and vocations. For instance, the MAKTABS had the priest in the masjid as the teacher who taught the Quran, some arithmetic and knowledge of alphabets. Beyond this stage were professions for which they needed to have separate institutions—the Madrasahs. Even now, Muslims the world over have Madrasahs. Their courses of study have been modified and stand modernized to some extent but they persist with their religious content and the teaching of Islam with all its fundamentalism. I shall merely give a small example of what they teach here. Islam too accepts division between tow types of scholarship. Scholars, according to Islam, are either Ulema-I-akharat who devote their lives to learning and uplifting the Muslim society or the Ulema-I-duniya who employ their knowledge for earning wealth. This is another way of dividing knowledge into higher and lower forms of learning or between the spiritual and the material. Just as the Hindus had designations for their priestly class like Ritvij, Chhandoga, Somini, Udgitha, Gayatrin, Adhavaryu, Brahma, etc the Muslim Ulemas too have their divisions into Imamas, Khatibs, Muhatasibs, Muftis and Qazis. The medieval curriculum of the Madarsah consisted of the following: Tafsir (Exegesis), Hadis (traditions) and Fiqh (Jurisprudence), Grammar, Literature, Logic and Muslim Scholasticism (Kalam).

In the modern system of education the major features of the education remain the same. Even today education must serve society and respond to the needs of its clientele. Today's society is more democratic than it ever was and the so-called common man is gradually becoming the king. The reach of education is no longer restricted to classrooms and mode of its delivery is not limited to face-to-face category. Changes are fast and have forced the teacher to the updating of one's information almost mandatory. Instead of knowledge it is the age of information. The selection of quality information has become the sole concern of modern education. It is not the quantum of information or learning that matters but its relevance and usefulness do.

Today the modern system of education is considered most important and useful education. It is divided into several stages. Each one of the stages can have its own mode of delivery and the curricula. Without going into details how it evolved, the modern system of education in India is almost parallel to the one that obtains in the West. The truth lies with the fact that what pays dividends is also responsible for its popularity.

The modern Indian education is divided into *several stages like pre-primary* (Nursery and Kindergarten), primary, lower secondary, higher secondary and higher education (college and university education). The *other division (equally popular*) lies in its *curricular distinction* like the ITIs, IITs, engineering colleges, medical colleges, etc. Each one of the stages of education has a specific curriculum because the same has been designed and regulated by a specified committee of experts. The third educational *category is in terms of intellectual abilities of children besides their physical capabilities*. For instance, *each type of handicap has its own category and provision. Physically handicapped* are generally treated as part of integrated education but within that also distinct variety of attention is to be paid to different degree of handicaps children suffer from. The goals of education, therefore, differ according to the category one belong. The *visually handicapped* are quite different from the mentally handicapped. Each physical and psychological category demands its own type of attention. In the past couple of decades all societies including the Indian society have come to realize that its normal, well-to-do children alone do not need to be provided with the best of education. Others demand equal, if not more, attention and care. Almost all other categories of children are able to contribute their mite to the development of society. The *last category of the educational division is located in financing education.* We have in India today three categories of educational financing: 1) the government 2) the aided or grants-in- aid system, and 3) self-financing or completely private system, though regulated by both professional and designated bodies like the UGC, AITEC and others including the MHRD.

Each category of children has its distinct requirements and therefore it is no longer difficult to define the purpose of education for each one of them. Efforts are on to include several of the erstwhile categories of handicapped children to be offered education in the ordinary schools along with other normal children. This is done to see that this category does not feel that it is being ignored as social outcaste. In fact, each category gets fitted into the general framework of the societal development. Ever since we have started to move in the direction of becoming a global society, we have our attention riveted on international standards and global quality of life. Educational advancement is no longer a national achievement for the local consumption. Our goods and services have to compete with the best, cheapest and by far the most competitive of economies. Education cannot fail to sustain and better its performance on each score. India's goals of education are evolving to define its educational provision in global terms. For the first time in the history of Free India, we have a combination of Prime Minister and the President, who are both far-sighted and goal-oriented and are focused to making India become world leader in scientific and technological sense. Such achievements are difficult to attain but the goals should be set high. And this is what is currently being done.

We have reached a stage of educational development when we find the latest policy decisions like 1986 the POA and its improved version of 1992 considerably out of step with the global educational developments. We need to have a pro-active system where policy decisions in education must be left to experts to decide with least interference of political parties and their ideologies. We must decide whether or not we are gradually moving towards a global society, and the inspiration for the same should come from the political leadership, because it is not in the hands of educationists, howsoever able and fore-sight gifted to sit on judgment.

MODES AND CHANNELS

Just as the judiciary operates through courts and its various legal functionaries even as the police have for their institutionalized operation such as police stations, jails and an independent machinery and methods of search and law enforcement, and their official cadres, education too as a distinct institution has its schools, colleges and universities and teachers giving it an identity all its own. Before technology came to disturb its even tenor of life, education had a simple structure for its operation. The village teacher symbolized it with his quite demeanor even as the urban teacher left his impact with his quietness and simple dull dress. Until the end of the World War II. the type and variety of schools were very limited. For instance, the formal schools up to primary/middle levels were run either by village panchayats, municipalities or corporations. A few private schools also existed but their clientele was very limited. Each district headquarter was endowed with a government run high school. Teaching in these places was face-to-face. The timing of the school could vary according to the area of its operation. The higher system had only two types of institutions—colleges or the universities. In the past couple of decades however things have started changing. Free India witnessed a massive demand and provision of education. In fact, this demand for education was stimulated by the government agencies too, which went on recounting the benefits of education.

The change did not occur only in the type and variety of educational provision but for the first time ever, the educational system itself started adding categories to its delivery modes. Since we are already familiar with the history of education in India, it is not necessary to go into details. Suffice it to say that in 1947 when India became Free we had by and large three types of financing schools—the government, totally private and grants-in-aid. The structure had three divisions—primary, middle and higher. While the higher had colleges and universities, the primary education could also be totally distinct category for the majority. Majority of students did not or could not go beyond this level. The rest finished at the high school. The Intermediate category added by Calcutta Commission to the secondary education was vocational in character and was intended to prevent students flooding higher education. For once, India started making efforts to vocationalize education. For a vast population like ours the number of vocations was highly limited. Since then efforts have not ceased to make it really effective but largely without success. The Indian universities even now attract very few young people unlike Europe or the

USA. The percentage of Indian youth going to universities and colleges does not exceed 10 per cent of its eligible group, whereas in the West their counterparts are crowding institutions of higher learning in such high percentages as 56 to 65. The situation as it exists today is unsatisfactory on several counts. But this is not the place to go into this aspect of the system.

Today we find that the type of education too is characterized by numerous categories. The number of professions has increased by leaps and bounds. A sudden mushrooming of professional institutions is reflecting this expansion. Financing of education is not a problem anymore, provided market response for its products warrants such a requirement. Alas, what was once a social service has now become a business proposal. Education today has acquired a new persona. The latest sobriquet Education has come to acquire is: *Big Business*.

Considering the variety of alternatives available for both the elites and the masses, the modes of delivery have also got transformed. In this process technology has offered a helping hand. While for the majority face-to-face mode of delivery remains the most used and popular, for a minority we have 'open' schools and 'open' universities. These universities are offering *online*, *e-learning* and the virtual classrooms modes. These modes have become possible only due to technological developments. They obviate the need of hiring regular staffs and building of additional structures. In the on-line teaching, one can now download specific curricular content and get answers from teachers located at distant places if the need be. This mode offers pre-prepared lessons or a whole lot of curricular requirement in capsule form. This mode is free of time constraint and the physical presence of a teacher even as it has the benefit of addressing million of students across all geographical boundaries without finding variations in the classroom instruction. But one has to have a computer, be computer savvy for being a student under these modes. For the virtual classrooms one has to go to a center where arrangements for a regular classroom type of instruction are made. Here the teacher is located at a distance from where he/she is taking his/her classes and he/she addressing simultaneously unlimited number of classes. But one can make arrangements for question and answer sessions. This mode is closest to actual face-to-face formal classroom teaching mode. But virtual classroom mode is expensive and needs huge investments. The same cannot be said of other modes. Therefore, currently numerous private and public institutions have adopted online and e-learning modes. This mode is extremely cost-effective. The traditional universities too continue with their face-to-face and correspondence modes of educational provision.

Open learning mode is becoming increasingly popular because its clientele desires convenience and the open time frame for covering courses of study. Surprisingly, this mode is more popular among those who can afford face-to-face, formal classroom teaching as well, but because of various reasons like time-constraints and professional requirements, students prefer the Open distance mode. *For the first time we have an educational mode, which demands more managerial gifts than academic competence.* With the coming in of 'country-wide classrooms', 'gyan bharati' NCERT's SIET programme, etc., the home television has also got transformed into being an in-house tutor. The easy availability of DVD, computers and their floppies and the discs we find that suddenly there is an explosion in the modes of teaching. For a moment it would appear as though the very existence and the familiar role of an ordinary classroom and its teacher have become totally irrelevant. The latest developments in the delivery systems, for instance, 24-hour curriculum-based countrywide classroom channel in all regional languages can easily be converted into an additional poser to the face-to-face mode. We must remember that at times extra-facilities do not augur well for the existing modes. They can and do become threats and challenges for some. But then this is something that always happens. The steam engine came as a challenge for bullock/horse-driven carriages but soon enough the former received challenges from automobiles and airplanes. But in sum, we find that today all modes of travel exist cheek by jowl. The coming in of a new mode does not necessarily be taken as the death knell for the old. Somehow we have learnt to live with them. Only, these inventions have come to add more classes to society. The same is happening with the coming-in of new gadgetry. Education is getting its own class-division. This division is clearly economic and quality-information driven. In fact, the speed with which knowledge is getting generated has created immense problems for all. The technology-savvy class is reaping benefits from their investment and aptitude. While around 30 per cent of Indian children are still struggling to get into some kind of school and receive some kind of literacy/numeracy, etc., a fraction of Indian children are going through identical courses of study as are being offered in the best of European schools. I suspect no society thus far has succeeded in being fair and just. India is also trying to be both. The hope is that majority of us will eventually get to arrive at our destinations.

CONCLUSION

One of the things that we should remember is that along with the priesthood, education has been the oldest institutions in each and every society. Even the Greeks could not escape having their Oracles and a substantial body of priests and priestesses. The first teacher in the world was a priest.

The next point worth remembering is that every society has taken time to realize that education can be used as a tool for perpetuating its cultural and material achievements.

It has taken time for education to grow into a powerful instrument for socio-economic change. It is only an irony of circumstances that the propagators of education themselves have remained an economically deprived/marginalized lot. A few societies have ever accorded status that teachers in fact really deserve. Part of this deprivation has something to do with the nature of work they indulge in. It takes time to get recognized and by the time some recognition comes one's way-one has already lost interest in it. Concentration and development of ideas makes them insensitive to recognition. Men of ideas have their own levels of satisfaction. Material achievements and development of ideas somehow never seem to agree. This single streak among the teaching community keeps them to remain a class apart. These days numerous prizes get awarded in all countries to mark singular achievements of distinguished teachers. But it is not always that merit gets awarded.

The nature of education is such that it presupposes need before it gets propagated. Need is the basic foundation of an education system. Each society deserves what it gets. A responsive, vibrant educational system requires a positive attitude of the ruling elites. Education is some kind of capital that grows in direct proportion to the investments one makes. Education helps institutionalizing innovations, discoveries and inventions. Without education societies remain both backward and negligible entities.

One must make a clear distinction between being totally deprived of education and being a tribe of unlettered people. Literacy alone does not make societies scientific or advanced. Even the so-called advanced societies are as superstitious and intellectually backward as the aborigines. It is possible for an unlettered nation to be ideationally advanced. For instance, a comparison between the Mohan-jo-daro people and the Vedic populace reveals that while the Vedic people unlike the Mohan-jo-daro people have left no monuments behind, their superiority in ideas and contributions to world culture are unparalleled. One must make a clear distinction between literacy and education. Similarly, one must also make a clear distinction between education being used as a means of economic development and an education as a means of establishing military superiority. The case of North Korea and South Korea can easily be cited in this regard. A military power can be socially backward and economically poor and one that does not have an army to match the former can be economically very powerful.

One must use education as an instrument of socio-economic progress and create conditions for its people to become development–oriented. Modern societies have to leave their baggage of superstitions behind. They should help people to dream of better days and match their dreams with their efforts.

REFERENCES

Basak, N. L. (1974) *History of Vernacular Education in Bengal* (1800-1854), Bharati Bookstall, Calcutta

Carrie Paechter, Margaret Preedy, David Scott & Janet Soler (2001) *Knowledge, Power and Learning*, PCP, London

Chauhan, C. P. S. (2003) *Modern Indian Education*, Kanishka, New Delhi

Oad, L. K. & Singh, R. P. (1975) *Perspectives of Indian Education*, Mehra & Co., Agra

Singh, R. P. (1969) *The Indian Teacher*, National Publishing House, New Delhi

———. (ed) (2001) *Teacher Education in Turmoil*, Sterling, New Delhi

———. (1985) *The Nature of Teaching*, National Publishing House, New Delhi

———. (Ed.)(1997) *Training of Teachers—Looking Ahead*, Neeta, New Delhi

———. (1991) *Professional Education in Ancient and Medieval India*, Arya Book Depot, New Delhi

———. (1987) *Non-Formal Education*, Sterling Publishers, New Delhi

———. (1996) *Future Classrooms in India*, Vikas, New Delhi

Steve Bartlett, Diana Burton &Nick Peim (2001) *Education Studies*, PCP, London

Part 2
Technology in Indian Classrooms

8

Technology in Indian Classroom
Introduction

THE NEW CLASSROOMS—EMERGING SCENARIO

For the first time ever the Indian classrooms are finding it difficult to resist change. The classical image of the teacher—ever so knowledgeable, is currently finding his authority being challenged—and that too in his own domain i.e. both in delivery of content and in the nature and quality of content. At times the teacher comes across a student who happens to be more knowledgeable than he/she. This awkward situation arises because the teacher alone is no longer the most knowledgeable of all beings. The quantum of knowledge is undergoing change and so are the sources of knowledge. The information that was once an exclusive preserve of the teacher is being made available by alternate sources—like the internet or ready to use CDs; and TV broadcast. In certain classrooms teachers feel insecure because of their ignorance or lacuna in their latest information repertoire. This is happening in a few Public Schools where children have access to theses facilities. This is one reason why recently the corporate sector refused to accept B.Eds being churned out of the incompetent system, approved and promoted by the NCTE. In fact at one time the government itself was informed in the Parliament that its own elite schools were unwilling to accept the 'unemployable' B.Eds.

It is no longer possible to prepare a perfect textbook or impart knowledge whose advanced form is not or cannot be made available in no time. Instead of learning in the classrooms where a single teacher could once answer all queries, the present times are witnessing a sudden change. Those who do not teach anywhere and are in fact not even aware how teachers are prepared or selected have come to produce material that undermines the authority of the teacher. The newer concepts like E: Learning; auto-teach/self-learning, virtual universities, countrywide classrooms, digital books and even virtual teachers, etc are no longer unfamiliar terms or ideas. Every passing day we notice the authority of the teacher is being challenged in one form or the other—especially in his all too familiar role of instruction in the classroom. Education is no longer the monopoly of any system—certainly not of the teacher—because the entire game of teaching has undergone change.

In the name of quality assurance we wish to give identical information to all and since it is impossible to ask anyone teacher to be available everywhere, the technology can help in this regard. In that case it is not the classroom but a 'virtual' classroom that could make this possible.

We must also acknowledge that social divide would continue to bother us. Even the advanced countries like the USA or EU have not succeeded in bridging the gap between those who have access to all the alternative sources to classroom teaching. A survey had revealed that in the USA everyone does not have access to telephone, and therefore it is understandable that inequality is inherent in all societies. This should not prevent the Indian system from adopting the best and the most advanced technologies in education. In this connection there is no need to bring in unnecessary debate like the question of basic equality of all or access to education for all.

We must not forget that lakhs of Indian students go abroad every year for higher education. It is now being realized by all that our educational system is fundamentally flawed. It is neither flexible nor forward looking. Yet we continue saying that this system is producing men and women whose caliber is in no way inferior to anyone else's. In this discourse what is being overlooked is the fact that these extraordinary boys and girls have to put in their own efforts into success. A large number of these brilliant products seldom come from within the system. Either they are born extraordinary or their families have put in extra effort to nurture them. The indigenous educational system itself is not very supportive. Our of a few, successes have to be analyzed threadbare to come to some kind of conclusion. Look at the success of Indians in the Silicon Valley but that should not mislead us to believe that the credit for all this goes to our ingenuity or our support. It is largely due to the individual effort and also to the challenges Indians faced in a foreign land where there were not many choices except the one 'either do or die" In a desperate situation like this the success of the few should not make us accept an argument that our educational system has come of age and become competitive.

The pitiable condition in which our system is made to produce world class material is simply unacceptable. Look at the government's own admission year after year that thousands of our schools have no buildings and millions no washrooms (toilets) and where a substantial percentage of teachers never goes to their classes; and, additionally our higher education is marred by the politicization of the educational content and behavior. Therefore for those who cannot afford to send their children abroad and still wish them to succeed or come up to the levels others reach because they are exposed to an academic climate that suits their talents, are matters that need hardly to be overlooked. Analyze why our IITs are so successful and you will know immediately it is largely due to the competitive nature of their admission policies and the challenge their content poses. Additionally, the academic climate that these institutions offer makes for all the glory their products earn. Children from ordinary schools cannot even dream of entering these institutions. Success in this country is not dependent on any single factor—be that economic, political, social, etc.

Therefore it is imperative that we address the problem of providing the best of education with lot of caution and well-planned design.

Let us start with an analysis of classroom instruction. A given class is definable in terms of its level, content, content quality and its relevance for future use. But the most important part of any education is the delivery of the content and the way students learn. It is not possible to standardize learning but it is nowadays possible to homogenize teaching techniques and the delivery of the content. We are all aware that changes occur frequently in the content because of the inherent nature of modern societies and the speed with which they are changing. The older societies were more or less static or they changed slowly. But this cannot be said of our societies any longer. Because our markets are dependent on our likes and dislikes and to suit our tastes and demands, the supply system has also to change. This brings in the role and the speed of earnings; hence of the nature of consumer societies. While a few continue to redefine themselves because of the possibilities they are able to generate for more and quick earning; it is not possible for others to do so. In between the growth of our economies comes into play the major role of scientific and technological development with their impact on education. Society therefore offers education because it finds education to be a tool for survival and progress. Competing with others and being able to maintain its position in the world order, could be an additional fall out. Individuals themselves start bringing in their own goals into this scheme of things. It is not necessary that these goals have universal approval.

The main players in the education system are: (a) individual child, (b) teacher; (c) society through its approved curriculum. It is the expert who divides the entire curriculum of a class into bits and pieces besides fixing the sequence of learning and teaching. The entire process looks simple but its complexity is also equally well-known. No system functions in isolation. Individual nations feel the heat of international competitiveness. This problem of competition brings in varying types of measures nations adopt to remain a step or two ahead of others.

We in India, therefore, must also adopt the best of the measures to remain in step with others; if not exactly ahead of all others.

India must look at the options it now has in the field of teaching, and what is more it needs to do so because we have to remain in contention internationally.

The choice before us is the use of machines in teaching for making the system efficient and economical. Let us now have a look at the history of the use machines in teaching.

TEACHING MACHINES

The main function of Teaching Machines or mechanical devices is to present systematically a programmed sequence of instruction to a student.

The first teaching machines were designed by the American psychologist Sidney Leavitt Pressey in the 1920s to provide immediate feedback for multiple-choice tests. Immediate correction of errors served a teaching function, enabling students to practice test items until their answers were correct.

In 1954 the American behavioral psychologist B. F. Skinner popularized the potential of teaching machines for academic instruction. Skinner held that classroom teachers, responsible for heterogeneous groups of students, could not be expected to provide individualized instruction for each student without assistance from mechanical devices. Teaching machines containing well-programmed sequences could provide step-by-step progress toward carefully defined instructional objectives, with each step depending on mastery of all the prerequisite steps. A good programme in a teaching machine could thus make efficient use of the principle of active responding by providing students with immediate feedback on success or failure.

The early linear teaching machines could not judge the student's response nor, indeed, even determine that the student had responded; they simply presented the correct answer on demand, providing a chance for the student to inspect that feedback before proceeding. Branching teaching machines, using multiple-choice questions, sent students to different next frames, providing either remedial information and a chance to try again, or confirmation of success and the next step in the sequence. Both kinds of machines were so simple in design that they were replaceable by programmed textbooks, offering almost the same control over learner's progress.

The potential of the computer as a teaching machine promises increasing design sophistication. Computers can be programmed to judge student input and to tailor lessons to each individual's level of mastery. In a tutorial mode, computers can present instructional input and require mastery of each step in ways that were not possible in the early machines. The sensitivity of the instructional designer to alternative patterns of student learning is the necessary key to full use of this advance in machine capacity. Simulation—using the machine to model a real situation—enables even greater sophistication, allowing realistic reactions to student input. Well-designed intellectual games can provide patient environments in which to practice important problem-solving skills.

Tomorrow's teachers will have to compete with machines like computers and information-mongering internet. Since the cost of these machines both for transmission of information and the speed for communicating knowledge is going down everyday. The alternative to classroom teaching is beginning to become a reality.

India too has made tremendous progress in this direction. It holds out a promise to offer instruction via machines and the internet and that too of international quality. The future teachers need to sit up and take notice of the challenges that are likely to come in.

Is this not the time when teachers' colleges start incorporating in their teaching methods suitable programmes for imparting instruction in learning a proper use of these machines and the technologies that are readily available today? Time has come when teachers must define their roles and face the reality to admit whether they would like to remain masters of the emerging technologies or would they prefer to accept the humble role of technicians in the classrooms. The digitalized knowledge in the libraries and the convenience of learning at will and at leisure are soon going to pose a challenge which may not be easy to face.

Change being the only constant in the world; are teachers not aware that a change is no longer in the offing, it is already knocking at their door?

Only those who hear the knock are likely to survive and the rest will have to wait until they receive a proper notice of having become irrelevant.

What we present here is addressed to those who are conscious of their obligations and are always wide awake to learn. A teacher not only teaches but is always ready to learn. And we are sure that the learners far outnumber those that have to be made to learn.

9

Countrywide Classrooms—A Teaching Alternative: Stepping into Knowledge Society

"I am convinced that the methods and approach of science have revolutionized human life more than anything else in the long course of history, and have opened the doors and avenues of further and even more radical change, leading up to the very portals of what has long been considered the unknown."

—From the **Discovery of India** by Jawaharlal Nehru

Never before could a student have imagined that some day as and when he/she needed help in learning, it could be made technologically available. The application of technology to classroom transactions has brought about a near revolution unmatched before. India—though a late entrant in its adoption, has succeeded in creating for itself a niche in the field. As we go through the pages down the history of classroom instruction, we learn that India has always valued her illustrious teachers, scholars and the seers. This of course did not mean that all teachers were uniformly knowledgeable or gifted and they were easily approachable. Indeed, to make an outstanding teacher readily available to everyone is beyond human prowess without extra-ingenuity. Knowledgeable teachers down the centuries have continued to command respect. Of them exceptional teachers consistently enjoyed nation's admiration and gratitude. The Vedas mention the attributes that a good teacher ought to possess. Not many attributes have since been added to the Vedic definition. We in India, like the ancient Greeks, have a long tradition of peripatetic teachers. The modern technological revolution demonstrably combines both these qualifications of good teachers i.e. knowledge and mobility, and makes possible the creation of an alternative system, which only a couple of decades back would have sounded imaginary. All this has come to assist student's learning at the pace and time of his/her convenience. It is beside the point that technology has met only a part of students' requirements. Many more spirals of progress have as yet to follow to meet universal needs. Perhaps we should wait for yet another stage in technological development to help us out even better in all areas of our educational concerns.

The present write-up is all about telling the story of the trials and travails of an exciting journey of educational media's presence in the Indian classroom. It would appear as though the tables have turned. For once it is the student who stands enabled to command the presence of classroom as and when required and the later readily acquiesces to such a wish.

We have long left behind the stage when 'the doubts surrounding the practicability of integrating ETV with classroom teaching,' has to be explained. Instead, we have reached the stage wherein we are being forced to listen to the complaints like the one that Philip Travis made on September 1, 1994 about the present day misery of the Westerner, where almost all jobs he used to do once have been taken over by machines—'be they talking machines like PC phones or car machines which run the automobiles, or business where storing and retrieving of relevant information are of considerable essence.' Remarked James S. Kinder (1959), "Television has literally captured the country. Its expansion has been much more dramatic than that of radio or the automobile. It has become an important part of our way of life, so much so that it is difficult to say whether it is a luxury or a necessity."

The world experienced first visual transmission by John Baird way back in 1924. Marconi too had succeeded in starting experimental television. But the BBC on 2nd November 1936 was the first to have begun television service with only 300 television sets. Berlin Olympics too were covered by television. However, during the World War II the service had to remain abandoned. It restarted the television transmission in 1946. Since then it has not looked back. By 1960 the television had bloomed into maturity. This is the time when the rest of the world too realized its potential. Unfortunately, all nations have not been all that lucky as the West or a few in the Asia-Pacific region have been.

In 1956, the General Conference of the UNESCO was held in New Delhi. The Conference recommended that India should start a pilot project as a medium for education and community development. In 1959 during the Nehru-vian era an agreement between the AIR and the UNESCO was signed to start the project on an experimental basis. The then President of India, Dr. Rajendra Prasad, inaugurated it. Thus started the experimental project at UNESCO's encouragement with 'experimentation, training and evaluation' as its defined objectives.

The initial efforts were modest. Indian skies were as yet to open up for satellites to orbit. But the significance and utility of employing Television for instructional purposes had dawned on the mental horizons of India's top leadership. They knew that the key to European rise lay in their classrooms, while Indian backwardness stood explained in their rarity. To begin with, only 21 community centers were started for adult education and social welfare services. Each center had to form a tele-club. This club was expected to promote organized viewing, conduct post-telecast discussions and convey back to the All India Radio the feedback consisting of their reactions. Each club had to have a convener. The telecast was for an hour only and that too only on Tuesdays and Fridays. The programmes were both informative and educative. The format of the programme consisted of talks, plays, ballets, interviews, discussions, music and documentary films, Besides important celebrations festivals like the Republic day, Independence Day, State visits of foreign dignitaries, Holi, Diwali, Id, etc. were also included.

The All-India Radio provided this television service. The television was broadcast from Akashvani. The range of the area covered was anywhere between 15 to 20 km. At its 21 centers some 150 odd persons could watch this program. In the initial stages during 1960-61 a series of social education programmes were broadcast. In fact, as many as 21 programmes were broadcast, covering topics like community health, good manners, traffic and road sense, and the rights and duties of citizens. Another series followed the first one. The nature of the programmes and their impact were evaluated by the National Fundamental Education Center and the Indian Adult Education Association, New Delhi. The findings were fairly positive. The impact had been substantial.

During January-March, 1960 the first step toward offering Educational Television was made by school transmission in New Delhi. The school programmes were beamed for an hour only between 3 and 4 P.M. This programme came in lieu of the community programme in the evening. This programme faced several glitches. There were difficulties in assembling children at the community centers where TV sets had been provided. Still, the results were excitingly encouraging.

The next step in the series of offering classroom teaching through television came with the help of Ford Foundation. The Ford Foundation entered into an agreement with Indian government for launching a regular educational television programme for four years. This was a historic occasion when Delhi's 600 secondary schools received television sets and were able to offer their students instructions through television. The programme was inaugurated on October 23, 1961. Eight ETV programmes of 20 minutes each were telecast every week. These programmes were repeated to benefit such students too who came to school in the second shift. The subjects covered included Physics, Chemistry, Hindi, English, Geography, and current affairs. The timing of the first telecast was 9.25 am to 9.45 am and the same was repeated from 11 am to 11.20 am.

The Agreement also provided for the supply of technical equipment, deputing AIR personnel abroad for training and making available experts from the USA. Initially, some 250 schools that had AC current received the television sets. But the proposal was for all schools in Delhi. As the number of schools with TV sets went up so did the number of students benefiting from the ETV increase. The number of students in science subjects peaked to 36,000 and with English to 96,000.

The interesting part of the programme was its evaluation. Dr. Paul Neurath, a New York City University Professor of Sociology, was invited to evaluate it. This evaluation revealed that the project had been highly beneficial. In fact, an Indian writer (G. C. Awasthy, 1965) found out on the strength of his personal contacts that the results were more encouraging than reported. Indian Radio also claimed that the performance of the students after viewing the programs had improved considerably. Not only had student's interest in science increased but the standard of classroom teaching too went up. Dr. Paul Neurath's evaluation endorsed these findings. "Teachers had found television to be a very useful aid in their teaching of science subjects. The level of learning among students improved since they were able to see on the television screen more and better experiments with greater detail than what teachers could provide in most of the schools. It was found that the interest in science among students also increased.

"Those who had television in schools felt that students would lose something valuable if it were taken away, and those who did not have it wanted it. Schools with television performed fairly better in tests than the schools without television."

Regular ETV started with its inauguration in Delhi on August 15, 1965. The next landmark was reached with the launch of Krishi Darshan programme for the farmers. This programme was run in collaboration with the Institute of Agriculture Research, the Delhi Administration and the Atomic Energy Commission. The roots of the programme were purely indigenous. The results of the programme were extremely encouraging and largely evident.

THE SITE PROJECT

Originally initiated during 1965—the Year of International Cooperation, (when the initiative was taken by the UNESCO), the SITE project took shape in a meeting of the International Committee of UNESCO on Space Communication. This committee eventually recommended after a close examination of the issue in its report that a pilot project might be taken up in India by using SITE (Satellite Instructional Television Experiment). The idea was to help Indian farmers with modern tools and information to overcome problems of food production. Besides mass illiteracy, India suffered from scarcity of food and lack of developmental strategies. The SITE was thus suggested to resolve India's basic problems of mass ignorance and lack of strategies to overcome well-known shortcomings. Mass Media like Television had done wonders in the USA by helping homogenizing a very heterogeneous people and improving the quality of their lives. It was to pay similar dividends to Indians in due course of time.

Smt. Indira Gandhi, the then Prime Minister of India, inaugurated the SITE project on August 1, 1975. The place was Ahmedabad, the hometown of Vikram Sarabhai. It was the dream of Vikram Sarabhai that television be used primarily as a vehicle for education and community development. The TV programmes could be telecast then through a satellite called ATS-6 (Application Technology Satellite), loaned by the National Aeronautics and Space Administration, USA. To begin with, the SITE programmes were related to Education, Agriculture, Health, Family Planning and National Integration. The duration of the telecast was for four hours—out of which, one and a half hours in the morning were devoted to primary education and the remaining two and a half hours to the adults in the evening. Also, the total time was equally divided into three segments for six States in India. This was done in keeping with satellite's capacity for telecasting on video with two audio channels.

The development of the rural community was the real focal point. Keeping this in view, 2,400 direct reception television sets were deployed in different linguistic, cultural and agricultural regions, located in 6 States. These States were Andhra Pradesh, Bihar, Karnataka, Madhya Pradesh, Orissa and Rajasthan. Within these States also the distribution of television sets varied. For instance, in Orissa alone 354 TV sets were installed in 3 districts. These districts were Dhenkanal, Sambalpur and Phulbani. The TV Base Production Center of Doordarshan and Indian Space Research Organization (ISRO) produced ETV programmes. Number of TV programmes for teachers were also telecast alongside a few for students. The programmes for the teachers were largely directed toward the requirements of science teaching. Several organizations such as the ISRO, NCERT, Ministry of Human Resources Development, the E.T. Cells and the universities engaged themselves in conducting evaluative studies on the impact of TV programmes on the rural population. It may interest us to know that the research findings were not only positive but they were found to be extremely relevant and useful. Be that as it may, the ETV had successfully planted its roots in the native soil of one of the most ancient civilizations.

The SITE was not the only medium, which defined the efforts of the government in the field of television transmission. The terrestrial mode was also available. After the SITE the Government took a decision to spread the wings of the programme. The Government of India, therefore, thought of providing TV viewing facility to 40 per cent of the SITE- served villages by setting terrestrial transmitters in the six SITE States. It was now easy for the Doordarshan to take up the SITE continuity programmes in these areas by setting up terrestrial TV transmitters. Samabalpur area in Orissa was selected for the terrestrial transmission of programmes, besides areas in the other SITE-covered 5 States. The programme in Sambalpur envisaged that some 260 TV sets would be installed in the selected areas/ villages within a radius of 40 km from the town. The project was known as 'community viewing scheme.' The system was to be made permanent. The idea was to extend the same facility to more schools in the area.

Today the revolution in the field of IT has made it possible to utilize to the maximum the potential of good teachers. Both enrichment programmes and syllabus-based instruction are currently getting beamed through Vyas channel. Indeed, the presence of 'open' school and 'open' universities system has transformed the entire classroom scenario. India is currently considered one of the superpowers in the field of information technology and one can see its impact all around.

It is against this backdrop that we recount the developmental tale of ETV for the Indian classrooms. In this context it is essential to remember that long before India thought of introducing ETV, 'non-commercial broadcasting' was already being used in several countries to reduce educational inequalities that existed for varying reasons. Non-commercial broadcasting is of two types: (a) community education television, and b) television supplementing formal education and offering non-formal academic education. The genesis of the non-commercial broadcasting can be traced back to the extension programmes directed toward farmers and health workers. The idea then was not to teach them any given courses of study but to help them learn new techniques and acquire relevant information for greater efficiency in their respective fields. For instance, farmers were offered help and given necessary information for raising better crops, better animals, better fruit trees, management of homes efficiently, etc. The health workers received lessons in rearing children hygienically, taking care of the family nutrition, and maintenance of cleanliness in the neighborhood, etc. This is how the foundation for instructional television had once been laid. What is now called Educational Television was initially known as Instructional Television. The usefulness of television gave birth to its manifold transformations. Its utility as a potent means of offering syllabus-based education was commandeered for its ability to reach out to people living across difficult terrain and inaccessible geographical areas. It was discovered pretty early in the day that syllabus based ETV could be used:

1. To improve the quality of existing educational services and to provide teaching materials that is not easily accessible to students,
2. To assist in curriculum reform, and
3. To give in-service teacher training.

Anthony W. Bates once made out a case for direct teaching through television and radio. The arguments have since proved their validity.

1. To expand the range of the school system, enabling pupils who would otherwise have had no formal schooling beyond a certain age to continue schooling. In such circumstances the government aims to provide education for all children in the relevant age groups in principle, but lacks the facilities for all such pupils. In this situation, lessons based on the standard national curriculum are relayed by television or radio to areas where there are no adequate conventional school facilities.
2. To improve the quality of instruction in places where there are schools, but due to the low level of education of teachers or their lack of other suitable resources, such as books, the quality of instruction is poor. Once again, programmes based on an existing national curriculum are transmitted, but in this case to conventional schools; and
3. To reform the national school curriculum in such a way that both the subject matter (content) and the method of teaching are radically changed, with television playing the central, direct

teaching role. Television is, in this situation, both the medium and catalyst for reform.

It is during this time that enrichment ETV got its definition, role and functions stated in definitive terms. The attributes of these programs are:

1. They do not deal directly with the syllabi of schools or colleges, instead provide a broad perspective on the enrichment of formal education,
2. Students view them irrespective of their own subjects of study since these programs are not syllabus-based and have their aims greatly diffused.
3. They rarely relate to specialized topics, instead they help in enriching the existing knowledge, provided they are used selectively.

Individual countries made their own choices in this regard. While most of the Western countries opted for the enrichment programme broadcast approach, others like China and (even Japan to some extent) went straight for using this medium for syllabus-based teaching for the benefit of those for whom it was not easy to provide classrooms. Recounted above are some of the reasons why in the developed countries enrichment programmes have scored heavily over the curricular programmes. Interestingly, while the advanced countries were well on their way to developing their instructional strategies and innovating classroom and out-of-classroom practices besides furnishing models for others to follow, India too showed an inclination to follow their suit. New educational terminology was in the formative stage of which 'Enrichment ETV' was one such defined component. In the early eighties enrichment ETV was conceived and introduced as something akin to "the styles of general broadcasts in the documentary and current affairs fields." These programmes, stated an expert, " tended to be loosely structured and tried to make use of the characteristics of general broadcasting that motivate and hold the viewer's attention." India followed its modified model. It followed its homegrown lecture-cum-demonstration model. It is immaterial which model one followed or a strategy one evolved, the crucial point was to make a choice of the approach that appealed to one's audience.

One might as well consider couple of additional points at this stage. For example, is ETV a mass medium? Perhaps, not. The number of viewers may be large but it lacks heterogeneity. Both the programmes and the audience share similar interests. Being a part of multi-media and for its cost-effectiveness, the ETV may have grown into a popular mode but a reference to some of its earlier successes and the reasons thereof in advanced countries may not be out of place here. It is unwise to look at this instructional-cum-entertainment medium without recounting the convergence of several disciplines that helped in promoting it. Extensive sociological researches in America have established that "the aggregate flow of reiterated formulae, formats and reutilizations 'cultivates' the social environment almost as farming cultivates the natural environment." In fact, because of the 'pervasiveness of television, characteristic images of the world become the most familiar aspects of the shared cultural environment within which minds are fertilized and nurtured'. Such is the power of the new media—an input from psychologists reveals that even toddlers are seen stringing sentences together to sing commercial jingles and older children incorporating into their attitudes and behaviors what they see or hear on the television.

Mass illiteracy, poverty and lack of general awareness about sources of information regarding almost all aspects of human development have forced majority of Indians to live in the dark ages. Knowledge and information provided through Television and Video enable them to improve their quality of life. This was the basis on which the enrichment programme was initially launched and also pursued. Since then several changes have taken place. While enrichment and general awareness among masses continue to constitute an important objective, the educational uses of the medium have ever since become hard to ignore. The provision of syllabus-based instruction in the virtual classrooms and E-learning are the two eventual goals that higher learning needs at this point of time to achieve. The CEC has to outgrow its past accomplishments. To remain competitive in the WTO regime, ever-newer strategies need to be evolved and goals set.

10

The International Scenario: The ETV—The World Experience

"So the reason ought to rule, having the ability and foresight to act for the whole, and the spirit ought to obey and support it. And this concord between them is effected as we said by a combination of intellectual and physical training, which tunes up the reason by intellectual training and tones down the crudeness of natural high spirits by harmony and rhythm."

—Plato's *Republic*

We recount here some of the stories of Educational Television (ETV) programmes outside India. The first one in the list is from Italy.

(a) It's Never Too Late

In Italy, from 1958, RAI attempted, to cope with the shortage of secondary schools by creating the Centro di Telescuola, which transmitted regular schedules of lessons, complete with course guides, to emergency classrooms where children were placed under the supervision of monitors. This initiative developed further in 1960 to create the famous series 'It's Never Too Late,' which used the same techniques with adults to help combat illiteracy. This series at one time claimed 1.5 million viewers, and 55,000 regular students. In examination pass rates between 75 and 84 per cent were recorded. (Hancock 1977)

(b) Sex Education

Effective television programmes can be produced by means of participatory approach as well. 'Living and Growing '(Grampian Television) in the USA is a widely applauded attempt to introduce sex education to children on the edge of puberty. Before the series was made, Grampian organized an extensive range of meetings with educational administrators, teachers, clergymen and parents. A second round of meetings included the showing and evaluation of pilot programmes. The television company justified this exceptional level of consultation because of the sensitive nature of the topic. And no doubt, the series has continued ever since. (Groombridge 1972).

(c) Knowledge Network

In 1980 Knowledge Network was established in British Columbia province of Canada. This is a provincial authority for educational communication, meant to act primarily as an agent for the various organizations in the province. It is thus available to any of the regional community colleges, schools, universities, institutes and other public agencies that wish to make and distribute television programmes.

Knowledge Network has the only educational channel on British Columbia cable systems and can, in this way, access more than 80 per cent of the provincial population, in addition to the narrowband cable network, which links three universities, five teaching hospitals, the British Columbia Institute of Technology and the Law Courts. This two-way broadband cable system enables material generation in any of the studios on each campus to be communicated directly to any other part of the broadband network.

The amount of time available as a result of a whole channel being devoted to education, and the comparatively low production budget, leads to a unique production style. For instance, a programme may be two hours in length and consist of several segments. A university lecturer may talk directly into the camera for ten minutes or so and then introduce all or part of a 'brought-in program.' This may be followed by a studio discussion between two or three guest experts. There may then be a break while students can phone in questions and have them answered on the screen.

Knowledge Network is a serious attempt to provide educational institutions with a centralized production and distribution system, covering a whole province. It gives some pointers to the opportunities and difficulties likely to be faced by educational institutions in other countries as a result of the introduction of cable and satellite systems. (Bates 1984)

(D) The Open University (UK)

Harold Wilson, the then leader of the Labour Party in Great Britain, first suggested the idea of Open University in 1963. He also presented an outline of a plan for starting a "University of the Air." He declared that 'we ought to have an educational system, which would make use of TV, Radio and Correspondence Courses'. While some people laughed at the proposal, the Labour Party in the UK included it as part of their national agenda. Plans were made well in advance and the first Open University in Britain took birth in 1970. It received a warm welcome all around and in the first year itself it received 40,000 applications out of which only 25,000 alone could be selected. The first courses were offered in the areas of Social Sciences, Arts, Natural Sciences and Mathematics. The first course was beamed duly on January 1, 1971. Since then the university has not looked back.

Students have to study at home but arrangements are made for interpersonal meetings among students and teachers. The material developed is self- explanatory. In these programmes conventional universities too co-operate. Students receive grades (1 grade = 10 hrs. a week) and get regular assessment reports. BBC does the production and broadcast of the Programme through a specially created section for educational broadcast purposes. Arrangements have also been made for research and feedback. It is recognized that research and feedback are essential components of any new venture. The Open University is no exception.

It might sound strange to some that in Britain too the cases of missed opportunities for education have always been plenty. Therefore, it is no surprise that the Open Systems found favour with a certain class of people. Of course, over a period of time the acceptability of the open systems has gone up tremendously. In fact, the U.K. Model has several lessons for India. These lessons are:

(i) The development of advanced, multi-media distance teaching methods

(ii) The introduction of degree courses for home-based students without formal educational qualifications

(iii) A comprehensive continuing education programme to meet the training and technical updating needs of industry, commerce, the professions and individuals.

(E) Media-based Continuing Education (USA)

American ETV/ITV experience dates back to the good old days when in 1931 the University of Iowa's department of Electrical Engineering displayed at the state fair an elementary closed—circuit television demonstration. On September 10, 1931, the university applied to the Federal Radio Commission for construction permit. They received it on January 8, 1932 and on January 25, 1933 the new Station, W9XK, in Iowa City, joined the facilities of the university's AM radio station, WSUI, to transmit its formal 'sight and sound' programme. During the next 7 years,

W9XK broadcast some 389 ETV programmes, including ' Elementary Art', 'Home Planning', 'Introduction to Astronomy', and 'First Aid' series.

By 1940, a number of TV stations, operated by large companies, such as a public service. On April 30, 1941, the FCC adopted rules to permit limited commercial operations, and the first grant for regular TV operation was issued in June 1941. By November, 8-TV stations had made the transition from experimental to commercial authorizations. Pioneer viewers with TV receivers in their homes enthusiastically responded to the broadcast.

When the USA entered the World War II, this 'miracle' was on the threshold, " revolutionizing the material aspects of civilizations... TV was destined to provide greater knowledge to larger numbers of people."

When the war ended in 1945, the expanding interest in television as an instructional medium influenced educators to such an extent that they began to consider the advisability of ETV reservations as early as 1944. Since then ETV has not looked back. In fact, since then the USA has almost 100 per cent homes that have TV sets and TV viewing has reached almost a saturation point. Currently, a debate is on whether ETV is purely business or a social service. No definitive answers seem to be forthcoming in this regard.

The Open University in the USA has been paying particular attention to the rapid advance of the Association for Media-based Continuing Education (AMCEE). It has assembled a formidable array of video-centered distance learning courses. Twenty-two universities were involved in the early eighties, offering video recordings of lecture courses in engineering, economics and management. Such materials can be studied at home or at work, and they are entirely up-to-date. AMCEE courses are particularly attractive to the participating academic institutions because they involve little interference with normal teaching—standard lectures are recorded in a lecture theatre at low cost. They attract clients and their employers because they involve fewer expenses than conventional retraining courses (no travel or subsistence allowance) and less disruption (no ego threat to the individual student, studying on his own at convenient times). AMCEE says that where a conventional lecture is ephemeral and restricted in audience, even a straight recording of the same lecture can be reconsidered, modified and/or incorporated in other material. (Moss 1983)

(f) Television University

China's Television University (1979) started with the clear objective to provide distance education, keeping in view the economic, demographic and geographic conditions of the country. Undergraduate degree courses began to be offered in subjects such as mathematics, physics, chemistry, civil and chemical engineering, arts, social science, English, Chinese literature, and industrial management.

The Central Broadcasting and Television University (usually called the Central China Television—CCTU) started preparing courses in 1978 and was launched the following year. The Beijing Television College (now connected to CCTU as the Beijing Broadcasting and Television University) opened as early as 1960. It's teaching was through television, correspondence material and face-to-face instruction. The establishment of the CCTU was the first attempt in China to set up a national multi-medium, distance education institution. CCTU is a central body, responsible for course design and material preparation but there are Local Television Universities (LTUs) too, one under each of the Municipal or Provincial Education Bureaus, which are responsible for the registration and organization of students.

The courses presented to registered students of the university are at the undergraduate level, though it is involved, along with the Education Department of the Chinese Central Television (CCTV), in some 'open broadcasting' aimed at other levels, for example, the evening course on English. The degrees are intended to be comparable to those awarded by conventional three-year colleges. A central coordinating system exists within the Ministry of Education, which lays down the syllabi and monitors standards for all universities and colleges. Entrance requirements are a special entrance examination, testing the capability of the student to cope with CCTU courses.

Television provides the basic mode of instruction, consisting largely of lectures, written out on a black (green) board, as would be found in conventional universities. Although programmes are pre-recorded prior to transmission, little use is made of pre-prepared material, and lecturers often write and explain what they need as they proceed. A 'lecture' typically goes on for 50 minutes and it is in doubles with 5-15 minutes break. The programme mirrors the lectures delivered at conventional universities in china in length and style.

The print component of the teaching package is largely made up of conventional textbooks. These books can be bought in the shops of national retailers—Xinhua Shu Dian. Some books have been produced on a trial basis by the CCTU for their courses. The others are the same as in the conventional universities. All courses are supported by printed supplementary material. This material acts as the guide to the course, containing the objective, a review of content, and assignments (not used to assess students). The original idea was that this material was to guide the tutors but it is now also sent to students. In view of the great pressure on television and its limitations (in both production and transmission), the university recognized the need to develop its use of print as the main medium of instruction.

Courses are designed in outline by a group of teachers, including some from other universities. A course team then draws up a detailed plan for the whole course and individual programmes. This plan has to have the seal of approval of the television director, especially of the production team. Thereafter it goes to academic section for approval of the academic administration. In a way the entire control is vested with the academics. The television staff is responsible for the production of the programme alone.

Television programmes are viewed by registered students, in groups at their places of work. A clear policy on the level and nature of student support has evolved over a period of time. The policy formulation lies with the central authorities. Therefore, the central policy covers television studios, directors, television sets, print, tutors, equipment and classrooms. It is the pass rates of the students that surprise. The rate is as high as 80-85 per cent.

(g) Aram in his book, referred to earlier, has listed some of the success stories in some other countries. In this book the first story to get recounted is from the USA. We do not need researchers to discover that no one likes to view a dull program, more so the youth. The first successful programme developed (1969) in the "USA was titled ' Sesame Street'. The main aim of the programme was to 'use popular television techniques to promote intellectual and cultural growth of pre-scholars, particularly the disadvantaged ones". The real intention was to reduce gaps in information on the class lines. This delightful programme, aimed to reach out children in the 3 to 5 age group and being fun-filled and highly informative, continues without interruption till this day. It may not have succeeded in addressing its target audiences alone since it is being viewed as much by the better class children as by the deprived ones. In conclusion it has succeeded in reaching out to its targeted audience.

(h) The next success story comes from El Salvador of a project initiated in 1968, which offered a unique opportunity to the world to witness the introduction of television into the school system. Here the television was conceived to be an integral part of school system, unlike other countries where it was made to play a role outside its boundary. The ETV here was a component of national school reform, embracing school curriculum revision, teacher training and the new concepts of supervision and student evaluation. The research on the programme yielded following conclusions:

1. The ETV can and does reduce the dropout rate.
2. It does contribute to learning.
3. It did have an equalizing aspect to it. Earlier policy decisions had benefited the urban schools more than the rural ones, the rich as compared to the poor.
4. Not only did it establish that television has the power to shatter established atmosphere, it impacted positively student-teacher relationship in terms of interaction.
5. And lastly, cost-wise it is both economical and efficient.

(i) The third story of success in the series comes from Japan, which offers a model worth emulating. The NHK (Japan Broadcasting Corporation) by 1983 had already entered 90 per cent of Japanese primary schools. It is the only country in the world, which offers an example of extraordinary investment in public service application of television. In 1985 it was estimated that Japan was using 2.2 billion U.S. dollars worth revenue to support a wide range of telecommunication services of which television constituted the largest component. Being a homogeneous society, in a way its near universal use in the classroom can be understood.

ATHABASCA UNIVERSITY CANADA

The conception as well as the birth of this university is as eventful as the courses it offers are meaningful and welcome. The early years witnessed the coming of age of the baby-boom generation, free speech movement in Berkeley and emergence of student power, a sudden consciousness of environment resources, the Vietnam War and rejection of traditional societal values by the younger generations. All these factors combined to bring about a profound change in the demand and character of universities. Students came in droves to seek admission in the universities, and instead of the traditional subjects like sciences and engineering, the demand arose for Humanities and Social Sciences. The student enrolment in Canada increased at an unprecedented scale. For a population of 2 million souls, the province of Alberta already had 3 universities. To ease the pressure on the university of Alberta, the provincial Government in its January 1970 white paper on post-secondary education policy, announced the establishment of a fourth university to be named Athabasca University, located in St. Albert, a suburb of Edmonton.

Interestingly, though the primary purpose of setting up Athabasca University was to accommodate the greatly increased admission pressure, the government authorized through its Order in Council 'to explore and to institute, if deemed necessary, new procedures in curriculum organization and instruction at the undergrade level. Clearly, the mandate itself was to be innovative. Though it took nearly two more years to come up because of change in government and politics, the new Athabasca University was established in December 1972 as an experimental institution. Initially, it started as a pilot project. With a tiny staff of 35 Faculty, the early years were characterized by frenetic activity.

Since then numerous major strategies in teaching and planning have been evolved. The fact that the Canadians followed the British Open University model, ensured its remaining in step with contemporary changes all around.

11

The Indian Initiative

"In social science there is certainly as yet no corpus of interdependent propositions, tested against reality, that can match the formidable body of systematic discovery in natural science."

—J. A. Barnes: Who should know what? Penguin Books, 1979.

Before embarking on the Satellite Instructional Experiment (SITE), the Government of India went into overdrive to see that it succeeded. Until then their experience had been limited to terrestrial broadcast. The Government already knew about the potential of the Satellite. Therefore, for the development and designing of the programme, due and detailed attention was paid. N. Bhaskara Rao made the intention of the Government abundantly clear, "The SITE programme should be an action-research effort, involving immediate development of target group profiles, deciding what sort of messages in what combination and context are to be delivered, and then actually producing these program. Television hardware capable of diffusing all over country by itself does not ensure a television service. Unless adequate priority and planned attention are given to producing target audience-oriented, educational/motivational/informational software from now onwards, the whole satellite experiment would become irrelevant. Feasibility and problems involved in producing such programmes need to be explored and studied. Finally, audience research and evaluation of the programme are an integral part of any broadcasting system. To avoid costly mistakes, research and evaluation should be given high priority alongside hardware and software development."

In accordance with a clause in the Memorandum of Understanding, social scientists were appointed by the Indian Space Agency to conduct relevant evaluative studies. Bella Mody (1978) even laid down the social science evaluation plan in the following phases:

Phase 1 (Pre-SITE) Context evaluation, Audience profiles, and Needs assessment.

Phase 2 (Pre-SITE) In-put evaluation, pre-testing of proto-type programmes

Phase 3 (During SITE) Progress evaluation, Programme feedback from the audience, and In-depth studies on specific programmes

Phase 4 (Pre-during and Post SITE) Global-evaluation, Sample surveys of adults, experimental studies of students.

India entered the modern age of Educational Technology by beaming a first time ever television programme for a year in 1975-76. In theory the preparation was outstanding. The outreach of the programme was 2400 villages, scattered throughout the country. It was called Satellite Instructional Television Experiment. The programme was telecast in four different languages, using different channels. The programme was largely viewed in the open air and mostly on community television sets, using low-cost dish antennas.

The broadcast consisted of four varieties of programmes:

1. National news;
2. Community education programmes consisting of news, information and guidance about agriculture, family planning, health and nutrition;
3. For teachers and their students;
4. And lastly, entertainment carrying social messages.

Community education programmes broadcast by SITE are believed to have succeeded because they had 'raised hopes of the target audience by highlighting their needs'. Hopes turned into disappointment, as means for fulfilling the heightened requirements were found to be unavailable. Only in the case of schoolteachers and students, some support in the form of practical handbooks, teachers' manuals, posters, etc. was forthcoming. The SITE programmes helped perceptibly to accelerate the process of change in education, agriculture, health and family planning.

Of the several projects started initially, the Kheda Communications Project of the Development and Educational Communication Unit under the Indian Space Research Organization (ISRO) in 1975, aimed mainly at development in agriculture, health and animal husbandry, besides touching upon social issues like untouchability and the status of women. These programmes addressed local problems in local dialect. It enjoyed credibility because for the first time in Indian history two-way channels were opened between the people and their administrators.

Bella Mody, writing for Educational Broadcasting International (September 1978) under the caption Lessons from the Indian Satellite Experiment gave her assessment in the following terms:

The first month's average evening audience of 300 settled down to about 100 per cent, and the audience was composed of about 30 per cent children, 50 per cent men and 20 per cent women.

The socio-economic status of the audience was found to be inversely related to TV viewing. The small farmers and labourers formed the largest chunk of the attendees.

Twice as many men as women were reported viewing.

TV viewing did not either replace or decrease the use of other media.

There was significant gain in the knowledge about preventive medicines. Also, the respondents favoured small family norms.

The other gains related to the knowledge of improved varieties of animal breeds and political events but there was no gain regarding farming practices. Those who gained the most were the lower castes, women, economically poor and illiterates.

It had no impact on school attendance or enrolment. The TV school teachers were excited about the programme being an aid to teaching but declared the going into details boring and uninteresting.

Yet another study found that programmes on familiar themes were generally more interesting and useful, but recitation of long poems or details of a topic failed to retain their interest.

The NCERT in its evaluative study found that dubbing of programmes made them uninteresting because dubbed programmes lacked synchronization of sound with the lips. A few programmes appeared too overcrowded with details. The NCERT group suggested that problem—approach would make programmes more likeable.

Several other groups also made their own evaluative studies. Their findings seldom agreed. But by and large the programme received the seal of general approval.

PREPARATION FOR INSAT UTILIZATION

The Sixth Five-Year Plan showed commitment to a linear expansion of education, reaching out to nearly 18 million of students in the age group of 6 to 14 and to reforming as well as restructuring the teaching- learning process to make it relevant to the national development. The Plan admitted, for the first time ever, that linear expansion was not possible within the existing system. The reason was simple. Firstly, the resources were not available. Secondly, even if they were it was not possible to build schools in the same proportion and speed as the growth in the number of school-going children. It was not the question of school buildings alone. The trained teachers also could not be made available in the same ratio, as was the need. Similar constraints applied to the procuring of school equipments as they did to the production of books and other services and support systems. All these factors and constraints did not however influence the pilot project directly. Therefore, it was found doubly imperative to call on resources of educational technology and the use of two INSAT that were to be made available during the Sixth Plan period.

The Ministry, therefore initiated action to prepare plans for the early operation of INSAT as early as in July 1979. The help and involvement of Space Application Center, Ahmedabad ware solicited in the utilization and expansion of TV programmes for the purpose. A document had, therefore, to be prepared for discussion, containing an outline of the human, institutional, technical and financial resources. In response to the Ministry's request, the Space Application Center prepared a document, outlining the INSAT capability, the ground segment requirements for the TV, the possible hardware for satellite utilization and an approach for developmental communication.

On 30th January, 1980, a meeting was convened to discuss the background paper and all connected issues, involved in the utilization of the satellite for the radio and television programmes. The Secretary, Education, presided over the meeting with representatives of the NCERT, SAC, AIR, Doordarshan, Planning Commission, the UGC and the Ministry of Education being present. The decision was that urgent steps were needed for planning software in connection with INSAT utilization by all other user, Ministries in general and the Ministry of Education in particular.

The Ministry of Information and Broadcasting set up a Working Group under the chairmanship of its Secretary on February 2, 1980. The term of reference was to draw up a plan for INSAT utilization. The group consisted of members from different organizations and the user Ministries. The report submitted in September 1980 recommended that each concerned user Ministry should develop its own individual programme production capabilities. The Ministry of Education took a decision that concerned educational authorities would be entrusted with programme production, and indicated to the Working Group that the major educational objective of the satellite television would be to promote alternative approaches to education for children, youth and adults. The thrust of the specific programme, according to the Report of the Study Group (1981) on INSAT

Television Utilization for Education and Development, would be to emphasize direct teaching, moving away from curriculum-oriented approach and aim at reduction of load in the classroom and improvement of the quality of programmes through training of manpower.

The Ministry of Education and Culture set up yet another group in May, 1980, to look into the entire utilization problems of the satellite for education. The Report of the National Workshop on Educational Broadcasting (1981) touched upon all aspects of the problem. It developed a policy for the use of TV for educational purposes. It identified approaches, priorities, target audiences and themes for programmes besides considering matters concerning infrastructure and manpower requirements. It also talked about the key areas for training and developed a few training courses in detail, suggesting in the end guidelines for further action. In short, the Ministry had made up its mind and provided a framework for the subordinate systems to work accordingly.

In April 1980, the UNESCO Regional Office for education in Asia and Oceania invited the Government of India to participate in their Asian Programme of Educational Innovation for Development (APEID) in the area of educational technology. All the participating countries were expected to organize National Workshops for the purpose. The Indian Ministry of Education in collaboration with UNESCO convened a National Workshop on Educational Broadcasting from December 1 to 6, 1980, at New Delhi. The basic reference document for the National Workshop was the Draft Guidelines on Educational Broadcasting. These guidelines were prepared by a Technical Working Group meeting on Educational Broadcasting, organized by the UNESCO in, 1979, in Malaysia. The Indian Workshop of 1980 received all the necessary co-operation and assistance from the NCERT, AIR and Doordarshan.

The National Workshop (1980) with 41 participants, representing various media and educational interests, took some crucial decisions with a bearing on utilization of satellite in the future. Until then the INSAT had not been parked in the orbit. The relevant portions of the Workshop for our purpose are:

1. The Workshop laid stress on the point that satellite would not be used for syllabus-oriented courses of study. This recommendation was highlighted as the new priority. Recognizing the new priority role for not adopting syllabus-oriented courses of study for non-formal systems, the Working Group advised to as much as possible, avoid dependence on the intermediaries.

2. Stressing team mode of production, making planning and production of educational broadcasts, a collaborative effort of the producers, educators and social scientists.
3. Calling for an integration of educational broadcasting within the total educational system and for the purpose of recommending autonomy to the Center for Educational Technology at the national level and creating autonomous Institutes of Educational Technology at State levels, which will be necessary professional and technical structures for Educational Broadcasting.
4. Laying more emphasis on research and evaluation as an essential component of Educational Broadcasting at all stages of planning, production and utilization.
5. Evolving a national framework, spelling out the priorities, broad areas, themes and objectives of the programmes.
6. Entrusting the responsibility of planning, production and use of educational broadcasting to the educational authority.
7. Urging immediate action on all fronts to prepare for the utilization of the television facilities under INSAT.

The Report of the National Workshop stated that the participants, representing a cross-section of varied professional background and interest, were able "to take a collective look at the problem of Educational Broadcasting, share their individual and group experiences and to pool their expertise in the creation of new approaches toward making broadcasting a meaningful educational tool the free script of which can cut across the barriers of syllabi, age groups, and traditional restrictive educational philosophies. It is to be hoped that the liberal thinking that permeated the Workshop will be instrumental in shaping Educational Broadcasting and pave the way for exciting educational horizon behind and beyond INSAT."

Around the same time the Ministry of Education and Culture also received a Report of Hardware and Manpower as well as of Software Group. The Ministry examined these documents very closely. What Professor Humayun Kabir had once stated about educational broadcasting was equally applicable to television that when made efficacious and meaningful, it can "serve as an instrument of human progress and a condition for human survival."

It may be recorded here that the greatest contribution of SITE was to prove that television is one medium that can enlighten people, living in all parts of country, be that part remote, inaccessible, backward, rural or highly developed and urban. The cost-effectiveness of the medium was its yet another plus point. The result was the nation's motivation to put a satellite of its own in the orbit.

HIGHER EDUCATION TV

Early in February, 1982, it was indicated that (a) when INSAT facilities become operational, it would be possible to ensure transmission time of one hour every day in the afternoon on programme for higher education; (b) the Ministry of Information and Broadcasting would also assist in identifying the hardware, needed by the centers, which would be responsible for the production of programmes, and (c) the priorities for various categories of programmes of higher education, their content, the language, and other details would be examined by a group, who would also advise on the production of original programs. Unfortunately, the INSAT-IA, which was launched on April 21, 1982, became non-operational soon after. Its replacement—INSAT-IB was expected to be available in December 1983. The higher education broadcasts had, therefore, to wait for sometime more.

In the meanwhile, besides the proposal from the Jamia Millia Islamia, which had already been accepted, the University Grants Commission received a few more proposals for the establishment of Centers of Mass Communication and Educational Technology viz. from the universities of Pune, Roorkee, Osmania and Gujarat.

It is against this background, the University Grants Commission set up in June, 1982, a Working Group to advise it on the selection, working and development and various aspects of the establishment of the Centers of Mass Communication and Educational Technology in the universities. It was agreed at a meeting that the desirability of using all the media for educational purposes and encouraging research in communication, as also the need for popularizing the culture of amateur production, might be referred to a Task Force.

In pursuance of the recommendation of the Working Group, a Task Force, on the setting up of Centers of Mass Communication and Educational Technology, was appointed on 25 August, 1982. An eight-member Task Force was set up accordingly.

The Task Force was expected to make recommendations on:

A. The structure of three or four Mass Communication Centers, which should function at the inter-university level and would be conceived as to avoid duplication.

(i) Nature and size of the Centers, and their programme of activities i.e. training, education and research; and the production of software, using various media such as film television, radio, print and other systems. One Center may specialize in one activity.

(ii) Type of software to be produced for restructured undergraduate education and extension services, after taking into account material already available from other resources.

(iii) Type of essential software to be imported so that the centers or university libraries move into the modern system of learning.

(iv) The Nature of the Centers and their locations, keeping in view the facilities already available.

(v) And, examination of the nature of the minimum hardware necessary and the cost involved, particularly for spreading the culture of amateur film/television/radio production in the universities.

After seven sittings and a couple of visits to a few universities, it made the following recommendations:

1. In view of past experience with educational media, where equipment or hardware played a dominant role, the Task Force recommended that equipment, along with space, manpower and budget should be designed and planned as a system on the basis of specific educational objectives. Educational goals should be the main thrust, and equipment and manpower designed to suit those objectives.
2. Designing and planning may be done by positive questions in the order:
    - What (educational goal)
    - For whom (target audience)
    - By whom (manpower and its training)
    - By what objectives (specific)
    - With what facilities (equipment, space, budget)
    - With what organization set up and administrative framework.
3. The Task Force recommended that instead of too many goals, efforts of each University Center should be to concentrate on one or two only where there is need and expertise. Too many goals tend to diffuse rather than strengthen a programme.

4. The members of the Task Force recognized the paucity of educational software in the country and recommended that educational institutes and universities toward production of software, its duplication and use as self- learning material as well as for transmission through broadcasting network, should make a major drive.
5. The Task Force recommended that the preparation of software should not be scattered in all subject areas for different target groups but be confined to producing material in the *form of a series* in a few universities.
6. From the point of view of simplicity of production, the Task Force recommended that the medium of slides, audio and videotapes would be the best for universities to undertake. The committee did not recommend the setting up of 16 mm facilities.
7. The Task Force recommended that the vital question of manpower for software development, maintenance and operation of hardware and the management of media would be carefully planned and executed because of its inter-disciplinary nature. The positions should not become just another avenue of promotion for the existing staff.
8. Because of the various tasks involved in the area of Educational Technology (information, planning, training, production, duplication, playback and utilization) the Task Force recommended that few centers would be set up initially to perform these different tasks. Instead of concentrating efforts on one center, the Task Force recommended setting up of several centers, to cast the net wider and to decentralize production and utilization.
9. The Task Force recommended setting up of three levels of centers in the universities—a national center for media in universities (for all tasks), few Educational Media Centers (essentially for production and utilization) and several Audio Video Centers (for orientation, utilization and electronic journalism), all to be coordinated centrally by the UGC Secretariat on Educational Technology. The budget, space, manpower and equipment required by each center depend on the educational tasks assigned to each one of them.
10. The Task Force recommended that a secretariat at the UGC level be set up to give impetus to this activity in its various centers. A Joint Secretary sould head it.

11. The Task Force considered the two cultures—that of feature films and educational media, divergent from each other. Introduction of the glamorous feature film culture in a university set up would tend to obliterate the vital growth of educational media. The Task Force observed that Jamia Millia Islamia University had been attempting to build a huge infrastructure of equipment (film and video) and staff strength of over 300 persons for its Mass Communication Center. It also belt that this Center in its present plans would become more of a combination of FTII, Pune and Indian Institute of Mass Communication (IIMC), New Delhi. Whether another Institute in addition to the two already in existence, was needed at present was to be considered by UGC. However, the Task Force recommended that Jamia Millia Islamia could not and should not be the model for Educational Media growth in universities even if it did take up work of producing educational software at some stage.
12. Setting up of Media Centers, the Task Force felt, could be done in phases. In the short term Plan, two universities could have the Educational Media Center while three would be given AVC. The National Center for Educational Media could be taken up in the VIIth Plan. In the meanwhile, the Task Force recommended that an Expert Group should be formed by the UGC Secretariat on Educational Technology to advise on the training of Manpower, purchases of equipment and programme production for INSAT.
13. The Task Force recognized the lack of Manpower in the field of Educational Media in the country. Each center could identify two or three persons in this area to be trained. It was recommended that UGC secretariat should work out details of their training programme within the country with the help of the Expert Group.
14. The production for INSAT should be contracted out by the UGC Secretariat for series of programmes, which could be produced on 16 mm film and video tape. The Task Force feet that there was a wealth of talent amongst young film makers in the country today, and recommended the use of this talent towards educational production on contract basis, the way it was done by Films Division, Bombay but by keeping strict control over the script. This approach was not by the Task Force as contradictory to its earlier recommendation that no in-house facilities be set up for 16 mm film production in universities. It

is quite conceivable that many filmmakers would turn into video producers as video facilities developed in the private sector.

15. After examining the potential the Task Force recommended setting up of two EMCs and three AVCs at the initial stage. That is to provide:

    - Poona University with EMC& AVC
    - Gujarat University with EMC
    - Osmania University with AVC
    - Roorkee University with AVC

16. —To—22 recommendations of the Task Force dealt with budget to be provided for each EMC/AVC.

This Task Force Report became the basis for future organization and arrangement of ETV. It may be recalled here that even before INSAT IA was sent to the orbit, the ETV was operational. The INSAT transmissions changed only the area-of classroom coverage and the outreach of the medium. Exactly what was happening on the ground came out a little more clearly in the review meetings of the Standing Committee of UGC-INSAT programmes. As already noted, the in-house reviews and evaluation of the INSAT programme were mandatory because in the very beginning it was made an integral part of the running of the project. Even otherwise the government believed in taking stock of the project work on the ground.

The UGC Project titled 'Countrywide Classroom' started on August 15, 1984. It had gone on air after a fairly prolonged spadework in advance. Interestingly, though the programme ran in the project mode but it was no longer a project.

It may also be noted here that this was one time when everyone seemed to be interested in education in general and higher education in particular. The Government was keen about knowing the reality in advance. Before the Government came out with its Educational Policy 1986, it took a step hitherto never taken before.

A Programme of Action was developed, which was adopted soon after by the Government of India. The Indian Parliament put its seal of approval immediately after National Policy on Education 1986 was framed (Later on in 1992 its revised version also came). This document carried the recommendations of the 23 Task Forces, appointed for developing Programmes of Action in each specified area. For the first time in India's history of education did a Government think of an educational action in practical terms and looked determined to implement a Policy it had adopted.

This was a departure from the past practices. The ground realities that demanded immediate action were duly paid attention. Consequently, improvements were suggested and presented to the Government for getting accepted.

In the following few paragraphs we present a picture, which emerged from the data collected by the Government. The quote though lengthy is both meaningful and relevant. Both the data and contemporary images stand frozen in time and space:

The Indian Scene (1986)

"Several efforts have been made in the past to use technological aids for improving the quality of education. Audio-visual units and film libraries were set up at the center and in the States for promoting the use of educational films and projection/non-projection aids. Educational Technology cells were also established in 21 States/UTs in a phased manner and a center for Educational Technology was also set up in the National Council of Educational Research and Training (NCERT) to stimulate the use of television and other instructional media. School radio broadcasts have been in vogue for more than 40 years. AIR's Education Programme Production Units, set up in 44 years of the network's 88 stations, produce radio programmes for primary and secondary schools, presently broadcast by 74 radio stations. General enrichment programmes of 15-20 minutes duration are relayed 3-5 school days per week for primary school children. Programmes for secondary school students are broadcast for 15-20 minutes on all school days. AIR stations at Delhi, Jalandhar, Hyderabad and all stations of Tamil Nadu also broadcast programs all 5-7 days a week, in support of the correspondence courses conducted by universities. 3-4 adult-education programmes are broadcast per week by 14 AIR radio stations.

"4 Doordarshan Kendras are presently telecasting curriculum-based school TV programs for secondary school students. Educational Television (ETV) of the general enrichment for children in the age group 5-11 years is engaged in telecast in the respective regional languages through satellites, six days a week, in the 6 INSAT States. Its programmes are being relayed by all transmitters in the 4 other Hindi-speaking States. A 1-hour general enrichment programme for University/College students is also being telecast daily. 2,000 VHF and 2,000 Direct Reception Sets (DRS) have been provided for community viewing in selected village clusters in the 6 INSAT States, installed mostly in the village schools. Under the 'INSAT for Education' project, launched in 1982, State Institutes of Educational Technology (SIETs) are being set up in the States of Andhra Pradesh,

Bihar, Gujarat, Maharashtra, Orissa and Uttar Pradesh A Central Institute of Educational Technology (CIET) has been established in the NCERT, with 100 per cent Central assistance, to generate educational software for children. Audio-Visual Research Centers (AVRCs) and Educational Media Research Centers (EMRCs) have also been set up in 6 Universities to prepare educational TV programmes for University/College students. Some facilities for TV programs production have also been developed in the Technical Teacher Training Institutions (TTTIs).

"Video Technology has also appeared on the educational horizon. The Electronic Trade and Technology Development Corporation (ET & T) has formulated a "TELETEACH" project to prepare educational software on videotapes. VCRs and viewing equipment would be provided in about 600 viewing centers to be established this year. The Ministry has also identified certain subject areas in which educational software would be developed by ET & T."

The Ministry of Human Resources Development's foray into this domain was relatively tentative as it was trying to take note of the changing technological revolution all around itself. The responses of the Government departments are herdly prompt because they have to take into consideration several factors. This is even true in a democracy.

What one ought to take a particular note is that the document in question relates to details of Computer Literacy and Studies in Schools (CLASS) project with TELETEACH in view and expresses satisfaction with computers entering the portals of school education. It mentions that some 750 secondary/higher secondary schools have received micro-computers to familiarize their students and teachers with the range of computer applications and their potential as a learning medium. It is against this background that one ought to see the targets fixed for the VII th Plan.

TARGETS ARISING AS AN APPLICATION OF THE NPE AND PRIORITY MEASURES TAKEN DURING THE VIITH PLAN

The following tasks have emerged from the NPE statements but only a few of them have a bearing on higher education

1. Expand the TV and Radio transmission network to:
   - (i) Provide minimum ETV and Radio programme coverage for identified target groups in all major language zones by 1990
   - (ii) Establish Radio stations in teaching universities/colleges during the VII th Plan.

(iii) Provide a dedicated educational TV channel by 1991-92

(iv) Create a dedicated satellite system for educational needs in the long-term.

2. Expansion of in-house programme-production facilities to generate adequate capacity in major Indian languages by 1990, and in other languages during the VIIIth Plan;
3. Development of facilities organizations for production, duplication and dissemination of curricular support material, using non-broadcast method/graphic teaching—aids during the VIIth Plan;
4. Development of training programmes/facilities for manpower generation for educational media during the VIIth Plan;
5. Provide Radio receivers in all primary/elementary schools during the VIIth Plan and TV sets to all schools by 1990;
6. Eliminating elements of consumerism, violence, etc. from media programmes without delay
7. Expand existing/initiate new programmes for computer – manpower Development during the VIIth Plan to reach desired levels by 1995;
8. Integration of computer-education modules in professional and general education courses at first-degree level and provision of computer facilities in these institutions—initiated in the VIIth Plan to be completed by 1995;
9 Introduction of elective computer-science courses at higher–secondary level during the VIIth Plan;
10. Extension of computer literacy programmes to cover all higher–secondary schools by 1991, secondary schools by 1995, and elementary schools in the long-term;
11. Establish a national Center of Educational Information during the VIIth Plan;
12. Mount a technology mission to develop a reliable source of electric supply to schools in remote areas by 1990.

The Programme of Action had envisaged strategies for ETV as well and thought of basic pre-requisites for success in achieving targets. It may be recalled here that the National Policy 1986 had emphasized, "In order to avoid structural dualism, modern educational technology should reach out to the most distant areas and the most deprived sections of beneficiaries simultaneously with the areas of comparative affluence and ready availability." This approach will, it was thought, intrinsically favour the broadcast methods, with their inherent advantages of greater reach, convenience of management and cost-effectiveness; over the non-broadcast methods largely oriented to individual learning. Because it is not possible to broadcast programmes for every class through radio or television, coordinated with their teaching schedules, it was felt that these media could be utilized effectively only for enrichment of the process, and to transmit course material for distance education.

However, the extent to which media like radio and television can be used in the service of education is, *inter alia*, dependent on the transmission capability of the network as well as the manner in which competing claims on broadcast time are sought to be rationalized. Large-scale use of Audio and Video programmes in broadcast and non-broadcast modes would also generate enormous demand for qualified manpower to work in educational media set-ups. In the long run, it would be desirable and probably essential that maintenance structures be decentralized, both organizationally and geographically, and local 'technician-entrepreneurs' could be trained for such responsibilities. Education requires media support, which is related to the curriculum as well as enrichment. Curricula-based education also requires materials, which the teacher can draw upon in the course of this teaching. This can be provided in the form of charts, slides, transparencies, etc. Video technology offers considerable potential for improving the quality of education especially at higher levels.

It was correctly envisaged that educational technology offered the means to reach large numbers in remote and inaccessible areas and remove disparities in educational facilities available to the disadvantaged and provide individualized instruction to learners, conveniently suited to their needs and pace of learning. However, all technologies require supporting infrastructure, and unless that infrastructure, such as trained manpower, competent and willing teachers, school buildings, etc., exists, no technology—direct or distance—is likely to succeed. One of the major hurdles in the way of introducing modern technology in the rural hinterland is availability of assured electricity supply. Providing a source of assured electricity is a pre-requisite for using technological options in the service of education, and needs to be addressed on priority. To a large extent, the ETV has achieved its major goals. This reality stands duly endorsed.

THE UGC AND THE SATELLITE COMMUNICATION

The entry of UGC in ETV had become possible both because of Policy level support and also because of India's growing technological muscle.

One without the other would have ended up in realizing nothing. The Project Report (May 1993) in its Foreword acknowledged, "With great foresight, the University Grants Commission recognized both the emerging needs and the potential of satellite communication, almost a decade ago. The result was the Countrywide Classroom, using the INSAT system and the network to broadcast "enrichment" programmes at the undergraduate level. Beginning (in 1984) with a preponderance of imported programmes, Countrywide Classroom programme today has indigenous content of 80-90 per cent, with selected foreign programmes included by choice rather than necessity."

The growing activities related to the Countrywide Classroom and various new initiatives (such as non-broadcast "video-lectures" for the complete undergraduate curriculum in 15 subjects, programs/transmissions in Hindi, a series for pre-school children, marketing of video-cassettes etc.) necessitated a proper institutional structure. The UGC, therefore, decided to set up a separate Registered Society (under Section 12 ccc of the UGC Act) so that this body might provide focus and thrust to the media activities, while ensuring flexibility and permitting new initiatives to emerge. The Consortium for Educational Communications (CEC) was therefore set up: first, in the transition phase, as a project of the Nuclear Science Center, which now exists as a separate Society."

THE CONSORTIUM OF EDUCATIONAL COMMUNICATIONS

The CEC document recorded details of the functions of the newly set up Society. It stated that the "CEC is envisaged as the nodal agency for UGC's media activities. However, by design, it will remain small in terms of core staff, and will have only limited technical facilities. It will do most of its work through the EMRCs and AVRCs, established in various universities (at that time 15) spread throughout the country. This decentralized mode of working requires considerable managerial innovation, but has been adopted by choice."

It was largely because of this reason that a formal Memorandum of Understanding was signed to "guide the functioning of the tri-partite relationship between the UGC, CEC and the concerned university." Earlier on too there existed a Memorandum of Understanding between the UGC and the university that ran the programme. The only difference now was that the CEC also became a party. Thus the CEC came into being on August 15, 1993.

The objectives of the CEC were broadly defined as:

The CEC will address the educational needs of the country through the use various media of communication. Its objectives will include:

1. Production of educational programmes (especially video and audio) and related support material, and the setting up of appropriate facilities for this. The CEC itself will have only very limited in-house programme production facilities—mainly capsuling/packaging programmes.
2. Dissemination of educational programmes, through both the broadcast and non-broadcast modes; procuring programmes, preparing integrated capsules for broadcast for this purpose.
3. Co-ordination and liaison with the broadcasting/distribution agencies (including especially Doordarshan and AIR) for dissemination of educational programs.
4. Close coordination, facilitation, overall guidance and direction to the activities of the Media Centers set up by the UGC in various universities.
5. Research related to optimizing the effectiveness of the programmes, through studies aimed at assessing audience needs, formative research including pre-testing of programmes, feedback from the audience, impact studies, and basic research related to distance learning and the use of media.
6. Programme utilization through organized viewing groups, clubs or other related activities that help to ensure the maximum utilization of the educational material.
7. Networking and collaborating with other agencies—in India and abroad- in the field of educational communication, including especially IGNOU.
8. Providing a forum for the active involvement of academic and other scholars in the creation of appropriate educational programmes, organizing Workshops, exchange of scholars (within the country and with other countries) etc. to this end.
9. Training and overall human resource development in the field of educational communication, especially for the staff and academics associated with the Media Centers.
10. Creation of Central library and database of educational programmes, with appropriate facilities/mechanisms for storage, duplication, access and distribution.
11. Vigorous marketing of the educational programmes/material, both in the country and abroad, undertaking necessary publicity

efforts for this purpose; generation of revenue from sales of programmes, and sponsorships, etc.

12. Studying, promoting and experimenting with new techniques/ technology that will increase the reach and/or effectiveness of educational communication, conducting studies and taking necessary initiatives toward the evolution of dedicated educational TV/radio channels.
13. General advice and assistance to UGC on matters related to educational communication, or on any other matter referred to the CEC by the UGC.

The CEC Project Report document also defined the nature of activities to be taken up in the future. The same were supposed to be undertaken in two phases.

FUTURE ACTIVITIES

Phase 1

6.1 Under the first phase of activities, the Consortium will strengthen the infrastructure of the existing Media Centers and also set up some more centers as envisaged by the Commission (UGC) in its sub-plan in the VIII Five –Year Plan. The ultimate aim would be to have a wide and well-distributed national network, so that the production may reflect the diverse culture of the country and be able to meet the complex requirement.

Phase II

6.2 During the second phase, the Consortium would undertake other activities such as production of programmes in Hindi and other regional languages and production of programmes on issues of national importance like environment, ecology, etc.

Technology Experiment

6.3 The Consortium would undertake experimentation in the use of state of the art technologies in educational media and distance education. This would include experiments in talkback via satellite and in creating library network (in collaboration with INLIBNET) of video programs.

Preparation of Video-Material

6.4 The production of educational video material (in non-broadcast, video cassette form) in various subjects would be further strengthened by the Consortium.

Marketing

6.5. A major effort would be made in the area of marketing, so as to ensure wider dissemination of the educational material and also to generate revenues. The Consortium would give a major thrust to this activity immediately.

Research

6.6 Research would be a continuing and important part of the Consortium's activities. The primary focus would be on research activities so as to enhance the relevance, effectiveness and quality of the programmes. Some basic research on media and distance education would also be initiated.

UGC COUNTRYWIDE CLASSROOM STATUS REPORT & VII PLAN PROJECTIONS (1990-1995)

The countrywide programme had been operational for the past couple of years. During this time on the basis of both Feedback Reports and continuous monitoring, a few shortcomings of the programme had become evident. It would appear as though the cause for some of these shortcomings lay in infrastructure and inadequate knowledge of ground reality. Following is the text of the relevant document:

"Although the quality of programmes, produced by the various centers has reached a satisfactory level, there is much to be desired in terms of quality and depths of the programmes. An effort in this direction is being made through special effort programs, in the preparation of which considerable effort, money and time is spent. For example, some of the special effort programmes are in the field of remote sensing, environmental degradation—an Indian perspective, Buddhist art and architecture etc.

1. There is need for research at the formative stage in order to improve not only the content but the overall presentation of the programme as well.
2. There is a need to develop a competent pool of academics that will contribute towards making quality programmes on a regular basis.
3. Audience research was initially limited only to analysis of feedback letters from viewers. However, with the appointment of Research Scientists in most centers' formative research and field surveys are now being undertaken (The post of Research Officer (Reader) was created for the EMRCs in 1984 itself. But at the CEC the Research Scientist could come only in the year

1987. This rank was common to all centers including UGC's SAT Cell/CEC/EMRC/& AVRC.)

4. A comprehensive study on the programme needs of the undergrads was also suggested.
5. Media centers are a new concept in the context of the traditional university set up. They are the electronic counterparts of publishing houses for the print medium. Since they operate in production-cum-transmission mode, a work culture different from the traditional university work culture is necessary. This leads to conflict; hence a considerable degree of autonomy for the centers within the university set up is absolutely essential.
6. For similar reasons as above, an appreciation of the importance of the CWCR experiment at the level of the UGC is crucial for success. This means a strong organizational support from the UGC in terms of finances for the day-to-day functioning of the centers, purchase of equipment, and providing additional manpower needs."

NEED FOR PLANNING

1. Any project with substantial input of manpower and money needs careful planning. While CWCR is executed in a project mode, it is not a project. It is a sensible experiment in the field of education, which requires planning not only of material inputs but also of ideas. This planning must be done on a short term and a long -term basis.
2. Short-term planning and monitoring of the CWCR is done at the Coordinators' meetings, which are held after about six weeks at various media centers. These are meant to be business meetings and are held with the specific purpose of overall coordination for the CWCR programme. Normally the agenda for these meetings consists of:

    1. Preview of programmes followed by discussion and critical evaluation of each programme, keeping in view the credo of the CWCR.
    2. Review and discussion on the feedback reports from all the media centers.
    3. Review and discussion on the production done at each media center in various subjects.
    4. Transmission schedules.

5. Production plans—short term (i.e. for the next three months as well as long term (i.e. for one calendar year, as in the case of special effort programmes)
6. Operational problems,
7. Financial and administrative matters
8. Plans for organizing workshops, seminars and training camps
9. Discussion of innovative ideas, new experiments, and findings in educational TV programs.
10. Technical matters such as purchase of new equipment in place of old equipment and maintenance of old equipment.

In brief, the status report and future Plan projections for the next Plan period did convey the message it carried. The note explained the working of the CWCR and difficulties it faced. Considering that this was a new programme with which no one was familiar. It started functioning fairly scientifically (but very slowly), taking everyone concerned into confidence.

12

The Media Centres—EMRCs and the AVRCs: Activating Support Systems

"O Men! Send the pigeon as messenger who is trained with your word. We enjoin upon you to send desirable knowledge through pigeons while having destroyed obstacles in the way. Send messages across the globe. Let the pigeon covering the path with message increasing our strength proceed onwards. Those who train the pigeon take its benefit, know the properties of fire, communicate the word of news and a message all round, attain fame among learned men. Who would dare conquer them?"

—*Atharvaveda* VI. 28.1&2

The history of CWCR is the history of Media Centers. History being a chronological record of cause and effect relationships, denies possibilities that freaks would prosper. Institutions need favourable conditions and hospitable environs to survive and grow. They must continuously adapt and change and respond to the challenges that come their way. Institutions like ideas have to take birth with some purpose at hand and must also function in a social milieu. The moment they become irresponsive, they die a natural death. Institutional histories reflect an evolutionary process and must discover their place in a socio-cultural context. In the present case, advances in technology, coupled with the vision of academic luminaries, eventually gave birth to a project called Countywide Classroom. If CWCR as an institution was unimaginable without the Media Centers, the Media Centers would be rendered virtually irrelevant without CWCR. Lord Reith some 75 years ago defined the purpose of the BBC as "to inform, to entertain and to educate." The new Director-General of the BBC in 1999 declared that he visualized its main role as that of the educator. "I want to bring education into the frontline," declared the new D.G. because 21st century was ushering in "Information Age." He further added, "I believe passionately that if Britain is to be a major player in Information Age, something must be done to help the large number of people, who have until now gained so little from our educational system. If we can deliver our vision, the BBC will have made a major contribution to the learning society."

India too stands on the threshold of becoming a learning society and its educational system too hasn't been either open-heartedly generous or welcoming to all. Parallels apart, the reality is that only those societies shall remain competitive in the coming days that have an educational edge over others. It is no longer the question of this or that type of provision. Each system has to contribute and lend a helping hand in seeing that every single individual functions in top gear in a world, which concedes nothing without a fight.

There is enough evidence on the ground to give us hope that India too can be one of the best educational systems in the world. Ideally, each system must combine autonomy with accountability. Nothing much happens in closed or regimented societies and neither such societies ever succeed in reaching the levels free societies easily attain. Fortunately, we are and intend remaining a free society.

This brief diversion is regarded necessary to point out that the Media Centers under UGC's patronage were conceived with almost identical goals as Lord Reith once put it for BBC. Like Britain we too are a functioning democracy. These Centers were conceived in India, as Professor Humayun Kabir once said, Television has the potential, "to serve as an instrument of human progress and become a condition for human survival." To cite the National Workshop Report (1980), the idea was " to integrate educational broadcasting within the total broadcasting and for the purpose of recommending autonomy to the Center for Educational Technology at State levels, which will be necessarily professional and technical structures for Educational broadcasting."

As we look back, exactly two decades after, we can see that the entry of the UGC into the field of ETV had become possible largely because of Policy level support and India's growing technological muscle. The Project Report (1993) acknowledged this reality in its Foreword," With great foresight, the UGC recognized both the emerging needs and the potential of satellite communication, almost a decade ago. The result was the Countrywide Classroom, using the INSAT system and the network to broadcast 'enrichment' programmes at the undergraduate level."

The growing activities of the CWCR resulted in the constitution of the Consortium for Educational Communication, set up first as a project of the Nuclear Science Center and later as an independent Society within the UGC Act. The CEC in fact is designed to fructify the dreams the founding fathers and early pioneers had dreamt. The list may be long but one name among the visionaries will always remain emblazoned in the history of CWCR is that of Vikram Sarabhai. It is he who had foreseen things to come and desired that India too should join the bandwagon the advanced countries had set in motion.

Currently, the CEC coordinates, facilitates, directs and guides the activities of Media Centers.

It will be interesting to look into the records to see how the UGC initially created an infrastructure for receiving its programmes in the targeted areas and among its pre-determined audience. The programme required numerous arrangements, including the broadcaster, the project staff and the audience, besides television sets, which the majority of its viewers did not possess. This arrangement was dependent largely on the electricity, which was endemically in short supply. The UGC had to change the timing of its programmes several times due to lack of infrastructure. It had initially to develop programmes, make plans and schemes and distribute the TV sets according to a well-thought out plan. It had also to develop objective criteria for functioning and adhere to it accordingly.

To become operational, the first task was to identify colleges that qualified for receiving TV sets. The size of the town and location of the colleges constituted the major criterion.

The second criterion included colleges located in Hill States like Himachal, J&K, North -East, etc. other than the States' capital towns.

The third criterion was that the colleges be located in the 6 INSAT-covered areas.

But the circular when issued (March 4, 1985) carried the information that the grants for buying TV sets were restricted to 4000/rupees only; and that too was a matching grant. The colleges had to shell out the rest of the money. The circular also mentioned that the schedule of the telecast would now be regularly published in the AIU Newsletter, besides Nations' leading Newspapers. The CEC took time to bring out its own Newsletter. It would appear that CEC brought out its first Newsletter some time in 1996, but in the year 2000, it was discontinued. It had started again after a gap of around 3 years. But all the while when the CEC had no Newsletter of its own, the CEC news was carried either in AIU Newsletter or the Gyandarshan outfit of IGNOU.

To continue with our story until June 1989, the UGC had not assured the EMRCs/AVRCs that the grants-in-aid to them would be regular. Circular-number D.O. No. F. 1-1/89 (J.S.-MC) dated June 6, 1989 informed the Media Centers that "The Commission has now agreed to continue the financial assistance to the various EMRCs/AVRCs for the CWCR programme beyond 31.3.1990 for the entire VIII –Plan. (It carried a condition as well.) However, the Commission strongly belts that the centers should take up steps to produce programmes up to the assigned targets i.e. 8/10 programmes per month for each EMRC and ¾ programmes per month for the AVRC. Because of our failure to reach the targets, the Commission had to repeat the programmes (either imported or prepared by freelance artists). This aspects needs to be carefully considered and solutions to be worked out."

THE LETTER STATED FURTHER

"The Commission would need a fresh MoU between the universities and the Commission for the continuation of the arrangements during VIII th Plan period. A copy of the same is enclosed."

The letter clarified,"As far as the revised pay scales for staff working in Media Centers are concerned, Government of India's 4th Pay Commission's scales shall be applicable along with the State/University's employees. For the Group A posts a separate communication shall follow."

The enclosed MoU carried details of the role, functions and duties of the EMRC/AVRC. The document stated:

1. Prepare and forward periodical programme plan to the UGC.
2. Produce and send the assigned target of programmes to the UGC/ INSAT Cell i.e. on average 8 to 10 programmes per month by the EMRC and 3 to 4 by AVRC.
3. Conduct appropriate research and send the same to the UGC.
4. Propose and organize training programmes to expose the academic staff to the electronic media and to motivate them to experiment with software making.
5. Ensure that all rules were scrupulously followed.
6. Ensure that no advertising type publicity is given to commercial or other organizational products.
7. Send monthly and other reports to the UGC on a prescribed form only.
8. Insure that the Coordinator/Director, or in rare case his nominee, attends the UGC-convened meetings.
9. Take active steps to encourage the participation of academics, practitioners and other resource persons in the programmes and compensate them at the UGC rates.
10. Prepare and forward budgets to the UGC through proper channels.

11. Ensure that all UGC guidelines are scrupulously followed in respect of facility utilization, programme production, equipment purchases and budgetary provisions.
12. Advise and guide official agencies in matters relating to the use of educational/instructional technology.
13. Ensure that all programmes are tested for accuracy and academic soundness.

Having seen how the Media Centers came into being and shaped up over a period it is time we knew about each Media Center. (The EMRC stands for Educational Media Research Center; MCRC = Mass Communication Research Center; and AVRC = Audio Media Research Center.) The Media Centers are as follows:

- AVRC, Osmania University, Hyderabad-500-007 (1983)
- AVRC, University of Roorkee, Roorkee-247-667 (1983)
- AVRC, College of Engineering, Anna University, Chennai 600-025 (1985)
- AVRC, Kashmir University, Srinagar (1986)
- AVRC, Punjabi University, Patiala (1988)
- AVRC, Manipur University, Canchipur, Imphal (1989)
- AVRC. Ahilyabai Vishwavidyalaya, A. B. Road, Bhanwarkuan, Indore (1993)

The EMRCs in the year 1996 were as follows:

1. EMRC, Gujarat University, Ahmedabad-380-009 (1983)
2. EMRC, St. Xavier's College, Calcutta 700-017 (1986)
3. EMRC, CIEFL, Hyderabad, 500-007 (1983)
4. MCRC, Jamia Millia Islamia, New Delhi 110025 (1983)
5. EMRC, Jai Narain Vyas University, Jodhpur 342-001 (1985)
6. EMRC, Madurai Kamraj University, Palkalai Nagar, Madurai-625-021 (1986)
7. EMRC, University of Poona, Pune 411007 (1983)

In the post-1996 period three more Media Centers came up:

1. AVRC, Manasgotri, Mysore 570-006,
2. AVRC, Dr. Harisingh Gour University, Sagar 470-003,
3. AVRC, Department of Mass Communication, University of Calicut, Kerala—673-635.

Before the 24 hr. Vyas Channel became operational, the CEC had undertaken several steps to see that their efforts did not end up in fiasco. In the dying years of the last century several committee reports were added to the list of surveys, which explained whether or not the CEC could be entrusted with the responsibility of a 24-hour channel like the one, which is currently functioning. These Reports include a 1998 survey of 150 students, 5 from each II P.G. & III U.G. of all departments) who were given a questionnaire on the following aspects:

- ❖ Academic inputs,
- ❖ Personality development,
- ❖ Teaching—Learning process, and
- ❖ Infrastructure.

The results of the survey make them interesting reading. The students felt that although the content of course appeared adequate, they would rather have practical and application-oriented subjects than the ones that were purely theoretical. A Committee in 1997 presented three scenarios for ETV in India:

The first scenario recommended that to continue with things as they were on DD-1 and in order to enable this educational programme to become commercially viable, it was imperative to have better quality programmes and considerably improved publicity than was currently being undertaken.

The second alternative was that if Prasar Bharati did not view the ETV as Public Broadcasting on DD-1, then it should give the MHRD 3-4 years time to set up an independent ETV Corporation and telecast its own programme through satellite and terrestrial system;

The last option was that in case the Prasar Bharati could not wait any longer and decided to off-load ETV, and MHRD decided to accept the Satellite Channel (which in its wisdom it should not accept), then it should be prepared to find the costs already worked out. The MHRD was expected to realize that they would have a delivery technology, which its vast but not rich audience was incapable of accessing it.

The 24-higher education channel was thus the culmination of initial efforts and plenty of planning that had already gone into for its eventual arrival. And come it did, and that too with a bang and flourish having put India in the comity of developed nations in the initial years of present century.

The 71st Coordination Committee Meeting held on 22nd January, 2004, brought to focus CEC's past achievements and a statement of its future goals. The participants were informed that a recent survey had revealed student viewers' preference for 25-30 minute video lectures. In future, the CEC proposed to develop subject-based programmes. These programmes should be based on the model syllabus of UGC. The CEC had already moved in that direction and number of programmes in different subject areas were already available. It was however suggested that necessary material for fillers and breaks might also be made. For once the CEC was focused and had plans to help out its target audience in the area where the help was needed the most.

The CEC has a highly developed system to get its programmes evaluated by external experts. For example, the University Grants Commission's model curriculum-based lessons in Political Science and Economics have already been evaluated. The same method Media Centers too are supposed to follow to get their programmes externally evaluated. The idea is that subject–based programs be so developed that full courseware, containing a lecture as granule, series of lectures as unit, and series of units as modules and finally series of modules as courseware could be developed. The content experts in all subjects should develop an identical approach in this regard. Camera focus may be effectively projected and manipulated. Rare simulations may be effectively projected. The scheme stipulated that granule should have introduction of courseware/ module/units and should end up with recapitulation and with at least two questions to be responded by the viewers.

In future the CEC intends to have a quality control (Q.C.) put in place and at the Media Center level Q.C. certification was imperative for each UVL to carry such a certification in future. It was made mandatory to get a Production Detail Report (PD) prepared and sent to the CEC for approval first. If one followed these steps everything else would fall in place and an all round improvement in the programs was bound to follow. The distance between the goals and the ground reality were thus being bridged.

It would appear that the earlier demand for change in the Credo currently stood at least partially fulfilled.

13

Packaging Knowledge—Quality in Quantity: Developing Insights

"O teacher! You are celebrated for knowledge. May I bring forth sweetness and wisdom? May I ask you to give me sweetness with good understanding in my life? I approach you; bestow upon me knowledge, splendor and vigor."
—*Atharvaveda* IX. 14

Since Time immemorial advancements in knowledge have originated either in human ingenuity or curiosity. Like food gathering, information gathering too is innate and instinctive. One of the major functions of education is to offer select information in appropriate dosages. The higher one goes, the greater is the selectivity in quality and quantity of information, mode and time of its delivery. As one grows, select information gradually crystallizes into knowledge, which in turn transforms itself into wisdom the moment one is able to coalesce all bits of knowledge through insight. Development of insight is the highest goal of life. It is a rare individual who is able to achieve it. Few teachers succeed in helping one achieve it. But that rarely prevents individuals against moving in the direction. R. M. Hutchins dreamt in the early 1950's of transforming the USA into a Learning Society. When the Americans did not approach anywhere near their goal, they came out in 1980's with a document called The Nation At Risk. Nearly all societies imagine that one day they too will join the ranks of being a Learning Society or a Knowledge Society. Logically, therefore achieving this dream is worth any effort.

The first reference to differentiating between learning and wisdom in the Indian context is traceable to the Chhandogya Upanishad. Here we see Narada, a great scholar of his time, approaching Sanat Kumar with a request that he be made knowledgeable. The teacher asks him about his existing level of knowledge. Narada says," Sir, I know the Rigveda, the Yajurveda, the Samaveda, the Atharvaveda as the fourth legend and ancient lore as the fifth, the Veda of the Vedas (i.e. grammar), Biology,

Mathematics, Augury, Chronology, Logic, Polity, the science of snake charming, and the Fine Arts. This, Sir, I know."

On hearing this, a long list of the subjects that his prospective pupil had mastered, the great teacher, Sanat Kumar remarked, that all that he had known thus far amounted to no more than mere 'words'. Since he had not acquired Atmagyan (the knowledge of the soul/self), he had not performed his duty as a scholar.

What is knowledge? What is its nature? When do we call a person knowledgeable? How do we impart knowledge? India's logicians have debated these questions for centuries on end, and the debate is even now on. For us this discussion is both relevant and necessary, or else what is the meaning of our 'teaching' today—something beyond the mode of delivery. If we are not aware of the quality, level, or nature of what we intend giving to our students, teaching shall remain a string of vacuous words. These issues comprise the subject matter of epistemological queries that lead to the formulation of a theory of knowledge. Beyond the skeptics and the dogmatists—the two dominant schools of epistemology, there are a few who believe that this question can be answered. While some thinkers hold that knowledge is an act, some others regard it as a relation, and if according to some it is self-subsistent, for others it is a quality.

Gautama uses the terms **jnana** and **uplabdhi** as definitive synonyms of **buddhi**, sufficient for understanding the nature of knowledge. This is neither the place nor the occasion to go into detail, but according to most Indian thinkers of yore, the term **tattva** stands for reality and the term **jnana** is considered a synonym to **buddhi.** which means knowledge or awareness of objects. This ascertainment entails investigation, distinction, classification, etc. and aims at giving everything a particular place in the scheme of things as a whole. The simplest test of the Nature of Reality is the type of evidence we can show to prove its validity/identifiable attributes. The subjects we teach are only a means to arrive at the Ultimate Truth that we can cognize. There are various ways to reach the goal. The goal is to be able to distinguish between the Truth and un-Truth. The Truth is not memory. Truth is 'experience'/'**anubhuti.**' We become knowledgeable when we are able to distinguish between the information that we acquire from books, which constitutes memory, and the **anubhuti**/experience that we attain of the Truth through intuition. The Ultimate knowledge is **anubhuti** or experience. Learning subject matter is merely a path toward that goal.

The Vyas channel leads one to become knowledgeable—by offering opportunities to learn subjects (Disciplines), enriching the store what one already possesses, besides learning the correct methods to learn—thereby leading one to eventually realize one's potential, i.e. having **anubhuti/** experience, which is indescribable in words. We come back to original function of the CEC, which is to 'enrich, educate and enlighten.' The Consortium is determined to achieving this goal with all the means at its disposal.

In one sense Indians are lucky to have more than one source of knowledge. While the West witnessed a linear scientific and spiritual development (on the strength of their sources of knowledge, dating back to ancient Greece) and peaked to become a dominant world power, the ancient indigenous wisdom of China and India is currently helping them to rise once again. They too are busy mastering tools of power—Western knowledge and modern industry, but additionally they have learnt to get back to the best of what was always theirs just for the asking—their ancient learning. In number of ways it would appear that in the days to come these two great nations are bound to reach the top. If one were to go by the areas of knowledge, which originated in the East, and which have attracted the attention of the West, their number is staggering. Indian music, dance, yoga, indigenous herbal medicines, philology, Indian art and architecture, oriental languages and literature, philosophy, various schools of painting, Indian logic and linguistics, science of augury etc. have of late come to find a place in some of India's best universities. One hopes this would be India's answer to Intellectual Property Rights (IPR) in the WTO regime.

One can notice a paradigm shift in the way the new CWCR programs are likely to take shape. On the one hand, it is going to continue handling classroom situation with subject-wise approach (organizing courses in terms of lectures as granules, series of lectures as unit, and series of units as modules and finally series of modules as course ware), on the other, it is thinking of introducing such programmes that only few universities or institutions in the country have thus far thought of introducing. These are:

- E-learning
- Up-gradation of technology
- W.T.O.
- Patenting
- Copyrights
- Women/gender issues
- Career watch
- Innovations in education, management and in other fields.

While quality control was always a matter of great concern for both the Media Centers and the CEC, the matter was gone into detailed discussion in its 71st Coordination Committee meeting. It is in this meeting that technical quality parameters were defined. It was reported in the Meeting that the number of programmes available with the CEC for broadcast numbered over 4500. The number of subject -areas covered stood at 47. What was missing in these numerous branches of subject-areas was specializations/honors courses that got initiated at the undergraduate levels. One expects that in future care will be taken to cover these branches and specializations as well. A CEC meeting also considered a few selected topics for subject-oriented programmes and assigned the same to different centers, keeping in view their specialization-strengths. The interesting point of presentation is Table III, which reports the list of syllabus-based model lessons in 47 academic areas, according to Model Courses developed by the UGC. Two subject-areas (Political Science & Economics) whose Syllabus-based Model lessons were ready, have reportedly received quality control certification as well.

Table III gives the list of completed Model Course Video-Lecture Series, alongside academic areas to which they belong:

Sociology	405
Mathematics	313
Psychology	300
Political Science	188
Home Science	220
Commerce	240
Economics	250
History	306
Physics	133
Botany	32
Model Course Video Lessons	
Geography	240
Chemistry	277
Philosophy	12
Zoology	114

This list provides intormation about the programmes prepared in all the subjects, mentioned above. Here we shall limit our discussion to model course video lectures on History, because the purpose is to examine the usefulness of its treatment. For those who have no idea in how many specializations History can be sub-divided, a close scrutiny of topics should prove to be very instructive. Paper 1 has 4 lectures on historiography the themes covered are: What is History? Philosophy of History, Ideas in History and Western Philosophy of History.

Paper 2 is Ancient Indian History and the number of topics dealt with here is 64. The level of expertise the speakers have is well established. For instance, what better names than those of R. S. Sharma, Romila Thapar, D. N. Tripathi, S. R. Goyal or B. N. Mukherjee can one find to teach ancient Indian history? The themes covered are not commonplace and surely the kind of expertise needed to teach them is not readily available either. I am referring to Itihasa Purana tradition, for instance. Similar would be the case of teaching the Vedic culture, the Sangam Age and the rise of the Janapadas, etc. It would be interesting to listen to an expert speak on Smriti social order, organization of guilds and the coinage in ancient India. Understanding a foreign traveler's account needs both depth and vision in historical writing.

The case of teaching medieval Indian history, Paper 3, is even more complex. Very few universities in India teach it better than the Aligarh Muslim university or Jamia Millia Islamia. Some of these video lectures have been delivered by the great names in the field For instance; these names include Satish Chandra, A. R. Khan, I. H. Siddiqui, N. R. Frooqui and Irfan Habib, S. M.A. Akhtar Hashmi, S. P. Agre and T. K. Subramanian. This is one period when we witness Indians coming in contact with the Middle East and the West and also see the decline of ancient indigenous social and political institutions.

Paper 4 is Modern Indian History. Some of the outstanding speakers in the series include Barun De, B. Sheikh Ali, K. C. Yadav, K. N. Sinha, Bipin Chandra, Ravinder Kumar, Aparna Basu, Aditya Mukherjee I. H. Siddiqui, S. R. Kidwai, Kapil Kumar, and S. Gopal. There are quite a few lessons that deal with modern historiography and none other than Bipin Chandra—a name to contend with in the field, has delivered all of these.

Paper 5 deals with Modern World History (Modern Europe) and the lessons delivered under this programme too have identical sweep and depth as one comes across in the other 4 papers, dealt with earlier. Some of the well-known names include Narayani Gupta, Aparna Basu, Meena Bhargave, Meenaxi Phukan, Sneh Mahajan and R. K . Trivedi. While two well-known experts, R. P. Kaushik and K. K. Sharma, have delivered five talks on American history. Madhavan Palat and R. N. Varma have made their contribution on Russian history of the Communist days.

Paper 6 is about Great Britain. The same authors as dealt with Modern Europe have also covered this paper by and large. It might sound strange but the British history does not extend beyond Disraeli and Gladstone, even as the Russian history seems to limit itself with the Bolshevik period. In paper 7, which covers Modern Asia the Chinese history starts with opium wars and the Japanese with Tokugawa system. The other countries covered in this paper include Turkey, Iraq, Iran and other oil-producing countries like Bahrain, Kuwait, Saudi Arabia and the rise of Arab nationalism. Both time and country-wise coverage are extensive.

Table II carries a list for the preparation of subject- oriented programmes.

These cover areas like Electronic Communication, Geography, Geology, Education, Home Science, Public Administration, History, Chemistry, Botany, Zoology, Archeology and Ancient History, Psychology, Issues related to important days e. g. United Nations Day, Women's Day, Children's Day, etc., Commerce, Physics, Hindi Literature, Sanskrit, Hindi, and other languages, Infrastructure development e. g. Roads, Telecommunication & Transport, etc., Mountains, Space Technology, Agriculture e.g. animal husbandry, irrigation, etc., Social occasions of the region, water ways, Education e.g. Sex education, Adult education, Adolescents, Traditional Medicines, Systems of Medicine e.g. Ayurveda, Naturopathy, etc., General Science topics e.g. why is sky blue/or cloud formation, etc.

Here too we have, as an illustration, dealt with History whose syllabus–based programmes are currently in use.

It is common knowledge that CWCR offers two types of programmes. While one deals with "enrichment", the other covers syllabus-based instructional material. The enrichment programmes have a tremendous variety and depth and suit all kinds of academic and informed taste. We shall consider here as an illustration one or two academic areas that fall within enrichment programme category and demonstrate how the two approaches impact their audiences through distinctly different treatment. I have selected from the list of enrichment programmes in History and Education for an analytical presentation.

The CWCR offers to enlighten its clientele about the scope and knowledge of History. Since this series is intended to enrich one's level of information, it is the sweep and depth that matter most. It has, for starters, a two-part talk by David Mac Dowell, Chairman of the Society for South Asian Studies, British Academy, on Indo-Roman export of glass bronze objects to South Asia. Then there is a programme on Egyptian pyramids, wherein the question whether they were mere tombs or observatories, too has been discussed. There is a programme on wall paintings in Rajasthan that are believed to be some 30,000 years old. An excavation site of a tomb in which some skeletons of proto-historic (1000 B.C.) times were discovered, too is covered in a programme. There is a series of programmes on Stone-Age finds in South India, which are called the Little Valley of Kings, as the place was supposedly a burial ground of local chiefs. Then there is a programme on the first city of Delhi called the Palatial Puzzles excavation at Lalkot.

We all know that art and architecture constitutes an important segment of History. Therefore, it is in the fitness of the things that more than 50 programmes on various types and forms of architecture are covered in the series. The series starts with Impressions on Learning Architecture, based on an interview with 4 students, who have completed their 5-year training in this branch of study. There is also a programme on the Introduction to Architecture, earthen architecture and interview with archeologists and architects, who explain the importance of their areas of learning regarding the march of civilization. Then programmes deal with living heritage of temple architecture of South India, which stretches back to several centuries. The architecture and sculpture of Hathisinh temple of Ahmedabad is also discussed. There is a series of programmes on Mosque Architecture, Hyderabad Residency Architecture, the Hindu Temple Shikhara architecture, Kashmir temple architecture of 6th-13th century A.D., and Martand or the Sun temple, displaying the craftsmanship of Kashmiri artists, the rock art of Warangal, the thousand door palace of Murshidabad, etc. While there is a programme on the architecture of Bahai and the architecture of Ghat kl Guni (Jaipur), there are programmes on archaic scripts of India. Besides India, other archaic scripts of the world have also been introduced.

Archeology is the science of reconstructing past; therefore it has a pride of place in History. Of the several types of evidences that History relies upon, archeology occupies a high credibility ranking. It is, therefore, important to appreciate various approaches to this particular branch of knowledge. The CWCR has several programmes on this aspect as well. As a testimony to the glorious rule of the Pallavas, the Kakatiyas and the Cholas, the temples and other architectural remains that these rulers have left behind stand recorded in several programmes. Similarly, the glories of Gujarat, Malwa region and the north India find a place in the programs of CWCR. Programmes have been made to show that the buildings of Bijapur left behind by Adil Shahi rulers bear an imprint of Indo-Islamic architecture. If the art and architecture of Harmandir Saheb is included in the list of programmes as are the Islamic remains in Bengal, the architectural treasures of the Holkars, Solar architecture, monuments of Gaur, and the temple art of Orissa. Then there are interviews of press correspondents who played an important role in the crucial struggle of India's independence, particularly during the decade immediately before independence i.e. 1937-47. It may be remembered that the above list of programmes could be covered under enrichment programme alone, because as a Discipline; a History course would have treated these themes very differently.

The CWCR also has an excellent series of programmes on Education too that have both relevance and sweep rarely found elsewhere. A mere glance at some of the titles will endorse this observation. It starts with An Agenda for Education—an interview with the Union Minister, about the priorities in education, as he perceived then. There are programmes on the Nature of Teaching with special reference to Social Sciences, Nature of Learning, study skills, plan your lecture, besides one that defines Teaching per se. Then there a programme on 'Learning to Be', an interview with a well-known teacher, who explains how education and learning are considered almost synonyms, while they are ever so different. One should feel interested in the series titled: Integral Pedagogy Process 1-4, which deals with themes like context, experience, overview, action & evaluation, reflection and learning. Then one comes across a programme that deals with the theoretical aspects of learning, besides several others that teach about learning through computers. There are several excellent programmes that explain the content and nature of future studies, education for equality, vocational education/training, distance education, education technology, computers in distance education, downloading, information technology, children and television, education through television, learning outdoor, experimental education, career guidance courses, guidance and counseling, values education (the ideals, the practice, and reaching out), teaching techniques, teacher education in India, etc. There are several well-prepared programmes that talk about higher education, and issues in higher education like financing, accountability, accreditation, NAAC, and interviews with some well-known teachers in higher education from both within and without, besides themes like health education, adult education, computer science courses, multi-media, e-learning, books in electronic age, internet, networks, a classroom from skies, media in formal and non-formal education, teaching shops and bazaar notes, etc. There is an instructive series on various disabilities and the challenged children. Besides the institutions that deal with visually challenges children, there is a series that deals with the methods of teaching such children titled: Visual Impairment 1-5, deaf, and the mentally challenged. There is a very interesting and illuminating series titled: Bharati Krishna Tirtha's System of Vedic Mathematics 1-5. In brief, the enrichment programmes have tremendous variety and depth, and therefore they deserve to be widely publicized and disseminated.

While all the above-mentioned programmes are in English, there are quite a few quality programmes on Education in Hindi. Let us recount some for the benefit of those who may not be aware about their existence. I am not quite sure that enough information is disseminated among the ones who are in real need of it. Be that as it may, here is a birds' eye view of the same.

The first programme in the list is on the importance of higher education. The next programme deals with all aspects/branches of higher education such as commerce, medical, engineering, architecture, etc. A three–part programme on admissions, teaching curriculum, extra-curricular activities, election and evaluation is also ready for transmission, besides another that deals with other components of higher education such as research, CEPT, etc. For teacher trainers there is one programme entitled: Models of Teaching—a concept popular in the USA. A programme explains Gandhi's concept of Basic education. Then a programme deals with communication channels for students. A programme dealing with the Rajasthan's success story in non-formal education called Lok Jumbish, has also been prepared. Education through Art, Why Environment Education? And, a five-part programme on integrated education, is the other highlight in the list already mentioned.

The CEC deserves praise for the outstanding work it has done thus far and if this is to be taken as a sign for the things to come, the future is bright not only for the organization but equally for those who are its beneficiaries. May be some teachers feel threatened by quality of the programmes but one must remember that there is no substitute for a good teacher, and the not so good shall always be wary of taking classes which they can hardly face. These lessons are good for both, for the better class of teachers they constitute a challenge and for the not so good they are model lessons to emulate. Whether these programmes are for enrichment or function as substitute syllabus-based lessons, they have a 'useful' end in view. In brief, they are excellent supplements and should be marketed aggressively as such.

14

The ETV in Higher Education: Reviews Within and Without

"*When we are young we are curious to know all about everything, why the sun shines what the stars are, all about the moon and the world around us; but as we grow older, knowledge becomes a mere collection of information without any feeling.*"

—The Penguin J. Krishnamurti Reader, compiled by Mary Lutyens

One of the CEC objectives mandated that the UGC-INSAT Project evaluation and review should be regularly undertaken. The UGC had for the first time started in 1984 tertiary level instructional programme mainly for the undergraduate students. Reviews were necessary to keep in touch with ground reality.

After 3 years of its existence i.e. in 1987, the project was evaluated for the first time. During the interregnum a Research Cell had been set up in the Consortium. It started research activities on the suggested lines. It was also the time when a Research Officer/Research Scientist was appointed. In fact, all Media Centers were allowed to have a Research Officer each.

The first survey was based on discussions, visits and consultation of all records that had been generated until that date.

The first phase review (as stipulated in the MOA) was done under the Chairmanship of Mr. Kiran Karnik. The terms of reference for the review were as follows:

The Review was supposed to examine:

1. The objectives of the Countrywide Classroom,
2. The approach adopted in production of programmes to achieve these objectives,
3. The adequacy of the infrastructure created in terms of equipment, manpower, etc.
4. The organizational structure and the managerial practices adopted, and

5. To make recommendations for augmentation/modifications in each of the above-mentioned areas.

It was stipulated that the review should be conducted in two phases. In the first phase, the specialists should visit all the EMRCs for a detailed review. Each EMRC was asked to prepare a detailed review document and submit it to the committee before its visit. The review committee would then prepare their own report and make recommendations.

In the second phase the final review would be held along with the Chairman, UGC.

In the first phase, each center submitted its detailed report on personnel, equipment, programmes, etc. The Report carried information about the infrastructure for project at the UGC level. It provided a window view of the facilities/functions too.

The UGC-INSAT Project had become operational with the focal point of providing one-hour capsule to Doordarshan and other agencies. The office performed the following functions:

1. Selection of programmes;
2. Procurement of programmes;
3. Coordination with UGC Media Centers, Doordarshan and other agencies;
4. Preparation of schedules for transmission;
5. Capsuling for transmission;
6. Coordination of research, besides taking up feedback studies; and
7. Organizing and coordinating training programs.

Initially, the UGC-INSAT office used the MCRC, Jamia facilities. Subsequently, it procured its own editing and previewing facilities. Administratively, the Project office was part of Jamia Millia establishment, therefore finances and appointments were processed there. The committee found that the Project involved undertaking:

1. Programme Production, but the idea was that Programme production should normally not become part of its functions.
2. Total number of programmes received by the Media Centers from UGC up to June 1987 was 632, while Total number of programmes telecast was 428.

PROGRAMME PLANNING

The Committee noted that present ratio of telecast of Indian programmes to foreign programmes was 50 : 50. It wanted that from now on, before such foreign programmes were procured, the titles should be circulated in the Coordinators meetings. Also in future a Calendar of important events connected with education, science and technology should be evolved for production, and telecast of special programmes. There was need to get a write-up (synopsis) on a standard format with each programme. Computerization of the library for easy access was necessary.

Technical Facilities

The Committee advised that additional equipment was required before the National Center was set up, which they pointed out included: Teletypewriter (character generator); dual DTBC with A/B roll switcher and measuring equipment/tools.

General Facilities

A vehicle was purchased for the project.

There was need for additional accommodation. Matter was taken up with the Vice-Chancellor of Jamia. It was desirable to provide a telex connection at the UGC INSAT Project Unit as well as at the UGC Media Centers.

Personnel Policy

Additional staff requirement included: (1) Tape librarian, (2) Production Assistant, (3) Accounts Assistant and a Peon. But the Committee had certain doubts; such as: Should a producer be employed for capsuling? Would he get job satisfaction? Therefore these issues needed to be considered, especially keeping in mind that Project Office's role was not to become one more production center.

Action Recommendations

The first recommendation was regarding the Credo. It was formulated merely as a starting point therefore it could not be the final product. A clear operational definition was required afresh. Credo of the telecast was initially kept fairly general and non-specific. That is why it said, "The broadcast will aim to upgrade, update and enrich the quality of education, while extending its reach. They will attempt to overcome the obsolescence of the syllabus and present the latest advances in all fields. The programme will arouse the interest of the viewers, whet their appetite and broaden their horizons. The aim is to stimulate and not to satiate."

It had stated further that, "(the EMRC programs) should seek to provide new insights, bring in new findings and take students on vicarious tours of places and laboratories they would never see. Inter-relatedness of various disciplines, and of development problems, would be highlighted, so that the sum is greater than the total of the parts—stress will be laid on the process of converting information into knowledge and hopefully—knowledge into wisdom."

The Committee recommended that on a priority basis all colleges would be supplied with television sets. The feasibility of providing VCR's in each college (along with the TV set) might also be examined.

The Report went on to record, "A much larger and continuous research effort is required. This must be aimed at determining viewing time and optimum programme duration (after considering all aspects like screen size, role of the teacher, size and composition of audience, and organization etc.), doing studies on specific programme series and on overall impact; need and effect of support (e.g. point) material; and on providing formative inputs to programme producers.

Research staff at the centers and/or Coordination Cell must be increased. In addition, greater involvement of university departments and outside agencies must be sought."

Programme Planning and Production

The Coordination Cell, along with EMRC Coordinators, required to clearly identify and delineate programme areas for local production and to be aware of what foreign programmes were being procured. A proper Programme Plan was required to avoid unintentional duplication.

Each EMRC must have a defined thrust area or a few areas in which most of its programming effort were concentrated. The EMRCs should not stray into non-educational or general topics, nor should they make programmes that were overly specialized and of interest to only small segments of the student community.

The possibility of providing fellowships to experts for extended periods in an EMRC needed to be explored. Contributing to programme making needed to be prestigious and accorded academic recognition. Workshops for orientation of experts were desirable.

Improvement was required in presentation. Over-dominance by experts must be carefully avoided. It was desirable to make greater use of professional scriptwriters and presenters.

Technical Facilities

All EMRCs required to be augmented with suitable computer graphics/

animation and post-production equipment. The latter should include one high-band VCR.

Greater emphasis on maintenance must be given. Adequate spares and test equipment must be provided to all EMRCs. A central data base on spares availability should be maintained.

A Microcomputer (PC) should be provided to all centers for multipurpose use in the Tape Library, spares inventory and research data analysis. Replacement of all equipment at all EMRCs needed to be planned. The case of Jamia was more urgent. The state of technology should be taken into account in deciding on choice of equipment. The new Jamia building needed close monitoring to ensure early completion, and very careful planning of lay out for studio, lighting, control room, etc.

Additional space was an important issue, especially in Poona and Hyderabad. Urgent action was necessary in both cases. In the case of Jamia, steps needed to be taken to continue their usage of the present 'temporary' studio.

Organizational Structure

Appropriate functional autonomy for the media centers within the overall framework of the respective universities, was essential. The signing of the MoU in this regard must be pursued vigorously. The relationship of the Poona EMRC to the School of Communication should be clearly defined.

The question of relationship (including the possibility of merger) between CIFL-EMRC and the RTVC department of CIEFL was thought to be closely examined and an early decision taken. The relationship between the Jamia MCRC and the Jamia administrative authorities seemed to be far from positive. Since this was seriously affecting the functioning of the MCRC, the issue needed to be resolved immediately.

In Ahmedabad, the long-term relationship between the EMRC and the Center for Development Communication needed to be discussed and defined, to stave off any possible future problems.

The UGC Coordination Cell must be completely independent of Jamia. [There were two reasons why the Report gave this particular recommendation was being made. (1) The Cell was located in Jamia; and, (2) The functions of MCRC &UGC-CC were and are very different.] It must play a greater role in planning and monitoring of programme production, conception and coordination of research activities; programme planning; training; information collection and dissemination; acceptance testing and planning of new equipment/facilities.

PERSONNEL PROBLEMS

The Report recommended that "the teaching or non-teaching status of the EMRC staff must be defined. All the positions needed to be made 'regular' and the staff given facilities accordingly for which other university staff was eligible. The staff must be given appropriate new scales, as and when their universities adopted these".

There must be career growth opportunities for the EMRC staff, at least commensurate to that available to other university faculty at equivalent levels.

A number of vacancies existed (the proportion of vacancies for Production and engineers in Ahmedabad is most alarming) and urgent steps must be taken to fill them immediately.

Except at Jamia, the Report mentioned, "high investment in equipment is underutilized in terms of the load on facilities. To use the equipment more fully and to improve both the quantity and quality of output, more Producers are needed. While ideally more free-lancers should be used, only Jamia has been able to do this successfully on a regular basis—possibly because of its location (Delhi). Therefore, the addition of a Producer and a Production Assistant possibly also a cameraman) at each center is desirable."

"Continuing and even greater emphasis on staff training is required, for both production and technical staff. Tailor-made courses could be organized and run for all EMRCs. While deputation for training abroad is also welcome, care needs to be taken in ascertaining the relevance of the course and the suitability of the candidate".

In the second phase, the Standing Committee meeting considered the report of the review committee on Educational Media Research Centers and UGC INSAT Project on 17.8.1987 under the Chairmanship of Professor Yash Pal.

During this review meeting all the 4 Directors/Coordinators/and Engineers were present. This number included representatives of the EMRC, Jamia Millia Islamia University. Sri Kiran Karnik, Chairman of the Review committee presented the report. He highlighted the achievements of the four centers that had been set up in the interregnum. Since they had been fully equipped and well lodged as planned, they had produced some 600 programmes. He was particularly appreciative of the dedication and hard work put in by the concerned staff. To cite, "for the first time high quality educational TV programs at the university level are available freely to all those who have an access to television." He was even happier with the viewership where his primary target group figures far exceeded the initial expectation. The reason was that the excess viewers came from beyond the targeted population.

He however expressed his unhappiness with the centers going beyond the defined boundaries contained in the Credo of program. In fact, Karnik was critical of the lack of planning of programmes. He expected that more research be undertaken and due credit to those who undertook research in the area be accorded. He desired that Fellowship programme be initiated in the area and they be put at par with other disciplines. He informed the group that systemic training for technical staff on sub-systems had now been initiated.

Professor Yash Pal, Chairman, UGC, did not mind deviations in the preparation of programs because the Credo was merely "an ambience and not a restricting boundary".

The Feedback Studies

A feedback study on, "UGC Countrywide Programme" was first mooted in 1986 when the programme was only two-year old. It was suggested that periodic feedback should be properly planned, since after the 1980s the expansion in the reach of the television had almost been phenomenal. The new programme addressed a much wider audience than ever before. It covered higher education students besides others located in remote areas. The programme was started on August 15,1984. It may be recalled here that since 1959, in the pre-SITE era, syllabus-based television programmes were broadcast on a limited scale for school children. Not only was the audience different this time but the objectives were also defined differently. This kind of television programme differed almost radically from the Chinese and the Japanese programmes. While the potential of the TV had been widely accepted, the UGC officials only hoped "that the UGC Higher Education programs (countrywide classroom) would successfully perform the complementary functions of colleges and university education." It was only to discover the extent and degree of success that the UGC planned through its newly appointed research official to systematize and analyze research findings. In pursuance of this objective the research staff submitted a proposal titled UGC INSAT TV Project.

The objectives of the proposed study were:

1. To provide periodic feedback to the UGC and MRCs about the UGC programme 2. To evaluate the programme preferences in terms of content, methods of presentation, topics and format 3. To measure comprehension levels in English language, utility and relevance to the course of study 4. To investigate into the viewing arrangements, student participation, periodicity of viewing and related difficulties, if any. 5. To

investigate the suitability of telecast timings 6. To analyze the viewer's characteristics, socio-economic-status (SES) and courses of study.

Sampling

The study was based on a random sample. The techniques adopted were interviews, covering some 600 undergrads from a variety of disciplines. 20 colleges in each EMRC/AVRC area were covered. Discipline wise college break up consisted of 6 Science and 12 Arts & Commerce colleges from each region of the country. The caveat was the TV viewing audience and the ones who have previously also been interviewed or contacted. (This was perhaps being proposed for assessing improvement in programmes during the interregnum).

The second research proposal came after 5 years of broadcast, probably by the same research scientist as the first one. The need for the Project was explained first. The relevant audience was informed that the Project Cell prepared monthly feedback based on the viewers' letters and fortnightly feedback from colleges. On an average the Cell received 200 odd communications per month. The content analysis usually formed monthly feedback Report. The Cell also prepared an annual report. Both these reports were then sent to the EMRCs/AVRCs and other concerned persons.

As one went through the research format already under use for feedback studies (since August 1989), one would notice that it ran into 9 mimeographed pages and has 3 main category captions. (Important to note is that according to the research-scientist of the Central Cell, the format for the feedback studies was not computer compatible with the ones under use elsewhere in other centers.) The format contained the following heads and sub-heads:

A. Total number of letters received	306
a) General viewers	147
b) Academics	28
Letters Replied (Total)	50
B. Feedback reports received from the centers	5
C. Comments on various aspects	
1. Presentation	5
2. Nature of the programs	9
3. Telecast Schedule/more publicity	20
4. Request for purchases/loan of programme Cassettes/catalogue of Media programmes	14
5. Request for at least 1 telecast in Hindi	8

6.	Telecast timings	31
7.	Request for new topics	61
8.	Request for repeat of specific programmes	10
9.	Specific programme appreciation	49
10.	Information on programme production	4
11.	Request for further information/transcript	63
12.	General appreciation	70
13.	General Criticism	20
14.	Specific Programme criticized	10

In November 1988 a detailed report was also prepared and duly circulated. It was felt then that since the Report presented" only a very limited picture (since it is based only on the letters received)" a few EMRCs desired that a properly planned- research might be undertaken. However, the concerned personnel at the Cell level had felt a similar need for a long time. Therefore, they now seized upon the opportunity to fill in the lacuna in the system.

The areas of immediate concern (as of 25.1.90) where studies were required to be conducted, stood identified; and they were:

1. Pre-production research (formative research),
2. Post-production research, and
3. Content analysis.

Interestingly, pursuing the policy statement contained in the CEC's Memorandum of Association (research related to optimizing the effectiveness of the programmes, through studies aimed at assessing audience needs, formative research including pre-testing of programmes, feedback from the audience, impact studies, and basic research related to distance learning and the use of media), formative research alone was officially advocated. The reason for this support was that formative research helped one define the "effectiveness of a programme." The formative research was supposed to include the following points:

1. Context analysis,
2. Need assessment—i.e. identification of needs,
3. Problem analysis,
4. Audience characteristic,
5. Delivery system constraints,
6. Communication contact strategies (selection of design & content) Input & feedback, and
7. Utilization factor.

In his paper Rajendra Mishra, Research Scientist, CEC (University News, Monday, January 1, 1996) informed the readers that except for one study (Usha Kumar's A report on IMPACT of UGC programmes on undergrads, AVRC, Roorkee 1993) there weren't any other impact studies conducted in the area. But plenty of summative studies however did exist.. For the CEC the Feedback studies were very useful. One could accept them too as part of formative-evaluative endeavour.

While giving details of the reasons why the research scientist thought about the need for undertaking feedback researches, it was stated in the proposal, "An attempt in this direction has already been made in the form of a format and a questionnaire prepared by the Cell and circulated to all the Centers in 1987. Sporadic attempts have been made and are still being made to elicit information from the audience, based on this format and the questionnaire. However, no concerted effort has so far been undertaken in this direction in a systematic, sustained and connected fashion." And the reason given for this state of affairs was allegedly, "the lack of opportunities for communication among the researchers in the different Centers and the Project Cell."

It was suggested in the proposal itself "that the researchers (should) meet at regular intervals to exchange and compare the findings derived from the field work done by them, to take stock of the situation and to incorporate any necessary changes in the format and questionnaire, if called for by their experience." The Research Group in the Cell, "shall then be in a position to coordinate and consolidate this work effectively." It was claimed that the proposed research plan was, "in conformity with the recommendations of the Karnik Review Committee, which had demanded that,' a much larger and continuous research effort is required and that the Coordination Cell must play a greater role in conception and coordination of research activities." Therefore, the present proposal contained the following points:

1. A mutually agreed upon format, which is computer compatible be evolved, so that the data collected by the Media Centers and the Project Cell can be compiled, updated and reviewed.
2. A common procedure be formulated for conducting surveys and gathering data from the viewers,
3. The feasibility of getting students involved on voluntary basis under the supervision of researchers be explored to gather information regularly from institutions,
4. The researchers meet at regular intervals to discuss the material collected, to evaluate its usefulness and to make recommendations,

if any, for future planning and to restructure the format, modify the data collection procedure, if necessary.

5. The Project Cell will summarize the main findings in the research reports from the Centers and circulate the same regularly.

The Cell also submitted along with the proposal a format for preparing status studies.

At this stage a few research and feedback studies can be examined to take stock not merely of the on-going activities in the Consortium but also of the Research Cell's effectiveness in the system as envisaged and cited above.

We already have a sample of a Feedback Study done at the Cell level. The other studies too followed the same pattern. All these studies have a few common features. The first page gives the title of the document (such as, Countrywide Classroom Report), the type of the document (such as monthly report), Months covered (specified), number of pages (such as 15), classification (such as Internal Circulation), target group i.e. to whom it is addressed (UGC, CEC, EMRCs/AVRCs, & selected agencies) and the name of the author. The format of the Report has usually 6 chapters. The order of the chapters is: Introduction, Viewer's Distribution; Part A chapter 3, Indigenous Programmes, General Comments on the Programme Telecast, Chapter 4. Topics Specific; Part B Chapter 5. Foreign Programmes, and the last Chapter 6 Summary A& B. While the first chapter is only explanatory, the next gives tables of the months and the zones covered, the number of students (zone-wise) who saw the programme, tables showing category and class-wise distribution, and also their urban-rural distribution. The analysis also indicates the type, category and class-wise distribution of the respondents.

The next chapter (3) gives a summary of the general comments. Here the requests, criticisms, etc. of the viewers are recorded and analyzed. Each chapter has its own importance but look at random, it would appear that the viewers prefer foreign programmes to the indigenous ones and their demand is always more than those of the latter.

To compare the internal feedback studies we could go through similar studies conducted elsewhere and by persons who could be termed outsiders. These researchers are mostly from the universities—Indore, Baroda, Bhubaneshwar, etc. the title of the book is Studies in Educational Broadcasting (Deep & Deep Publications, New Delhi, 1998) and the author of the collections is Jagannath Mohanty. This publication carries write-ups of persons like S. C. Behera, a senior IAS officer, S. P. Mullick—An IGNOU Professor, Ila Joshi, an EMRC employee, B. K. Passi, a UNESCO chair occupant, etc. The format they follow is no different from the one we have just seen. The results of the analysis are, however, different. The reasons for this difference are also obvious. Employees within a system cannot afford to be as critical as the outsiders normally can. It is also possible that proximity to defects blocks one's vision. The outsiders spare no efforts to locate defects first. Also what others say can be occasionally very instructive.

Here is what one might like to call an insider's view. Ila Joshi from the EMRC, Ahmedabad, is taken up first. In the volume cited above she has given three write-ups. The first one is titled: Making Educational Television Programmes More Effective; the second one is titled: Countrywide Classroom Transmission: A Comparative Study; and the last entry is: National Talkback Experiment, Ahmedabad. 1992. These three papers put together give a fairly comprehensive view of the situation on the ground.

In her first paper she defines the objectives of the CWCR by citing Chandra Kulkarni and Ray, 1986:" For upgrading the quality of instruction uniformly across the urban and rural areas, the colleges have to be equipped with adequate learning resources—teachers, books, equipment, etc. Since all these resources are costly, alternative methods of teaching through electronic media will have to be adopted." She then describes the objectives of her study as: to evaluate the programme being transmitted. The target audience for data collection is undergrads from Arts, Science and Commerce faculties. The methodology adopted is stratified sampling. The total is 120 i.e. 40 each from Arts, Science and Commerce faculties. The sex ratio is balanced. The tools used consisted of (1) Profile of the Students, (2) Viewer's feedback, (3) Non-viewer's feedback and (4) Acquaintances of the core target audience. Now the results: (Suggestions) (a) talking heads should be avoided, (b) advertise more for creating awareness of the programme, (c) make programmes available in other languages too. (d) Have more participation of the viewers, (e) there should be a separate channel for educational programmes, (f) improve programme quality be including more visuals and graphics, (g) there should be more quiz and competition, current affairs and the programmes, covering vocational guidance, h) avoid details, they bore and lastly I) telecast schedule should be formatted. The students appeared to favour slot programmes over serials.

It is not known how many of these suggestions were incorporated but one could safely say that many of them perhaps did figure in the CEC agenda for improvement. The next study, however, almost negated these attempts, if ever they did take place. The second study of Ila Joshi, which compared the programs over a period of time—1987/88/89/90 seems to affirm the general contention that improvements are rare in a bureaucracy. The title of the paper could easily have been 'a developmental analysis of the programme.' The study concludes that a) no systematic change took place over the years though the stock has increased quantitatively. Also, the ratio of the Indian and foreign programmes has not changed significantly, and the trend appeared to address both rural and urban audiences simultaneously. The lecture-based programmes continued to be as boring as ever. Surprisingly enough, the earlier awareness programmes that had aroused considerable enthusiasm no longer appear in these slots. The judgment is: there is decrease in the effectiveness of the programme. And the last paper of Ila Joshi is Talkback Experiment, Ahmedabad, 1992. The experiment is to study the feasibility and difficulties in creating network for talkback facility that was conducted by UGC.

An elaborate research was designed to find out the impact of the experiment on the learning process.

The methodology adopted for the study is well known. The results of the study were: the talkback has been a beneficial method because it allows interaction. The pre and post-tests showed that the knowledge gained was significantly noticeable. Technical hitches and constraints of time, telephone facility, etc. apart, the programme per se was well received. The English knowing audience seemed to be a greater beneficiary than the others. It also reflected class structure.

B. K. Passi *et al.* (IGNOU academics) in 1991 surprisingly reported identical findings. There were only two different suggestions. The interlocutor should also speak Hindi. And, more time should be given to this arrangement. The suggestions that needed note were; a) expert should explain rather slowly. While teachers should be available on hand, post talkback discussion would be a welcome effort.

The same volume also carries a paper titled ISRO-DECU-IGNOU Talkback Experiment, 1994: A Report. This 12-page report prepared by Abhilash Kumari & Vijayaluxmy Bose is comprehensive and helpful in getting an authentic official view. It also reflects upon the way UGC behaves. This report confirms the hunch that before embarking upon a new programme, the UGC is always cautious and therefore examines all the pros and cons of the new venture. It prefers, like an experienced householder, to prepare well in advance for all eventualities. As a prelude to incorporating Talkback as a programme in the CWCR transmission on an operational basis, the UGC in collaboration with DECU and SAC (ISRO, DES units) conducted an experiment in November 1991.

The major findings of the study were:

The feasibility of teleconferencing was to be evaluated at different levels—technological, organizational and pedagogical. An evaluation to measure the knowledge gains as a result of Talkback Experiment was conducted by a research team of the UGC. This evaluation aimed at exploring broad techno-social factors, influencing the use of Talkback facility. On the other hand, except for the initial technical problems, the experiment proved successful and it did impart some learning. Besides showing general audiences appreciation for this form as a method of increasing participatory learning processes, the result of the experiment also revealed that the induction of teleconferencing as a part of CWCR telecast, in the long run, would result in an increased and more dedicated viewer-ship. If we were to assess the greatest gain of the experiment, it was perhaps to popularize CWC programs among students who till now had little or no exposure to these broadcasts. Students liked it and responded positively. Students gained too, and at times, substantially. It was felt that although the selection of the programme itself was not very appropriate for the experiment (i.e. question and answer mode), the results were encouraging. Therefore, a suggestion was made that programmes for this mode may be separately designed and shown.

Almost everyone—the experiment producers, anchorpersons, subject experts and students alike, felt that this programme needed more time slot. They all complained that enough time was not given for thinking before execution.

And the last in the series that we need to take cognizance of is a paper titled: ISRO-UGC Talkback Experiment in India. The authors of the papers are: D. R. Goel and Kiran Jaiswal. This paper is small but written with precision. To cite:

"To study the feasibility of two-way communication in CWCR programme, the ISRO-UGC experiment was conducted from Nov. 25-30 1991. Later on such a system can become operational. 12 CWCR programmes were selected for telecast. For conducting the experiment UGC-SAC-DECU-ISRO and EMRCs, AVRCs & Doordarshan collaborated. In this experiment pre-recorded programme was beamed from the ISRO, Delhi earth station to INSAT-ID Satellite and then received back by a normal TVRO and easily transmitted by a TV transmitter on VHF or UHF. Students sitting in the classrooms received this ETV programme. The centers selected for Talkback were: Ahmedabad, Calcutta, Hyderabad, Madurai, Roorkee, and Patiala. Two of these centers were linked with the studios at Delhi through the satellite INSAT-ID, whereas the remaining 6 centers were linked through the Public Switching Telephone Network (PSTN). The students of Jodhpur and Imphal asked questions back through the talkback terminal. The talkback from the remaining centers was facilitated through Straight Trunk Dial (STD) of public switching telephone network. The responses by the TV teacher to the questions asked by the viewers, were communicated through the satellite and then received through receive-cum-relay transmitters and VHF sets."

The researchers saw all the programmes beamed from 25 to 30th November, 1991. The study was undertaken through an experimental tool specially designed for the purpose. The findings numbered 16 out of which a few questions also propped up. For instance, what is the optimum ratio between the talkback and the actual teaching? While 91 per cent questions put were precise, well structured and focused the remaining 9 per cent were not. There were centers where the programme was not properly audible. Most of the responses took less time and were prompt, some 18 per cent were not.

The general observation was that the programme proved a success. The selection of the programmes was also good. All the persons involved— the scriptwriter, anchorperson and the expert, performed their job well."

Be that as it may, the UGC took far too long to start (in the year 2003) the 24-hour CWCR. Independent observers had declared long back that it was both capable and technologically well supported programme.

The Consortium produces two sets of documents. One is titled: Countrywide Classroom Television News and the other UGC Countrywide Classroom Feedback Report. Both are regular publications. The first one is as important and interesting a document as the second one. As the name of the News suggests, it carries information about the title and timing (besides the summary) of the programmes that CWCR beams. Most of the time it also carries an informative paper from some well-known source/ author. On the back of the cover, it carries a Mailbox and an invitation to subscribe to CWCR News. The cover page carries a kind of Editorial— an information-cum-policy related small write-up, titled: From the Director's Desk. The Newsletter is so designed that it can use both sides of the cover i.e. the front and the back for sending messages to its targeted audience. The front cover carries the logo, the extended title of Newsletter along with the name of the funding agency, the names of the members of the Editorial Board and the Editorial from the Director's Desk, and some useful quote.

Similarly, the back of the cover carries the Mailbox and at times the profile of some eminent person in the field. The utilization of the cover to the maximum is a tribute to the designer of the cover. As a sample of what goes under News 'N' Views, one can go through some of the issues that carry highly informative papers written by senior academics.

VIDEO COMPETITION

The Consortium for Educational Communication (CEC) being an Inter University set up of the University Grants Commission is given the responsibility of utilizing electronic media in education. Countrywide programmes are produced by 17 Media Centers, also set up by the UGC. These programmes produced in Hindi and English are telecast over the national channel of Doordarshan. The CEC is vested with the responsibility of coordinating the management, research and production of the programs at the Media Centers. Once a year CEC also organizes Educational Video Competition. The first competition of the series was organized in 1988 in Delhi.

The annual UGC-CEC Educational Video Competition is meant to nurture, encourage and recognize excellence in educational video programme production in India. The following features are taken from 2003 Competition.

CATEGORIES OF THE AWARDS

Awards would be given in the following categories:

(a) Educational Programmes (for General audience)
   1. Best programme of the year
   2. Best series of the year (any two parts)

(b) Educational Programme (for undergrads)
   Best Programmes in
   (i) Social Sciences
   (ii) Life Sciences
   (iii) Physical Sciences
   (iv) Earth Sciences
   (v) Mathematics and Technology
   (vi) Humanities, Literature and Communication
   (vii) Fine Arts and Culture
   (viii) Sports and Health:
   Subject expert or Resource person in the above categories of the award winning programmes, will also be given awards,

(c) Educational Programmes (Other Categories)
Best Program
(i) For children
(ii) For teachers
(iii) For adults
(iv) On Child and Women
(v) On Environment and Development
(vi) And Human Rights

(d) Excellence in
(i) Formative Research
(ii) Script
(iii) Camera work
(iv) Editing
(v) Sound
(vi) Graphics/Animation/Special Effects
(vii) Presentation/Anchor

(e) Best Amateur Video Production of the Year
This awaxrd is instituted with the objective to encourage Amateurs to produce educational programmes. In this category, three prizes will be given as per below:
(i) Students studying in Mass Communication, Journalism, Film/TV and allied professional courses,
(ii) Students studying in any other course/discipline than in (i) above,
(iii) Institute/NGOs/Individuals.

(f) Educational Programmes (for general audience—Asian Countries)
1. Best Asian (foreign) Educational Video Programme of the year.

General Conditions for Entry (A to F)

A. (i) A video programme produced between January 1, 2002, and December 31, 2003, will be eligible. All the producers or production agencies shall have to give an undertaking, on a Rs. 10/- stamp paper regarding the production date of the programme, without which entries are liable to be rejected.
(ii) Only one programme in each category is permissible
(iii) The duration of the programme should be between 10-30 minutes.
(iv) Programmes should be either in English or in Hindi. Dubbed programmes will not be eligible.

(v) A separate entry form should be filled for each entry accompanied by the following:
  (a) One copy of the programme in Betacam format.
  (b) In case of Amateur Video Production VHS/Betacam can be sent.
  (c) A copy of the script in English or Hindi. In case of series synopsis of other episodes.

(B) Conditions for entry to the category [4D (I & ii)]:
  (i) *Formative Research*: Research reports along with tools used for data collection should accompany with entry form.
  (ii) *Script*: Only pre-production script will be entertained (programs not produced)

(C) Conditions for the entry for Amateur Video Production Category (4E):
  1. A student should submit his/her programme under this category along with a certificate issued by the Head of the Institute, certifying that the programme has been produced by him/her.
  2. An individual NGO/Institution, submitting a programme in this category, should declare on a Rs. 10/- stamp paper that the programme is not produced by a professional.

(D) Conditions for the entry for Best Asian (foreign) Educational Video Programme (general audience—Asian Countries) (4F):
  1. Independent production agency, educational institutions, broadcasting agencies outside India but within Asia
  2. Programmes should have been produced between 1st Jan, 2004 to 31st December, 2005
  3. Language—English –dubbed or sub-titled
  4. Should be submitted in Betacam SP PAL/B
  5. 6 copies of programme script
  6. 3-4 photographs from the programme with any other publicity material, if available.
  7. Duration of the programme should be between 10 to 30 minutes
  8. Undertaking that the programme does not violate the copyright/intellectual property right law

(E) Last date for receipt of entries:

All entries for the 17th UGC-CEC Educational Competition for the year should reach the CEC between 1st and 10th Feb. 2005

In case UGC-CEC Media Centers have already sent their cassettes, they are required to send only the following before 10th Feb., 2005:

(i) Entry form duly filled for each category
(ii) Script in English or Hindi
(iii) Title of the programme
(iv) Tape number

Cash Awards

All the above categories will be given Cash Prizes as follows:

(a) Best Educational Programme of the Year (4 Ai) Rs. 50, 000/-
(b) Best Programme for each category (4 A ii, B, C) Rs. 30,000/-
(c) Subject experts will give cash Prize of Rs. 15, 000/- for the best programme in the category 4B only.
(d) Rs. 15, 000/- for the Technical Excellence in each category (4D).
(e) Best Amateur Production of the year 20,000/-(4E i, ii & iii).
(f) Best Programme of the year –Best Asian (foreign) educational programme (4F) an amount of Rs. 50,000/-
(g) If more than one entry are adjudged for an award, in a particular category, a certificate and a trophy shall be given to each of them but the cash prize will be shared equally (not more than 2 entries).
(h) The award winners for the category 4F will be invited to participate in the Award Ceremony at their own organization's expense.
(i) Trophy & Certificate: Trophy in the form of Veena, will be given to all award winners along with the cash prize and a certificate of Excellence.
In case of appreciation award only certificate will be given.
(j) CEC reserves the right to reject any entry on technical or any other ground without assigning any explanation.

Such then are the rules followed by the CEC for the organization of its Educational Video Competition. It has developed all the necessary paraphernalia for improving the quality of its programmes. The additional advantage it gets from organizing a Competition like the one we have just described is that it helps them wide publicity both for the programme and the participants besides the CEC gets a proper expert–certified programme. In fact, there are many more advantages in organizing such an event than can be discussed. The implication is that while one could highlight the tangible benefits that flow from the aforesaid programme, it is not all that easy to define the intangible ones. However, one could define one or two intangible benefits too. It brings in fresh air from the undefined, unknown sources. It is not exactly incidental that the entire activity leads to an up-gradation of certain techniques and technologies for the all-round good of classroom instruction.

As part of regular assessment a Committee headed by Prof. E. V. Chitnis, submitted its Report in 1994. After viewing the programmes produced until then and having discussed relevant issues during their prolonged in-group discussion, the Committee presented its Report in which it made the following recommendations:

1. There is a wide range in the quality of programmes. While a few were excellent from all points of view (contents, presentation, aesthetics, effectiveness, general conformity and credo), some were rather poor. This indicates that while the system does have the potential to turn-out world class programmes, there must be much tighter quality assurance and control processes so as to ensure that all programmes are above a minimum threshold of acceptability. Internationalization of the quality-imperative by each member of the team is essential; however, even after this, systematic quality control mechanisms are required in each center.
2. The Committee observed that the senior and experienced Centers whose programmes once served as models for the new Centers, have failed to sustain their past production-excellence. With their experience, it was not desirable.
3. The Committee noted that a substantial number of programmes use the interview format. While purely talk-oriented shows generally tend to be dull and do not fully exploit the visual power of the medium, there are occasions when interviews can be interesting and intellectually stimulating. However, to achieve the latter, not only as the topic and the interviewee ought to be appropriate, but it is essential that the interviewee be fully briefed about the target audience and the credo. The interviewer has also to be first-rate.
4. The programme that merely records the talk of an expert (or even a talk with slides) should be used only as a source material, which can be utilized for making a proper programme with visual support for illustrating what the expert is saying and to interpret the concepts used by the expert to suit the need of the audience and the CWCR credo.
5. It is imperative that in the presentation of any topic, especially those relating to agriculture, environment and development, taking into account the variety and the complexity of Indian situations offered and statement made should be presented as

valid for the areas and conditions mentioned in the programme. The general point is that such programs should not promote a particular point of view. The aim should be to provide desired viewpoints and let the audience decide what is most appropriate.

6. It would be worthwhile for each Center to develop its area of specialization on the basis of availability of experts and resources in its catchments area.
7. The technical qualities of the programmes were generally good but not uniform. It has been observed that while choosing a topic, students' needs are often not kept in focus. The programme must operate at different levels, beginning with a popular level that ensures communicative ability.
8. There was conspicuous absence of women in all levels of activities: e.g. there were very few women experts. In fact, gender problem was present throughout: e.g. references such as 'mankind' and 'his'.
9. The background of a set should be made more interesting. The background music needs to be reduced while using more of ambient sound. Television programmes need specially made graphics, and use of existing (readymade graphic should be avoided.
10. There is a need to watch for the clarity of audio. In many instances, not enough attention seems to have been paid to framing, composition, visual appeal, etc. There is much scope to improve script, camera movement, smooth visual flow, etc.

When read with care, the Report furnishes insights into the working of the Consortium and shares its anxieties about the quality of the programmes. It is obvious that many a programme lack proper attention and biases impact programme presentations. The concerns of the Committee are both genuine and reflective of the ground reality that media producers often lack both vision and care.

Again in the year 1996 Professor E. V. Chitnis headed a Committee, which presented its Report reviewing Audio-Visual Research Centers (AVRCs). Professor M. M. Chaudhari presided. After detailing the work these centers were engaged in and the contribution they had made thus far, the Committee went on to make highly insightful observations and a few recommendations:

Members of the Committee discussed each center at length.

1. The discussion was based on the performance report and other feedback, which was made available during the discussion. It

was brought to the notice that it took about three years for the UGC-CEC to frame and approve the personnel policies for the recruitment of the staff in the AVRCs and EMRCs. And after framing these policies the UGC communicated to these Centers not to recruit any staff on regular basis. In fact, the ban on the recruitment has only recently been lifted by the UGC after its enforcement for a period of 3 years.

2. The members of the Committee observed that the 7 AVRCs under review had at present a staffing strength as low as 5 and a maximum of 16. The suggested number was 25. The members felt that the Centers could not give a better performance in terms of production of programs when they were having as low as 1 or 2 production staff. It was felt that the ban on recruitment perhaps was the single major cause for the Centers' poor performance. That this was beyond their control stands recorded.
3. It was observed that the Group A Centers, namely AVRCs of the Osmania, Madras and Indore, had as of now, built most of the infrastructure, required for a working production Center and capable of growth. It was felt that after recruiting the approved staff these Centers had the potential to produce quality 4 to 5 programmes a month. Therefore, it was recommended that AVRC Osmania, AVRC Madras and AVRC Indore be funded permanently by the UGC.
4. It was observed AVRC Roorkee had so far not signed MoU with the UGC and CEC, pending with them for the past 2 years. The Committee recommended that the Center be communicated, and in case the University of Roorkee failed to sign MoU within 3 months the Center be closed. (This warning to be given to EMRC Ahemadabad too).
5. In case of AVRC Roorkee and AVRC Patiala, which fell under the group B category, it was observed that these Centers needed to strengthen themselves with a better management and infrastructure to produce quantity and quality programmes. Taking the plea that both these Centers had only a skeleton staffs, the AVRC Patiala invested heavily on the building and the studio, and the AVRC Roorkee had a high academic infrastructure available around it. The Committee recommended that for the present both these Centers be continued to be funded by the UGC, subject to the fulfillment of the Clause 9.4 above; It further recommended that the progress of both the Centers be monitored

and reviewed after every 2 years and a decision to be then taken whether or not these Centers be closed down.

6. In case of Group C Centers, AVRC Srinagar and AVRC Imphal, it was widely acknowledged that the insurgency had effected both the States and in turn had affected the performance of the Centers. It was felt that these Centers had to perform a role in the development of the much-neglected part of the country, which needed to be encouraged against all odds. The Committee recommended that a) these two Centers be also transferred from the plan to non-plan of the UGC budget, and b) the progress of both these Centers be monitored and reviewed after every 2 years and then decision be taken about their continuance or otherwise.
7. Members of the Committee felt that Center assessment criteria be re-looked into and a method to fix Center Performance Index be evolved. It was also recommended that the Performance of all Centers be monitored and recorded annually by the CEC.
8. The Committee recommended that the Center Performance Report be communicated to Directors of the Centers and especially to the Vice-Chancellors, whenever there was decline in their performance. In case the Center still did not perform well, such a Center was to be given a chance to improve within a specified period. Feedback and warning should precede before any drastic measure was taken against them.
9. The Committee felt that a communication gap exist between Director, CEC and the Vice-Chancellors of the universities where the Centers had been created. Therefore, the Committee recommended that Director of the Consortium should organize once a year Conference with all the concerned Vice-Chancellors of the Media Centers and discuss problems they faced and tried resolving them. Such a session should be presided over by the Chairperson of the UGC.
10. It was also recommended that production targets of each Center be clearly defined and the Centers be asked to pursue them without deviation.
11. The Committee felt that in the past and as well as in the present the selection of the AVRC building lacked vision. The Committee recommend that unsuited buildings (e.g. older than 20 years) for the AVRC studio should not be funded. The Committee recommend that in all such cases a prior approval of CEC was obligatory, before any release of funds by the UGC.

12. The Committee observed that when a new Media Center was established by the UGC, it was placed to operate in the 'project mode'. However, considering the fact that the time they took in becoming operational, and the investment required for setting up the Center, the Committee felts that the system did not permit them to be set up in project mode. Therefore, the Committee recommend that the remaining AVRCs and new AVRCs (likely to be set up) should be put on UGC's non-plan budget. In case such Center/s failed to measure up to expectation within say 3-4 years time they be closed down after due warning.
13. The Committee observed that new Centers would take long periods of time to become operational. The reasons for the delay lay a) in procuring necessary audio-visual equipments and, or b) universities tended to divert the allotted funds to some other heads. The Committee recommended that henceforth the AVRCs would not buy any of such materials themselves, instead follow strictly the advice of the CEC about configuration, model, prices, places, etc.
14. The Committee raised certain doubts and raised basic questions, e.g. a) Why must the Media Center be invariably located in a university? b) If giving of equipment necessary? c) Could they be given funds for getting software produced through free lancers? d) Shouldn't UGC-CEC involve institutions (IITs, TTIs etc.) and several others in the field to contribute to CWCR? The Committee expected that all such issues be raised at appropriate forum and answer sought for future guidance. This was necessary the changing nature of the Media scenario.

In the year 1997, a National Viewership Research Survey was undertaken. The study was part of the CEC policy to gauge from time to time the effectiveness of their programme. This study was conducted in 50 towns and cities with a population between 10,000 and 1 lakh from each of the 6 regions (N.E., W, S &Central and North-East); and towns in 2 categories (1-10 lakh and over 10 lakh). A total of 18.927 persons was interviewed. The process of selection and the sample size was such that the results could have been generalized for all towns and cities of 10,000+ population of the country. Also, the viewers too stood classified as dedicated, casual and the frequent.

The findings of the study revealed that the CWCR viewers accounted for 11.5 per cent of the population of these towns, which might be around 218 lakhs. Of this number the proportion of regular viewers in the North East was the highest with 6.8 per cent followed by East, which was 5.0 per cent among all respondents (at all India level). The North East (10.6%), West (11.4%), East (8.2%), North (6.6%), Central (5.5%) and South (4.9%) also had relatively high proportion of once/less frequent viewership.

UGC CWCR VIEWERS—ALL-INDIA

	All India 10,000 + population towns	*% Lakhs*
1815	Universe of 14+ population	100
73	2-3 days per week	4.0
145	1 day or less per week	7.5
1597	Non/Never viewers	88.5

Profile

A large majority of CWCR viewers are students from non -Metropolitan towns, which, according to CEC definition, is the primary target population. Besides the students, other viewers include academicians, senior citizens and young adults. Given the level and dominance of English as the language of transmissions, the viewers belong to higher income, higher socio-economic and in most cases with English medium background.

Timing

Most of the viewers (65%) watch 1-2 p.m. programme. Others follow (31%) watching 6-7 a.m. programme and (19%) watch 6 a.m. to 6.30 a.m. programme. There are marked differences among the viewers as well. Those from the North East (58%) prefer 6-7 P.M. programme rather than 1-2 p.m. programme. The Hindi slot 6.0 a.m. to 6-6.30 a.m. is more popular in the West (47%) and Central (30%). The inappropriateness of the slot timing should be evident from these preferences.

Language

Majority of the viewers (85%) watch English medium programmes. The remainders prefer Hindi slots. Hindi slots are popular both in the West (32%) and the Central (44%). In fact, it is discovered that there is general non-awareness about Hindi programmes. However, Hindi as an option is generally liked.

Cable

Incidence of cable/satellite TV viewing has positively impacted the viewers. The cable viewers are about 485 and the majority of them are located in the South 70 per cent.

While this Committee did raise some very relevant questions, it was not known how many of their very pragmatic and helpful recommendations were actually put into practice.

However, when Director, CEC circulated a message (No. 7, 19-7-1999) to all Media Directors, seeking their advice regarding the Role, Function and Structure of ETV system, funded by the UGC, the content of responses received proved both instructive and revealing.

The terms of the reference were as under:

1. Redefine the role and relationship between UGC-CEC-MEDIA CENTERS.
2. Should we continue transmission at the mercy of Doordarshan? should we not think of an alternative?
3. Is was necessary for the media centers to continue to produce ETV programmes? Could they not become agency to commission programmes?
4. Would it not be desirable to convert media centers into regional centers on the lines of SIETs?
5. To create an academic atmosphere in the media centers, would it not be necessary to restructure its resources?

There was general agreement that the existing system had become dysfunctional. The reasons given for the present state of affairs also did not differ radically. For instance, the general complaint was that the UGC considered itself merely as a grant-giving agency and beyond that it refused to involve itself. The second reason for the general decline was that the staffs at the media centers constituted disinterested mediocrity. Thirdly the centers were overstaffed and consumed more than 90 per cent of the grant in salaries. There was not much left for programmes. Fourthly, the media centers being located in universities were subject to a variety of laws, regulations and control. Fifthly, the university authorities to satisfy their narcissistic requirements used the resources of the media centers.

The differences of opinions between the media centers and the universities in day-to-day administrative matters were such that even the intervention of either the CEC or the UGC was unlikely to succeed.

Besides, the heads of the Centers had no idea what broadcasting was and even the Credo needed redefining. They found it highly unsatisfactory a position in which they had to merely inform and enrich the audiences' experiences. The able and highly professionally competent staffs thus left for want of challenge.

The general complaint was that the media centers, if they desired to function independently and professionally, found it difficult to do so.

A few important recommendations were:

1. The CWCR could run not one but two satellite channels. They could run for 12 or more hours with specified hours of repeats. The role and functions of the CEC had to be reviewed carefully. Its earlier role to enrich and inform must be reviewed thoroughly. The operation of two channels would answer part of the requirements.
2. Channel 1 would telecast only syllabus-based programs (the UVLC type). More of such programs would be produced to cover as many subjects as were taught in the universities. This channel could be used for training purposes. Regular talkback programmes would run from this channel. The ultimate goal was to transform this channel into a Countrywide University.
3. The second channel would then be used for enrichment and general education programmes. After selecting social, economic and other relevant issues like pollution, water resources, etc. they might show number of episodes in a serial form. The model for this was currently available in the Discovery and the National Geography Channels.
4. Another suggestion was to centralize programme preparation and the media centers would be asked only to produce them. In fact, one of the suggestions was that the media centers should not produce these programmes either. Instead, they should arrange their production elsewhere and just check whether or not the production had met their requirements.
5. At the center the UGC should create a Cell with a professional broadcaster as its head for coordinating programs, delivery of programs, purchase of equipments for all. This person should be able to interact with the universities. But the most important caveat was that the Head of the central Cell of the UGC should be able to take bold decisions. Under no circumstance whatever no irregularity in fund utilization should be allowed. The use of staffs and material resources for the purposes other than for what they have been designated was not to be permitted.
6. As the media centers had grown obese in terms of staff, a workable exit system needed to be evolved. Number of category staffs had no function left for them to perform e.g. Junior

Assistants, Floor Managers, Carpenters, Helpers, Drivers etc. were some such positions that had become redundant. They had to leave. But for that the terms should be reasonable and humane.

7. Programmes like Science Olympiad, quiz programs on individual subjects, tele-counseling, etc. should be added to the existing list of programmes. Interactive programmes that helped in creating rapport between the CEC and audience should be encouraged.
8. There was a recommendation to make the CEC totally commercial. This aggressive salesman mode was offered to the CEC to adopt.
9. Somehow the staff of Media Centers should not only feel being proud of being associated with the UGC, instead additionally be encouraged to develop a spirit of camaraderie.
10. The CEC and the media centers must become conscious of the challenges that had of late emerged in the post –Satellite era. This called for the evolution of a new aggressive policy and a well-thought vision statement.

These recommendations reflected two realities: (1) there was a possibility to function much better than was the case and (2) the CEC should always take imaginative decisions to meet future requirements.

The CEC has reached a critical point in time and was on the verge of taking a long and high leap into future.

A recent survey (October 2003) yielded sufficient information to help build a realistic picture of the existing status of Multi-Media as well as IT education in the Indian colleges and universities. Of the 320 universities and colleges contacted only 65 of them responded. The idea behind the survey was to find out the scope for developing synergy between them and the CEC to work together in the area of E-learning. The synergy was supposed to cover organization of a course sometime in October, 2004, to provide training in multi-media for E-content development. The CEC was developing facilities for offering such training.

The internal reviews and external assessments had succeeded in making CEC a first-rate institution with plenty of possibilities. In a highly competitive world such institutions provided a cutting edge to those who were willing to change and were forever on the lookout for improving their performance. Resilience, goal setting and the desire to win made institutions perform well and outshine others. The CEC appeared to be all set to conquer.

15

Looking Ahead: From a Vision to a Mission

"*We are today at the convergence of nano, bio and information technologies. This age, I feel, will create a historic revolution and we must be in the driver's seat to contribute towards this societal change.*"

—President A. P. J. Abdul Kalam

(Reported in *The Hindustan Times*, August 1, 2004)

We live in Information Age. Those who today have no access to any source of information would soon find it difficult to lead a decent life. Information is the fist step to gaining knowledge. All information may not be knowledge but without information, acquisition of knowledge is impossible. With maturity and insight knowledge gets transformed into wisdom. The Consortium aims at making India a Knowledge Society. "The Vision 2020 envisages India to be a knowledge super power." It is quite logical, therefore, to take concrete and calculated steps to achieve such a high goal. The Consortium is ready with a concrete plan.

Accordingly, for the achievement of such a Vision, the first step in CEC's Mission "would be to find out knowledge-needs of the people through research and address the same by developing 'knowledge resources' with the help and support of research facilities available in the universities and colleges of the country."

Considering that higher education has grown phenomenally over the past couple of decades after Independence (9 million students in 13000 colleges and 234 institutions of higher learning), in terms of its quality there has been sadly no significant corresponding growth. The reasons are not far to seek. In most cases the non-availability of textbooks, journals and even good teachers constitute the stark reality behind national aspiration.

The Consortium intends "to bridge this gap by making quality knowledge packages, delivered by the best teachers available and those too to everyone who desires to benefit from them."

The Consortium acknowledges the reality behind the scene. As compared with the advanced and fast developing countries in the world where the enrolments in higher education ranges from 20 to 85 per cent of its university going population, India has no more than 7 per cent enrolment of the comparable population. By the end of the Tenth Five-Year Plan this percentage is most likely to go up to 10 per cent. The critical number for a nation to become Knowledge Society is around 15 per cent enrolment in higher education, which is likely to be reached in 11th Plan period. It is, however, not very wise to wait that long. The CEC already had the means to provide knowledge through 'open' systems and during the time when people are still engaged in the pursuit of their avocations in life. The third and final, the Mission is to make knowledge freely and seamlessly available to all those who need it.

The target audience is not likely to be students alone. Instead the aim is to widen the viewership to include family-viewing as well. The Vyas Channel is not going to limit its activities to beaming curriculum–oriented programmes. The programme will so position its enrichment component that it interests students as well as their families.

Two steps in that direction need special mention. The first step relates to objectives and the second to the approach. Both steps stand clearly defined. The objectives of Vyas Channel are as follows:

- Lessons relating to academic subjects, prepared by eminent teachers and developed for visual presentation in a manner that will hold learners' interest,
- Keys to effective retention of the core concepts in a given lesson
- Discussion type of presentation giving real life applications of the core concepts in a lesson, and new advances taking place, relevant to the lesson,
- Specific subjects placed against the inter-disciplinary backdrop,
- Selecting appropriate methods of production and delivery such as simulation of lab conditions, and other innovations,
- Concepts of precision, quality, measurement techniques, norms and standards related to the subject area,
- Suggestions for additional readings, easily available sources of information,
- Skill related subjects to be presented in a manner, enabling the learner to try practising the skill,
- Help-line for certification, and
- Interactive programmes with students through one-way video two way audio or both ways video audio.

APPROACH

To achieve the targets and to fulfil the objectives already defined, the CEC has outlined the approach of the channel as:

- The Channel is designed to be student–friendly. Here the students can register for a certificate, diploma or a degree level programme. The programmes will be so organized that proper sequencing of the lessons is followed by a repetition schedule. With this end in view the Channel will enter into specific arrangements with several mix-mode learning programmes, currently being offered by Indian universities. The programmes on this Channel will be seen as a high-value supplement to the students registered in the various university centers.
- This Channel intends to choose those subjects, which are in high demand but lack adequate number of competent teachers. It will also select such subjects, which are difficult to be explained optimally by conventional classroom tools but can effectively be covered in the visual multi-media animated form.
- Apart from being a subject-specific Channel, it will also beam programmes of motivational nature, general awareness and should aim at building the horizon of students and teachers alike. Some programmes will address staff development aspects at higher education.
- While some programs will focus on educating general public in the areas of health education, policy matters, etc. a few will focus on developmental issues, and lastly.
- Some of the popular programmes of the channel will also be made available on the Internet site of the CEC as well as being made available on the CD-Rom.

The Vyas Channel has come very close to achieving what President of India proposed for India to accomplish. India, he said, "is essentially a land of knowledge and it must rediscover itself in this aspect. Once this rediscovery is done, it will not require much struggle to achieve the quality of life, strength and sovereignty of a developed nation."

In the past one or more years, the CEC has made a few modest attempts to transform itself and aim high. The areas that in future are going to receive special attention cover E-learning, multi-media training, digitization of the media library, human resources development (manpower capacity building), infrastructure development, and the annual video-competition.

There are two specific reasons why the CEC has thought of bringing about change in course. The first reason is obvious. The CEC proposes to remain in step with the changes elsewhere in the world. The second is the realization that the organization has failed to utilize either its resources or the manpower to their maximum potential. Without going into the details, the fact is that the CEC has been able to concretize both its vision and the mission. Indeed, there can be no mission if vision is unavailable. Therefore, the CEC has come out with a document, outlining a few schemes and resolutions. This document is at once the organization's statement as well as a guide.

For record a few details of the concerns mentioned above are outlined. With a 24 hour Vyas channel, the CEC is in a position to become more interactive with its target audience. The CEC proposes to develop quality multimedia inter-active e-content with the cooperation of 17 Media Centers, located in the universities. With software currently available for more than 4000 hrs and a technically competent software production staff of more than 500, the CEC is poised for a forward leap. As it is, several universities have already started multi-media education departments. All this leads to strengthen the belief that there is plenty of scope for developing a mechanism for training in multimedia and e-content development. And this is precisely what the CEC aims at. Also, the CEC can meaningfully and quite easily coordinate with other inter-university centers through networking.

The other area where the CEC is about to transform one of its key institutions is its library. The media library has already evolved an elaborate programme with the help of subject matter expert to convert its present analog library to Digital Media Library. The idea is that after identification of subject matter the current form of VHS, U-matic, Beta ways will be found to enhance its quality to meet the growing and ever-changing requirements of both students and teachers. By using digital system, content editing is going to be both easy and efficient. The graphic designers can then play their role and the subject matter expert will have his/her final say. Eventually, a version from the video server will be made available to the cataloguing system, which will be enabled through a proposed CEC portal for its use in the institutions around the world.

Manpower requirements and capacity building are another thrust area, which has attracted the attention of the CEC. Besides training the existing staff for upgrading knowledge and skills, most of the future personnel requirement will be arranged contractually—an arrangement, which is at once economical and purposive.

The CEC is presently housed in NSC campus but very soon when its own building comes up on Nelson Mandela Road, it will move out. Efforts have been made to get appropriate funds for the purpose. Already one crore rupees have been advanced to the building account.

The organization has a regular Newsletter of its own besides having developed a logo for the institution.

Considering the amount of the work that has already been put in and a vision evolved there is no reason why the CEC will not become a class institution and be able to fructify its dream of becoming a center for the world to sit up and acknowledge its contributions. No one can predict about what lies in store for the CEC in the future but one thing is certain. It is going to grow from strength to strength. In the coming couple of years when the demand for quality higher education grows by leaps and bounds across the third world countries, India's superiority in this area will come in handy. It may not be forgotten that we shall soon be the only country in the world to have a Satellite wholly devoted to education. Today we have three channels—Eklavya for engineering students, Gyandarshan for general students and Vyas channel for higher education, but soon other highly specialized channels may join this club. In the age of WTO and the Intellectual Property Rights regime and also against the backdrop of the setting up of India's first Knowledge Commission in 2007 under Sam Pitroda, who aims to changing the very approach to spread knowledge and value traditional learning and their sources, India must exploit its vast potential and stand up to the challenges that are likely to come up.

INDIAN TEACHERS—CONFRONTING FUTURE

Virtual Teacher Goes Online

You can now get in touch with teachers and students across the country to seek help in studies, compare notes and give pre-board exam like test several times at leisure with a click of the mouse during preparation for the crucial Xth and XIIth CBSE examination starting from March1, 2008.

Last week a team of entrepreneurs in Delhi launched a web-site service that was a cross between social service website and a handy tutorial for CBSE students and teachers. Named cbsetutor.com this website contains the entire NCERT curriculum in toto, the extensive CBSE prescribed reference material, specially designed notes, and loads of tests on each chapter covered by the syllabus.

'In the next three months, thousands of students will need value-added study material to prepare for the boards. They will need to know where they stand on an all India basis. And they need not to distress themselves under pressure of examination. The website tries to cater to these needs'

To begin with, the company has a panel of experts who are professional tutors, former educationists, etc. who have designed the tests and the content. In the UK virtual leaning is mandatory but not so in India because here we have not been able to provide intrinsic value to students and teachers. The best part of the facility is that it is absolutely free.

The Hindustan Times (Dec. 31, 2007)

Seen against the above backdrop is the remarkable fact of continuously reducing the eligibility qualifications for teaching B.Eds in the institutional-mushrooming scenario the NCTE has created; and now in its reformist zeal it has further brought down the marks percentages of future teacher-trainers from earlier 48 to 45 per cent. In the past one year or slightly more, we have learnt the reactions of both the Government and the corporate sector. Even the present day products are totally unacceptable (when being taught by M. Ed.s & Ph.Ds), then where does the NCTE think it will make these 'unemployables' acceptable? Is NCTE playing tricks with the gullible lot? Also, it remains to be seen what impact it may have on the university departments of education that produce 'meaningless' M.A/M.Ed. s and the Ph.D.s.

There is a lot that has been happening in the field of education, specially in the classrooms but thus far I have not come across any serious academic paper on the direction in which we are moving. Despite the NCTE (or, maybe because of it) we are nowhere near preparing 'effective' teachers who are knowledgeable as well as 'reasonably good' communicators. After all, the main function of a teachers' college is to produce teachers who know how to communicate and present the updated subject matter in a manner that is easy to understand. But are we preparing teachers with these twin ends in view? I doubt it.

In fact, all the indications are that we have miserably failed on both counts. Communication is a skill and skills can be developed only with practice. One has to see the functioning of a present day teachers' college (even among the so-called best ones) and realize that there is nothing in the teacher education programme that ensures this type of training. Apart from a meaningless debate on the theme whether or not practice teaching should be based on 'block' basis, there is no model available for us to fall back upon. We have yet to come across a single university department of education in India where this question has been taken up seriously and some empirical research finding is made available for guidance. This obviously implies that generally teachers' colleges are not serious about imparting this 'skill'. If they were serious, the reality should not have belied the truth. The perfunctory and mechanical way teaching practice is conducted makes a mockery of the 'communication' skill. Remember we do not bother about this skill. At the time of selecting a candidate for teacher training, marks in an academic examination are considered and they are based on testing one's memory. And with the so-called management quota in self-financed colleges, all academic and professional considerations are thrown to the wind. Who will or who will not become a teacher is dependent on the fees one can afford.

There are essentially two problems with this ongoing callousness about the neglect of this basic skill. Those who know nothing about how to speak or communicate are not merely under-rating the value of this skill, and additionally they are corrupting the youth from the homes where purity of language is still considered a value. It needs to be taken care of. Obviously for all others the choice of words, the syntax and the correct pronunciation have lost meaning. We seem to have forgotten that in the oral tradition one does not have to remember only the text but the pronunciation as well. In the print era too, the value of the text and its pronunciation have not lost importance by any chance. A whole lot is dependent on the quality of spoken language. A single mispronunciation can spoil the meaning in a poem or impact adversely the good taste. A bad communicator is unlikely to be good teacher.

The other point that needs to be paid special attention is that developments in technology have brought us to a stage where it looks as though we do not need to train teachers at all. Even otherwise teacher education is no more than two hundred years old. It has no philosophy or psychology of its own. Indeed all that we teach at this stage is merely derivatives from the basic disciplines. Everything that we teach at the teachers' college is borrowed—the entire content and all the methods. Therefore to claim that teachers colleges teach something that they have themselves created or evolved will be unreal. Those who survive on borrowed knowledge can not be called scholars or innovators. After all only very few teachers are creative and teach what they have evolved themselves.

To recall Kendal, "things outside classrooms matter more than within the four walls of the classrooms" has acquired new context and meaning. For example, teachers' colleges are supposed to be teaching values but surprisingly they have not been able to evolve any tool to assess whether or not the training has been demonstrably successful. Linked with this failure are its other failures also. Read any national daily and find out how many teachers are found morally deficient and criminally inclined. I wonder whether any university department has ever tried to unravel the phenomenon and suggested corrective measures. These lacunae speak volumes for the failure of the system and suggest that those who should be responsible for guiding others are in fact basically unthinking and lack the 'Will' to resolve some of the basic problems this sort of training curricula faces. It is possible to argue that all management courses do not equip or ensure every manager of either success or honesty. Yet the fact is that the majority of the products does succeed and management skills can be easily showcased.

Teachers' colleges can be accused of being both unimaginative for the way they select prospective teachers for initial training and being totally irrelevant for the courses they offer. Regarding the first allegation, one can easily state that no one has thus far done any empirical research to suggest that the method evolved for selecting candidates for initial training are either predictable or demonstrable. There is also no proof to show that the cut-offs adopted in one university match with the norms followed in the other; or, for that matter the quality is or can be homogenized. In fact, talking about the quality of the products, this is one area where the quality of the products is so uncertain that nothing can be ensured. 'Quality assurance' is an unheard of requirement and few, if at all, can guarantee that their products have matured to some level of quality. One rarely comes across a teachers' college which enjoys the reputation of producing consistently good teachers. In fact, both the corporate sector and the Government of India has recently admitted that these products are not even employable.

After the arrival of the self-financed colleges on the scene, the overpowering greed among both the managers and the Inspectors drawn from the universities and from amongst the teachers' colleges has more than established that teachers' colleges are no more corruption–free than the other government departments, and the claim that teachers are above material considerations because of their high-ended values fails to describe the reality. Teacher trainers can be shown to be as susceptible to common weaknesses as anyone else. The fact of the matter is that even the universities are found to be guilty of money making via teacher training. The twin universities of Annamalai and Rohtak have for the past several decades gone on scandalously minting money from teacher education courses, and financing their other faculties is equally known to both public and the regulatory body called the University Grants Commission. The

NCTE, an apex body for teacher education, is equally guilty of not adhering even to its own declared norms anywhere in the country and for creating confusion by leaving several important areas and terms undefined. It has failed miserably in assuring quality control and preventing the unscrupulous elements from entering this area.

The meaninglessness of the teachers' courses can be shown by pointing out that even the NCTE finds it hard to explain why tailors and panwallahs (also, non-existent colleges) have come to offer teachers' degrees or prevent the absentee candidates from getting university degrees. This is one single cause that devalues teachers' degree or diploma that qualifies one to teach. It would be interesting to collect data after undertaking a proper comprehensive survey of teachers' colleges and learn about the real face of the owners of these teaching 'shops'. And if a test is conducted on the staffs of the these teachers' colleges and the university departments of education about the subjects they teach and the quantum of new knowledge they have acquired in the field. I am quite sure the appalling lacuna in their knowledge will be more than apparent. The most miserable part of the finding is that we will know for once that the content they teach became obsolete ages ago. The 'airy nothings' they produce in the name of educational research are mostly woefully short of real relevance and utility. Because of the lack of seriousness, attached to the areas of research and the way areas of research are identified, make it much easier to obtain a Ph.D. in education than to pass a high school examination. Thus far there is no proof whatsoever that any doctoral research in the area has led to any policy change or the creation of new knowledge. I have yet to hear of a finding or the name of a professor of education in the country whose work has evoked public admiration or received widespread applause.

One of the major functions of universities is to be repositories of wisdom and the centers for the creation of new ideas. The great universities of the world function as the vanguards of change through innovations and creations of 'new' knowledge. If nothing else, they at least give us new interpretations to age-old ideas. One will like to inquire and collect data on these scores from Indian departments of education, where its present day functionaries are generally known only for their net-working and mutual back scratching—in brief, for everything except for their academic excellence. I wonder whether anyone functioning in this field has ever produced an original piece of research and can stand up to a comparable scholar in any other university discipline within this country or abroad. I am not sure whether it is possible for this professorial class to find out the relevant or the irrelevant course of study and offer guidance for the posterity to save on time and energy.

Now I come to the basic point I wanted to raise. The point is that these departments of education are not even thinking of the days ahead wherein the whole variety of knowledge will have become a marketable product. The day is already very near when 'packaged' knowledge will be made available on the supermarkets. Already numerous agencies have entered this area and their products are available in select areas. This I believe holds out a challenge for the survival of teachers' colleges. The 'old' horses will have to learn 'new' tricks to remain in business/ competition. I want some one to show concern about the challenges that modern technology is posing for teachers in the area of classroom instruction. Way back in the late 80's I had talked of *Future Classrooms in India*—a book brought by a Delhi publisher. At that time no one had thought of a day when most of the tutorial functions of a classroom teacher could be transferred to a machine and it would be possible to teach inexpensively across the nation without much ado. That these machines/ products will one day make revision of a lesson easy and at one's own pace was absolutely unimaginable then.

One needs to think seriously about the future course of action vis-à-vis modern technology in terms of what we are currently teaching and what will be taught inexpensively with the aid of internet, virtual classrooms and with multi-media techniques.

This thinking will have several dimensions. For instance, the first dimension of the problem raises the question of relevance of the theory papers that we are teaching. Additionally, the items under each course of study have to be seen against the backdrop of examination that we wish to conduct. We have to identify not merely the subject matter but also the tools of testing for ensuring that the same have been learnt. And this could be done only after we have devised methods and tools to examine the candidate against the backdrop of the aims that we had originally thought of and devised ways to teach the same properly and scientifically. The main question is that teaching has a purpose. And the function of examination is to ensure that the efforts have yielded results. There is thus a direct linkage among the goals identified, subject or the content fixed according to the laws of the possible, and eventually the examination to ascertain that the goal has been achieved. This triad in teaching is well-known. I will like this to be specified for each course of study. If supposing one has aimed to teach a given candidate to be able to communicate or acquire some values or learn techniques and canons of logic then the examination should be able to demonstrate one's success or failure. Where do we stand in this regard?

Look at the syllabus of a teachers' degree. What do we teach here? We teach Philosophy of education, Psychology of Education, History of Indian Education, Sociology of Education and Teaching methods. Besides, there are numerous optional papers offered to specialize. The names of the papers or their content may be different in individual cases but by and large this is the common pattern. Think again and decide if we need this syllabus.

Part 3
The Nature of Teaching

16

The Nature of Teaching

Introduction

Developing a theory of teaching or understanding its nature is a difficult job. One faces a tremendous lot of complexities in trying to unravel the nature of teaching. If on the one hand teaching needs to be distinguished from learning, on the other one has to take pains to distinguish between what one acquires through the process called 'trial and error' in one's natural setting or through maturation. We tend to learn from our environment. For example, if we grow up in a Hindi-speaking area, we may learn Hindi effortlessly. But if we wish our child to learn some other language besides the mother tongue or beyond day-to-day spoken Hindi, we must create conditions, in which we may be able to fulfil our cherished desire. "But in those cases where the ordinary day-to-day environment does not itself offer conditions ripe for particular trial and error leanings", holds Donna H. Kerr, "we sometimes resort to the creation of environment or opportunities for particular experiences that foster specific leanings-environments such as rooms with pianos, sheet music, and opportunities for and expectations of particular kinds of repetition and the like. That is, we resort to teaching."

Even under these circumstances, the complexity of the nature of teaching does not diminish. 'Teaching,' not unlike 'loving' or 'hating' remains both complex and abstract. For example, when we say X 'hates' Y we can imagine several conditions under which this 'hatred' will be noticeable to us. Yet we may never be able to assess the exact depth or dimension or even the extent of 'hatred'. It is quite easy for us to describe the conditions under which teaching is supposed to be taking place. We may, if we so like, describe the school building, the background of the staff such as their academic qualifications, social status, the emotional stability of a given teacher, the prescribed courses of study, etc. It is also possible that the profiles of students may be got ready. Still, several aspects of these phenomena may not be known to us or may elude exact quantification.

Let us take an example of teaching mathematics in Class VII in the USSR and the USA. The external environment in both countries may be quite similar to each other. It is possible that even the qualifications of teachers in both countries may also match. In a subject like mathematics one has to explain equations. One need hardly be subjective about it. Therefore, it is difficult to say that there can be anything like Soviet mathematics or the American mathematics unless one talked of the variations in the standard of the subject or of the teachers or of the facilities associated with teaching in either country. And yet there is a chance that the subtle distinction in the teaching may exist which we may or may not be able to quantify or define.

We do not know exactly why there is a distinction between different students in a classroom when the teacher in a given subject does not distinguish between X or Y. In the same class X who passes out with average marks and Y with distinctions. Yet it reverses their roles in life. X attains such heights in the subject that he qualifies for a national or international award and Y with all his distinctions does not exceed the mark of mediocrity in life. If this fact can be attributed to the industry, perseverance, inherent talent etc. in the case of X and not of Y then the teaching in the classroom as such will be relegated to playing a very minor role. However, this is hardly a tenable proposition. We recall certain teachers whose teaching leaves a permanent impress on our minds. We remember a poem taught to us some two decades back. We also recall the meaning the teacher had given to a difficult word or imagery. This sudden recollection brings back to us everything from the past, including the teaching with such vividness as though the past had overtaken the present. It is possible to explain this phenomenon by ascribing all this vivid experience from the past to the gift of memory and to the situations which have impacted this memory, although neither reduces the value of teaching per se.

We may take yet another example. We find that a teacher is taking a class. He tries to explain the subject matter that he is teaching, and as he does so he transports only one of his students to a different realm from his immediate environment. This student of his excels his own teacher in the understanding of the subject matter. Why does the teacher strike a sympathetic chord only in one student and not in all? Are there patterns in teaching? Does teaching do different things to different persons?

The complexity inherent in the concept of teaching lies in the conditions which enable teaching to take place. We have to have a teacher, a student and a given level of subject matter ready for transmission. Who shall teach is a question that has a range of answers. We have the concept of teacher as defined in the Upanishad, in the Smritis, in the Mahabharata, etc. to the modern times where Education Codes define the eligibility conditions for being a teacher. Similarly, who can be a student is not easy to define unless one took resort to the Acts of Legislature, Ordinances or Education Codes, etc. The biggest problem of all arises when we arrive at a point where one has to decide; what shall be taught to a student?

Teaching is also an abstract concept. While one does associate teaching with schooling or for that matter, the presence of an environment in which we assume teaching may take place, the fact is that teaching and schooling are not identical. Societies and cultures exist and perpetuate without any schooling but not without teaching. It is, therefore, significant to appreciate that the nature of teaching would vary from society to society, and also that teaching by itself will be identifiable not so much with the process but by the end product. There is always a possibility that one may or may not know that teaching is taking place i.e. by observing the process we may not be sure about the fact that teaching is taking place, but we cannot mistake its impact by gauging the degree or the extent of its resultant modification either in our cognition or behaviour. We must take precaution while completely identifying the end-result of teaching with teaching per se because in the former case we will be identifying teaching with learning. We know for sure that they are different even if they converge on a given point. If learning gives us an idea of teaching, it will be possible only if it were successful in achieving its goal. In a class of twenty students, only very few would learn wholly in the manner the teacher wants them to learn. Does that mean that the teacher has taught only these few students? We will be interested to know what happens in the case of others who fail to learn that well. Also we should feel equally interested in learning about the unintended results of teaching. How does one explain that?

The question whether or not we should be taught at all also requires some kind of answer. If simple maturation, environmental setting and the 'trial and error' method can be deemed to be sufficient in the case of millions who have never faced any formal teaching; then why do we want them as well as others to be exposed to any type of guided 'Teaching'? The only answer we have to this query is that teaching leads to individual growth and development and therefore societal advancement. We learn how to learn more. We assume therefore that learning to learn is a desirable product and therefore teaching is essential for social and personal progress. It is true that we cannot easily define the term 'progress', and even if we do, there will be no universal agreement about it. Still we do want to teach the young ones and the not-so young ones because even besides sustaining the sources or national comforts available to us, we shall not have sufficient food to eat without matching the means of increasing food production with the growth of population. It is quite beside the point whether or not we have any universally acceptable definition of 'progress' but an all-round increase in the knowledge of the means of production and their efficient utilization is the minimum our society requires to perpetuate and sustain itself in the face of ever-increasing shortages all round. Therefore, we not only want to teach but also need teaching—a certain type and quality of teaching for our own survival. The quality in teaching under the circumstances is of paramount importance. Of course there are several dimensions to 'the quality' we are trying to define. The range can be 'a quality' which helps us to survive to growing powerful and remaining at the top in everything. The question of its quality can not be settled easily. The Russian quality of life and goals will determine teaching in their context such may be in the case of the USA or India. Teaching therefore can not be considered apart from its national context. We have to accept that teaching has as its goals for both the individual and the society and both in their turn are independent and also interdependent. The moment we accept this proposition we have also to concede that teaching can be defined and distinguished in terms of its context.

If we examine the concept of teaching from the point of view of its range and quality, we may also attempt considering its definition by distinguishing 'teaching' from terms like 'propaganda' 'initiation', 'instruction', etc. Each of these terms has its own connotation and if on one point it converges, on the other it has its distinctive attributes as well which make it so different from any other similar sounding term, Even a superficial comparison of the individual attributes of these concepts will help us realize that 'teaching' is a distinctly different concept i.e. it is quite unlike others. If 'teaching' resembles 'instruction', it does so because both have a similar setting and yet they are different because 'teaching' aims at helping an individual learn how to learn and thereby liberate himself of any authoritarian or formal setting. If instruction is narrow in its perception of goals, teaching does not bind itself with any such narrowness. Similarly, 'teaching' and 'initiation' are very close to each other because both aim at providing their clientele with sufficient knowledge to survive in their immediate environment. Whereas 'initiation' limits itself with attaining a given goal, teaching encompasses much more than a small range of objectives.

We could thus define 'teaching' as a concept different from several others which employ its setting, purposes or goals and yet stand markedly different from it. We may also remember that teaching per se has a range and quality and in turn each range and each quality attribute is distinguishable.

We have in the West a number of distinguished scholars who have attempted to grapple with the problems connected with the concept of teaching. Some of these scholars are: R. S. Peters, Israel Schaffler, P. H. Hirst; and D. J. O'Connor. This team is now expanding and many more scholars are joining in. Somehow in India we have not had this good fortune. We have to depend upon these Western scholars for our edification which, to say the least, is very welcome. My own humble attempt is being made to present an Indian standpoint which one hopes may help people acquaint themselves with yet another dimension to the philosophy of education in general and to the concept of teaching in particular.

For us everybody and anybody is not a teacher. The present day working in our schools and colleges allows only a few to qualify as teachers and thus makes them teachers- in-law. They meet the legal requirements of the State. For us a teacher is much more than a learned man. A teacher mends the way of his wards and leads them to the realm of knowledge. A teacher is wise and is someone who has seen the limitation of temporal learning. This teacher may structure his knowledge; and even sequence it and try reinforcing the same according to the predisposition of his disciple. But his job is to impose strictest conditions on his wards so that they are disciplined. Unlike Bruner's contention, teacher does not discard old knowledge because 'true' knowledge is ageless, and also teacher does not have to "re-enter the field of education in order to contribute to man's further evolution" because he is already there.

The fundamental question is where are such teachers who may help the mankind in the social task of creating an Ethical Man. How do we propose to nurture them? Do we not want them all? Teachers should be imbued with the spirit of social service. It is precisely this quest that has made me discuss and define the nature of teaching. I have no answers to all the questions that confront me. In any case I do make a clear distinction between 'teaching' and 'preaching'. A teacher may exhort his pupils but he does not preach because functionally preaching is the job of a priest or a saint. A teacher is neither. The purpose of this brief discussion is to clear up the cob-webs of ignorance regarding the use of term 'teaching' as distinct and distinguished from several other terms; which to my mind are unjustly taken to be its synonyms, and also hopefully present an Indian viewpoint.

I propose to conclude this part of my writing by a long quote from Professor R. S. Peters, who rightly holds that there is a lack of philosophizing on several educational concepts as a whole and a few in particular. Perhaps this would help Indians to join in a very meaningful discussion. And now the quote:

"To call philosophy of education a specific branch of philosophy is not, however, to suggest that it is a distinct branch in the sense that it could exist apart from established branches of philosophy such as epistemology, ethics, and philosophy of mind. It would be more appropriate to conceive of it as drawing on established branches of philosophy and bringing them together in ways which are relevant to educational issues. In this respect the analogy with political philosophy would be a good one. Thus use can often be made of work that already exists in philosophy. In tackling, for instance, issues such as the rights of parents and children, punishment in schools, and the authority of the teacher, it is possible to draw on and develop work already done by philosophers on 'rights', 'punishment' and' authority'. In other cases however, no systematic work exists in the relevant branches of philosophy-e.g. on concepts such as 'education', 'teaching', 'learning,' 'indoctrination'. So philosophers of education have had to break new ground in these cases in the philosophy of mind. Work on educational issues can also bring to life and throw new light on long-standing problems in philosophy. Concentration, for instance, on the particular predicament of children can throw new light on problems of punishment and responsibility. G. E. Moore's old worries about what sorts of things are good in themselves can be brought to life by urgent questions about the justification of the curriculum in schools."

Until we know what these terms really stand for, they remain 'words'. To us in India 'meaning' is more important than the 'word', whose meaning it is. Sanat Kumar called Narada's knowledge 'words', because the latter hardly knew the value and import of what he had learnt. Shakespeare comes very close to Sanat Kumar's standpoint when Hamlet replies to the query "What are thou reading, my Lord?" "Words, words, words" We, therefore, hold the view that teaching is complete only when, besides learning a set of new information and goals enables one to meditate upon the Reality whose manifestation 'words' are. Teaching is thus guidance to know the truth which in its true sense is never its content. Teaching in the ultimate analysis is one of the instruments of discovery of the Reality, and that these identified instruments themselves are a creation, which in turn lead to a step-by-step analysis of the making of a new creation.

REFERENCES

Newsletter, RCE, Bhopal, October-December, 1981.

Brubacher, J.S. (1966). *Toward a Theory of Education*, pp. 39-72, Harvard University Press, Cambridge.

17

Towards a Philosophy of Teaching

"TEACHING', as distinguished from terms like 'instruction', 'initiation', and 'indoctrination', etc. lends itself to the possibility of being conceived as independent and distinct from the 'process and consequence of 'learning'. In itself this statement questions the validity of interchanging 'teaching' with 'instruction' or 'indoctrination' for the simple reason that 'teaching' in this context has a built-in bias of incorporating within itself 'purposes', purportedly added to it by 'society as a whole or a group of individuals'. In other ·words,' the moment teaching takes on the shape of indoctrination it gets vitiated by an external agent (otherwise not included in the process of teaching). The major problem, therefore, constitutes in developing a theory of teaching which can easily be discernible by those who have something to do with it. D. J. O'Connor raises the point of 'usefulness of theory in the field of education: "But since education is not (and is not claimed to be) an exact science 'and does not even rely to any large extent upon the findings of such sciences, the word 'theory' is used in educational contexts in a derivative and weakened sense" Even so it is not futile to discuss the word 'theory' in the context of Education. Taking the cue from natural sciences where the word 'theory' is used without any ambiguity we talk of theory as: (a) a hypothesis that has been verified by observation and, more commonly, (b) as a logically interconnected set of such confirmed hypotheses.

Accepting this as the basis for proceeding with our examination and formulation of a theory of 'teaching', we may at first try to clear the ground by defining the distinction 'teaching' has from words like 'instruction' or 'initiation' or 'indoctrination', etc.

As already suggested both instruction and initiation have a built-in purpose. One cannot think of 'instructing' another unless one has: (a) a definite body of knowledge, and (b) a strong reason for handing over this body of knowledge to another. In the case of 'initiation', besides these two grounds, i.e. (a) and (b), some kind of perpetuation of values also appears to be involved. We can examine these words by citing two examples. For instance, a teacher instructs a child in the English language. There is thus a definite body of knowledge, i.e. English language. The strong reason or reasons to impart this instruction may be because: (a) English has a market value, (b) English holds the key to a vast ocean of knowledge, (c) it is the language of our former rulers and wields a charm of its own, (d) it helps us remain internationally aware and alert, etc. This sort of 'instruction' can go on from generation to generation or terminate immediately after the first pupil or batch of pupils has acquired command over it. In the case of 'initiation', the process must go on because it implies inheriting a value system besides a body of knowledge. One is initiated into a profession which has a code of conduct—all its own. Therefore, unlike instruction which may or may not lead to this sort of a continuous process called 'initiation'? The latter cannot be imagined of without a continuous process. If this 'initiation' can be an initiation into the mystery of an honorable profession, it may equally be true of beggary, prostitution or thieving, etc. R. S. Peters has discussed the word 'initiation' in detail:

> 'Initiation' too, even when connected with various ceremonies or rites, suggests an avenue of access to a body of beliefs, perhaps to mysteries that are not revealed to the young. One is not initiated into something that involves a mere know-how or knack. To liken education to initiation is, therefore, consistent with the second group of criteria of 'education', which connect 'education' with some depth of understanding. Furthermore 'initiation' picks out types of processes leading up to a successful outcome, which are consistent with the third criterion. For just as 'education' requires that those who are educated should be brought to this state by various processes which only have in common the minimum requirements of willingness and voluntaries, so too does 'initiation' convey the same suggestion of being placed on the inside of a form of thought or awareness by a wide variety of processes, which at least involve some kind of consciousness and consent on the part of the initiate.

Therefore, for Peters education and initiation are equally general terms and have no distinctive marks or features. It will, however, be difficult to agree with him because of their typical usages. One is initiated into family mores or social customs through a process more intimate than the formal schooling. If both terms arc general, as Peters suggests they are, one may be tempted to agree with him only on the ground that 'education' as a word means different things to different persons but not so 'initiation'. An educated person can be initiated into a smaller group for a specific end.

Similarly, an initiated person could be educated through a formal system. The examples of an educated man will be the 19th century concept of an English gentleman and of the initiated will that of a disciple of Acharya Rajneesh or Sai Baba. Even if the two are not that easy to delimit, specify or define, they surely are not so general as to be considered identical. Similarly, one can be more ritualistic, secretive, etc. in being initiated, which may never be true for receiving education.

The word 'indoctrination' has generally been used to connote additionally certain political overtones. It does for that matter cover by implication that meaning, which the words 'instruction' and 'initiation' carry within themselves. In all these terms there is a common link that runs through which is that of authority. One has to have an authority besides superior knowledge to instruct, initiate or even indoctrinate. It is quite irrelevant to say that the source of authority must always be external. In numerous cases indoctrination has the genesis in an individual's will'. The authorization for the exercise of this 'will' is a matter of time when the followers of that leader refuse to permit others to exercise their right to political choice in preference to what they have been commanded.

R. F. Atkinson discusses both these terms, viz. instruction and indoctrination and points out that his use of the term 'instruction' is a little broader than that of Schaffler in the Language of Education. Then he goes on to state: 'Instruction', though probably not 'indoctrination', is perhaps most naturally applied to theoretical teaching, to teaching 'that' as opposed to teaching 'how'. But the distinction we are concerned with can perfectly well be drawn with respect to teaching 'how', which cannot in any case be wholly separated from teaching 'that'. Quite apart from the fact that, so far as language goes, it is very frequently a matter of choice whether we speak of 'teaching' 'how' or 'that', it is clear that academic teaching as ordinarily understood is not exclusively theoretical, nor vocational but purely practical.

'Instruction' for Atkinson is "essentially a rational process" both at the giving and receiving end. He makes a distinction between the two by saying that "imparting and acquiring of an understanding of 'what' is taught is consequently involved in its realization. Because of this, and in so far as it succeeds 'instruction' puts its subject in the way of making progress, in the field by his own efforts. 'Indoctrination', on the other hand, need not; it is subject to no such restrictions". The main distinction in terms of end-product will be that whereas the one who has been instructed will know what he has been instructed in and will have a justified conviction about the instructed fact or skill, the 'indoctrinated' will have no such benefit.

Where one tends to agree wholly with Atkinson is that teaching is different from training or instruction even when in each the ultimate aims are knowledge and its intelligent practice. He regards it as inevitable that certain teaching methods have to be non-rational. In other words, he concedes that irrespective of the term one uses, i.e. training, instruction or indoctrination, etc. there continues, to be an undercurrent of irrationality and authority about them. It simply means that as soon as 'instruction' becomes externalized (here term 'teaching' or its variant is. irrelevant) the element of authority becomes ever so much evident. The same has been echoed by J.S. Brubacher:

"Every education system makes use of indoctrination. Children are indoctrinated with the multiplication table; they are indoctrinated with love of country; they are indoctrinated with the principles of chemistry and physics and mathematics and biology, and nobody finds fault with indoctrination in these fields. Yet these are of small concern in the great business of life by contrast with ideas concerning God and man's relation to God, his neighbor and himself, man's nature and his supernatural destiny".

We have no intention of justifying the use or practice of one against the other word. The idea is to make this fact evident that 'teaching' traditionally has existed cheek by jowl with authority. In the process of defining the term 'teaching' this variable, therefore, stands out quite clearly. This is so even before the learner appears on the scene or is noticed.

The major difficulty in defining the term 'teaching' and its parameters is that it has hardly, if ever, been thought of without 'learning'.

Among its parameters teaching has always been thought of being a part of 'learning'. Not much work has been done in the west on its definition and none at all in India. 'Teaching' seemingly overlaps several other concepts of the same genus with minor variations in their actual end-products. At one place P. H. Hirst and R. S. Peters come quite close to the stand I should like to take:

Usually educational processes involve not only learning but teaching as well. There is, however, no logical connection in this case. Education can go on without any (teaching). We can say it is a 'real education' for someone to take a boat out on his own implying that he learnt something desirable without anybody having been there to ram home the lesson. There are many forms of learning that go on without teaching, and 'educative' learning does not imply the additional criterion that the learning must take place in teaching situation. It may be a general empirical fact that most things are learnt more rapidly and more reliably if the situation is explicitly structured by a teacher. But it certainly is not a conceptual truth that either 'learning' or 'education' implies 'teaching' (emphasis added).

Also they hold that whereas 'learning' is logically necessary to 'education', 'teaching' is not. And while trying to answer the poser: What characterizes teaching and how are we to distinguish its activities? They say: It implies that the teacher intends to bring about learning. "This necessity for teaching activities indicates or expresses to some extent that pupils are intended to learn, serves to distinguish clearly those activities which are essentially teaching, from many which are not, however valuable they may be in the circumstances". The second characteristic of teaching will, therefore, be that at least in terms of intention it has its end-product as learning. Indeed, one of the major goals of education, which in several respects has been identified with 'teaching', is to see "character traits are internalized (as also) social rules such as honesty, punctuality, truthfulness and selfishness." We find the child at this age is being initiated; instructed, indoctrinated, etc. all at proper time and in a sequence as he is gradually growing into a socially acceptable person. For example, he is being initiated into· certain family 'mores'. He is taught to recognize persons and exhibit varying degrees of familiarity. His ablutions and bowl movements and food habits and dress, etc. fall under the category of instruction. As the child grows up a little more and is ready for movement in social circles he is given a set of rules. These sets of rules are covered by the term 'indoctrination'. A child is warned not to mix with certain groups of children or, for instance, not to· discuss internal matters concerning one's household. To be able to move about in an unknown world, the child is protected by the shield of 'do's' and 'don'ts'. The entire social fabric will crumble down if all the children start behaving as they like. The most well behaved child is regarded as a very well brought-up person. But the reality is that he has succumbed to certain tricks played by his family on him. True, he has thereby earned the 'goodwill' of his family and approval of the society but at the same time he also betrays the deep impress of the social or family indoctrination. (See: *The concept of indoctrination* by Patricia Smart in the volume *New Essays in the Philosophy of Education*. Editors Glenn Langford & D. J. O'Connor, R. K. P., 1973, pp. 33-46) She holds the view that education and indoctrination overlap as concepts. 'Indoctrination' means teaching of beliefs held by the system/individual but if they are challenged, indoctrination will be eliminated.

When a society as such starts indoctrinating on given points it indulges in propaganda. Schools through their regular courses of study attach values to national behaviour and the dictates. Such and such social system or an idea stands approved or disapproved which has a bias in logic in its favour or disfavour. On a national scale, for example, the USA condemns the political set-up in the USSR. People in the USSR hold the view that they have a democracy in their country. As a people, therefore, they have come to agree with whatever they have been taught through their social system or political institutions. This means the logic advanced in favour of their institutions and disfavouring the others, is in itself such a proposition that a child grown into an adult has no rationality left in him to question what he has been taught or made to believe. It also means that besides the arguments for or against a certain system, the propaganda perpetrated in the classroom is the most well-organized and sustained, resulting in the dulling of one's rational bases of independent thinking. Persons like lllych and Reimer seriously object to an unproductive educational system operative these days. Due to built-in inequalities in society "the mere existence of school discourages and disables the poor from taking control of their own learning. People are warned against being manipulated by schools. (Ivan D. Illych, *Discoloring Society*, Calder and Boyars, London, 1971 p. 65, See also, Everett Reimer, *School is Dead.* Penguin, Harmondsworth). The working class and the oppressed are generally not prepared for accepting the values of the ruling class and of the consumer and capitalist society. But they are forced to agree because they have no alternatives. By making this reference I am merely trying to point out that besides confusing schooling for education, the present system assists in perpetuating inequalities and the value-system of the few over that of the majority: 'Schooling' is not 'education' and neither does 'teaching' correspond exactly to 'education' nor 'learning'. The classrooms of a democratic country, therefore, have as little scope for enabling a properly indoctrinated child to think differently from others as the one which does not supposedly have such a system. The standards of living and behaviour are as much a part of classroom propaganda as any other manner of life. The 'tribe' gives an urban child an idea of a backward community. The urban child has no other way of measuring one's advancement except in terms of per capita consumption of electricity, gas, fruits, etc. For example, he has not been told that what matters most is the 'quality' of one's life and not the number of goods one has that determine the degree of 'progress' or 'backwardness'. People come to hate or love a person from another caste, community or country on the strength of what they have been taught or told either through books or public platforms including family mores. These distinctions, though subtle, help us identify the parameters of teaching. Surely no one would like to regard teaching as indoctrination or propaganda, etc. Maybe one might approve of part instruction or part initiation. We have, therefore reached a point where we would like to face the question:

What exactly do we mean by 'teaching'? Is it a process or just a designed activity? How does one try to define it? Does it end in imparting skill? The serious question in this regard is whether or not 'teaching' is a synonym of 'education'? I should like to say that this is not so. 'Education' may have 'teaching' as one of the purposes but they are not synonyms. One can teach a child a skill or a specific job but then education, skill and a job are three different things, and each one is dependent on teaching or instruction to materialize. Teaching like instruction which is inseparable in this regard, therefore, is an instrument for some end. It has an instrumental value. Perhaps it has an intrinsic value too but to that we shall come later. In a relative sense teaching or instruction can help one acquire a skill. For instance, one can be taught to read or write or ride a horse. To this extent teaching, while overlapping with the term and concept like 'instruction', may be a highly specific affair. By itself it perhaps does not give the impression that it is a value. One cannot be very sure about it. In order that teaching is not considered much different from a kind of job or "the work or occupation of teachers" it has been distinguished from the work parents do or for that matter siblings or peers do. It is not teachers alone who teach skills or educate. Parents teach such skills like walking, talking or personal hygiene or table manners. True, there are such activities that are dependent on the process of maturation and built-in mechanisms. Neither maturation nor teaching can help much a disabled child. Even otherwise someone has to guide a disabled child into learning ways to overcome its handicaps. There are several things which only peers do. For instance, peers teach one slang and make a child socially (group-wise) acceptable. Siblings teach family secrets. In other words, formal teaching may only be a commissioned 'occupation' of teachers. But as we all know they alone do not teach and are neither particularly very effective. Indeed, others may be more specific and effective than the teacher who gets paid for a job, howsoever irresponsibly may he perform it.

Teaching would thus appear to be a specific occupation *directed toward achieving a highly specified end.* It could be viewed both particularly and holistically. This means that it may result in providing one the bases for being considered educated. Perhaps because of this reason alone that 'teaching', 'instruction' and 'education' are generally and broadly considered equivalents or even synonyms, whereas they in fact are not. 'Teaching' has an end in view, e.g. handing over or transmitting a value system but so has 'instruction', which gives more authority to the instructor because he supposedly has the last word. His authority cannot be questioned with impunity. In the case of teaching, however, the authority emanates from social sanctions but somehow it is not so unequal an affair as in the case of instructor and instruction receiving child. It will be interesting to note that in the 'initiation' process no hostility or disbelief are anticipated but in 'indoctrination' which is also a one-way traffic like 'initiation', questions and doubts are anticipated and answered in advance. This is something which is completely foreign to the concept of teaching. Herein not only doubts are expected, but they are welcomed. The moment, therefore, 'teaching' refuses to welcome doubts it is reduced to the level of 'indoctrination' and therefore, ceases to be teaching, which is said to be true in 'non-free' or 'closed' societies (to use Popper's terms).

In fact, it is possible to show that all these terms have a rank order and can be placed in a row with levels of importance attached to each. 'Propaganda', which has political or business overtones, is engaged in on a massive scale but is at the bottom of this rank order. 'Indoctrination' is not as diffused and general as 'propaganda', and also one has no options in the former case. For example, the advertising agents of a certain commodity sell better because of their 'effective' propaganda. There are many who pay no attention to it. Even in the heyday of Nazi power, all Germans had not accepted the superiority of their system, and even in democracies there are people who somehow refuse to agree that democratic system can be any better than the crushing power of the ignorant over the elite (See, *The Revolt of the Masses*, Ortega Y. Gasset). In both cases propaganda can be countered by equally strong logic. By dinning something into one's ears day in and day out, it is not easy that the indoctrinating machine will fail to have desired results. There is an element of terror and choiceless submission involved in the indoctrinating process like, in a seller's market. Revolt in this case may amount to high treason. No wonder 'indoctrination' is accompanied by power to crush the doubting Thomases. In terms of effect, it rates better than propaganda. Indeed, propaganda may also be a means to indoctrination. Propaganda is a merciless attack on the gullibility of the less rational. This should then be put at a lower level than instruction which also carries with it the power to put down any rebellion. Troops and police, not unlike children at home or school, are both 'initiated' and 'instructed' at the same time. They are initiated into the mysteries of their codes of conduct and instructed not to disobey. An army officer or a policeman, even after retirement from active service, cannot easily forget what he was instructed once. Similarly, a child asked to commit to memory a multiplication table will remember the same until the end of his life. I would like to suggest here that 'initiation' should not be put in the same category as 'instruction' or 'teaching'. Teaching thus occupies the highest rank in this category as it appears to be more free an affair than instruction. (see, *International Dictionary of Education*, Page, G. Terry, Thomas J. B. Marshall A.R., Kogan Page, London, Nichols Publishing Co, N. Y., 1977, p. 338)

It may be apparent by now that I have tried to rank-order these terms according to the level and degree of choices and freedom it grants to the one being exposed in each of these cases. Someone disliking 'choices' or 'freedom' can put them differently. In this classification, therefore, I have attached values to these attributes. Indeed where these terms differ even more dearly is in the content of what is transmitted under each situation. The overlaps in each of these situations are so colossal that any precise tag-marking is virtually impossible. Even so 'choice" and 'freedom', (though interdependent) will be the hallmark of the concept of teaching which, as already suggested, can not be true of other concepts like 'indoctrination', 'initiation', etc. because no one willingly accepts either of these. To the extent that teaching is 'open' and 'free', it remains at the top in the rank order. But it can soon enough degenerate into something quite different as and when tempered with.

We come across a major difficulty in regarding 'teaching' as something which tries to meet a socially created need. Depending on the nature of society even 'indoctrination' may pass as 'a socially created need.' For instance, a one-child family norm in an overpopulated country may easily fall into this category. Teaching apparently does serve a useful purpose but this 'use' is something one cannot anticipate and define. The quality and content of teaching can thus be determined by its end result. Teaching, for instance, aims at transmitting a value system very close to helping maintain the status quo. The skills and the media of communication offered as 'teaching' can never hope to be so revolutionary as may lead one to subvert the social order. 'Teaching' in this sense when offered through socially acceptable institutions will always be 'conformist'.

R. S. Peters comes close to defining the concepts we have been considering, e.g. "the business of a teacher is to teach, not merely to instruct and certainly not to indoctrinate.' Teaching' involves the passing on of knowledge, skills, or modes of conduct in such a way that the learner is brought to understand and evaluate the underlying rationale for what is presented to him. Indoctrination, on the other hand, involves either merely the inculcation of beliefs or the addition of a rationale which discourages the evaluation of beliefs, e.g. the appeal to authority as a backing". He goes on to giving very specific examples: "In the early stages of education, however, teaching in a strict sense may be impossible, for there may be very little possibility of getting children to grasp the reason 'why' of things. They may have first to learn that metals expand when heated, or that electric wires are dangerous, without being able to understand why; similarly in the moral sphere they have to learn that certain things are wrong, such as lying or breaking promises, without grasping fully the reason why they are wrong. There is a place here for instruction as a preliminary to teaching proper. Such instruction will degenerate into indoctrination if it were done in such a way as to discourage the probing into principles at a later stage when the child's mental development is ripe for it. *A child will tend to* believe what an authority instructs him in an authoritarian or doctrinaire manner. This may make it very difficult for the child to pass from reliance on authorities to the acquisition of the underlying form of thought or awareness". (*Ethics and Education*, *op cit.*, p. 261).

What may interest us most is the implied hierarchy of values attached to each of these terms. Surely the value attachment is relative and in another set-up all this defining may turn out to be a fruitless endeavour. For example, to a tribal inhabiting a dense forest all these concepts may appear irrelevant. For him what Peters suggests is degeneration, viz. 'indoctrination' may itself be the only meaningful term. Questioning of authority or probing deep into some problem area anticipates the existence or the 'knowledge' of alternatives. For example, if the authority of the word of a priest is questioned, something quite common in modern urban world, there is another authority ready to take on that mantle. Similarly, one probes into scientific or philosophical problems because: (1) there is reason to believe that an alternative may be in existence and finding of the same may be worth one's while, (2) that the confidence one reposed in the earlier teacher was misplaced, and/or (3) that one has not enough knowledge or skill to test the word of an external authority against one's own which one may have acquired either experimentally or intuitively but in any case· through one's own efforts. In other words, the hierarchy of values suggested by Peters and others is valid for a democratic country where questioning of authority by itself implies advancement of learning and acquisition of ability to compete internationally besides personal recognitions and benefits that accrue from this recognition. No such conditions are imperative in the case of the hypothetical tribe we have been discussing. Also, this hierarchy of values expressed through these terms suggests the presence of a variety of knowledge. There is knowledge that may be questioned, and there is that one may not. For example, one does not question the birth of a child whether human or animal through a process and the need of father and mother in either case (even where artificial insemination is now possible). The same is not true in other cases, e.g. Birth of a day is not dependent on the periodic rise—and-setting of the sun in the arctic zones—something which has been accepted in other parts of the world as the gospel truth. A tribal would be horrified at the suggestion of questioning the authority of the word of the priest or head of the family or even that of the head of the tribe. Firstly, for him, there is no point in seeking alternatives, secondly, the tradition is the law, and thirdly, the quality of life is not quite the same in the tribal and non-tribal settings.

The fourth and fairly important characteristic of teaching will thus be in the variety of its meaning and definition, depending on the context it is used in. For a tribal 'initiation', interaction or even indoctrination may sound much the same but surely not to a non-tribal. In an urban-setting, however, 'teaching' has quite a few shades of meaning. Where classed as 'formal teaching' it generally means classroom instruction (curriculum, teacher, students, examination, etc. all thrown in under the broad term 'instruction'), but in other cases such as in case of non-formal conditions 'teaching' may mean anything ranging from mother's instructions regarding certain personal habits to being told to conform or not to conform by siblings, peers, posters and the other mass media. It is perhaps this loose usage of the term 'teaching' which has led to the confusion of 'teaching' being used almost as a synonym for 'education'.

Whatever these terms may mean to a Westerner, for an Indian these two terms stand clearly distinguished by their end-products. We distinguish between an 'educated' and 'learned' person. A learned person is he who has been taught several standard works, but he cannot be regarded as an educated man unless learning accompanies wisdom, sobriety and a sense of discrimination. This dilemma is evident in the case of Narada who approaches Santa Kumar's attaining peace of mind. "To Sanat Kumar's question, 'what have you studied?' Narada replied that he had studied all the branches of learning—"-art, science, music, and philosophy, as well as sacred literatures". In other words, he explained the nature and quantum of his learning which Sanat Kumar qualified by saying: "Whatever you have read is "only name". This 'name' could be equated to Sartre's 'word', i.e. Narada could pass as a learned man but he was not so learned that he could discriminate and distinguish between various terms like speech, mind, intellect, etc. This knowledge he received from Sanat Kumar who, while distinguishing between these terms, gave him the knowledge he sought. For Sanat Kumar the hierarchy of these terms in the ascending order would be: name, speech, mind, will, discriminating will, concentration and insight.

Even if one does not wish to consider the religious aspects of these terms, they are useful for the purpose of our classification. The dialogue we just referred to appears in the Chhandogya Upanishad. In the Taittiriya yet another distinction is made: "Let your conduct be marked by right action, including study and teaching of the scriptures, by truthfulness in word, deed, and thought; by self-denial and the practice of austerity; by poise and self-control, by performance of the everyday duties of life with a cheerful heart and an unattached mind". These conditions have been imposed on a lay student. The following terms should give us a clue to what we have been considering thus far: *study* and *teaching* and *unattached mind.* Here 'study' and 'teaching' have been used in two different senses. Study here means 'self-study through concentration and insight, i.e. swadhyaya'. An unattached mind is free from fear, bias, love or greed. It is an important condition for being able to learn the truth. Teaching, of course, had religious and moral connotations, i.e. teachings. The Katha Upanishad details the pre-conditions for learning. "The senses of the wise man obey his mind, his mind obeys his intellect, his intellect obeys his ego, and his ego obeys 'Self'". All these terms used here have different connotations in English language but in Sanskrit these terms have other meanings. Once again in the ascending order the terms mind, intellect, ego, and 'Self' have been used.

What is being suggested here is that teaching in the Indian sense is restricted to the imparting of knowledge to 'mind' and this knowledge could never be more than 'names'. In the Western sense perhaps teaching mean training of senses and of intellect because for Plato 'mind' was superior to 'intellect' and also somewhat abstract. Education in both senses is different and superior to 'teaching' because 'education' is the goal and 'teaching' the 'instrument'.

Teaching, we as view it, is a process which involves several activities such as reading, repeating, demonstrating, etc. However, the end-product of this process can never be the learning of a skill. Skills are the results of either instruction, or initiation. Dancing, singing or pick-pocketing are skills. They may form part of one's education or personality. Teaching goes much beyond helping one learn a skill. A narrow, 'specific' goal can be ascribed to 'instruction' alone, or at times to 'training' but not to 'teaching', which is much broader in scope than either term mentioned earlier.

To an Indian 'education' makes man wise and discriminating and relieves him of his animal characteristics. No suggestion is intended to making reference to the so-called 'Darwinian theory' of human origin. What one means here is the efforts to rise above the animal requirements common to both man and the animals such as hunger, sex and competition. Modern life is characterized by these requirements, more particularly by its competitive Nature. Competition and the game of 'survival of the fittest' are being played these days in the fiercest sense of the term. A discriminating person will know that man can rise above this level and still survive. A well-taught person may also learn this but will never be able to practise it or even experience it. Parrot-like repetition is about all that he shall be able to perform. To enable one to look beyond is the purpose of education wherein 'teaching' with this specific goal may help a lot.

There is yet another way of looking at the activity called 'teaching'. Assuming as we always do that 'teaching' implies transmission of knowledge or skills—howsoever broad or specific these may be. Considering that 'teaching' results in making the taught becoming an educated man or is able to transform or bring about noticeable changes in the behaviour patterns of human beings the following possibilities of this transmission are suggested for consideration:

KNOWLEDGE OR SKILL

↓

Transmission Through a Teacher

(Whether Informal or non-Formal Situation)

↓	↓	↓
Whole	Part	None

Reception

↓	↓	↓
Whole	Part	None

This diagram shows clearly that a teacher (whether' in a formal or non-formal situation) can succeed in transmitting all that s/he knows of a unit of knowledge or skill or part thereof. The teacher may fail miserably in his attempt because the taught is not ready for reception. The cause may lie in lack of maturity or motivation. There is a possibility that the teacher himself may not know all that he needs to know about the knowledge he has chosen to transmit. In fact, he may not know anything at all and yet he be assigned the job of transmitting what he himself does not know. The possibilities would thus be like:

Transmission	Reception
1) Whole	Whole
Whole	Part
Whole	None
2) Part	Part
Part	Part (part of a part)
Part	None None None (i.e. whole)
3) None	Minus or Confusion

The serious questions that one may like to consider here are: (I) is teaching (1) inter-personal or auto-teaching? (2) Is teaching static or dynamic? (3) Does it get transmuted before it is transmitted? (4) Is teaching non-linear? And (5) what are its specific attributes?

In a way we have thus far been trying to answer these questions in a broad frame. It has been suggested that 'teaching' is an instrument for given purposes, wherein its nomenclature also changes according to the value-assignment. If at one place 'teaching' is 'initiation', it may be 'propaganda.' in another situation. It is carried on as an activity whether the recipient is agreeable to it or not. In certain cases, even the transmitting agent may undertake teaching unwillingly. Under these circumstances one must concede that the mode of 'teaching' is inter-personal. It will, however, appear that even before it becomes inter-personal, to be able to succeed it must become an auto-process in which the learner or recipient himself takes on the role of the teacher. This sort of process is more evident in the case of children, though among adults also it can be easily discerned.

It appears that there is an intermediate stage between 'learning' and 'teaching'. The term currently being used for this process is 'internalization', which implies that 'teaching' appears to take time before it becomes 'learning", and the period in between is covered by the term 'internalization' or 'assimilation'. Herbart come the closest to describing this process, (See, Brubacher, J.S.; *Modern Philosophies of Education,* McGraw Hill Book Company, N. Y., 1950, p. 46. "This view of mind leads to definitely different educational objectives. Guided by a theory of mental states, the aim of educational psychology is to determine the structure of the mind by analyzing the complex affair of consciousness into its various elements. The whole is explained by the parts. On the side of learning, learning consists in putting parts together. It leans heavily on the psychological theory of associationism. Following this theory, the teacher organizes the lesson and presents it to the pupil so as to correlate and achieve the sequence of ideas or passing states of mind, which will ensure understanding and retention in memory. This process is strongly reminiscent of Herbart and not a little mechanistic in spirit.")

I am however suggesting that teaching besides being inter-personal is essentially self or auto-teaching. The teacher attempts to transmit knowledge but this knowledge will never be assimilated or learnt until the learner reduces it (this knowledge) to a familiar vocabulary or an already learnt behavior. For instance, we watch the child learn to speak a word or repeat a skill. This the child cannot easily do, therefore, he produces sounds, which finally match the word he is supposed to learn. In fact, what he already has is a repertoire of sounds, given to him by Nature. In other words, if he is normally healthy, Nature bestows upon him the capability

For speaking a language, a normal child by manipulating an ability inherent in him attempts to learn words, ·concepts, and skills, depending on his process of maturation and social requirements. The child's attempt at learning a new term is similar to an animal's effort of digesting his food, in which the latter regurgitates his food which he had swallowed earlier. To me what appears most significant is the fact that child will not learn anything which does not help him directly to become socially acceptable as an individual. He starts deviating from the norm for acquiring a distinctive personality, which, of course, is dependent on the level and type of maturity. Conformity is as essential to human beings as deviation is. Be that as it may, the child learns to speak a word by repetition of sounds close to that of the word until he is satisfied with his attempt. 'The same will be true of a skill like walking, jumping, etc. This process will in no case be different for an adult trying to learn a concept or a skill. One can assess the distinction between the learnt behaviour and the behaviour to be learnt as and when a person is aroused emotionally. In the place of rational behavior, something one puts on like a mask, any angry person may exhibit manners and use the tongue which he learnt first as a child. This will be the foundation on which the superstructure of approved behaviour is built and a fashioning of distinctive designs carried on.

Considered against this background, a certain amount of learnt behaviour is basic, and is not subject to any change. If taken in part, each individual effort of teaching is dynamic but after it has been learnt it becomes static to a degree. 'Similarly, no matter how and what one learns the effort is dynamic. Interestingly enough, this process is not unilinear in the sense that there is no such thing as a neatly packed 'concept' or 'skill' and, therefore, it cannot be transmitted like the transport of an item of furniture.

18

Conditions for Teaching

WE have thus far considered several aspects and dimensions of 'teaching'. We would here consider: (i) pre-conditions and (ii) post-conditions of teaching, i.e. the outcomes. There is abundant material available on the outcomes. Indeed, the procedure of adjudging the outcome has also been detailed. For instance, "Knowledge as defined here includes those behaviors and test situations which· emphasize the remembering, either by recognition or recall, or ideas, material or phenomena"[1], besides defining knowledge, the stress here is on memorization of ideas or phenomena. In other words, the outcome of teaching is held out to be learning of ideas or phenomena or material, etc.

Let me reiterate here that by itself 'teaching' is motive free. Motives or goals are attached to it. Irrespective of the agency that determines and sells 'motives,' 'teaching' itself exhibits no 'will' of its own. 'Teaching' is like a natural spring whose water can be used for any purpose ranging from quenching one's thirst to cleaning utensils or motor car. Being a process it is as motive-free as a garden-fresh rose ready to adorn the hair of a beloved or be offered to one's Deity. We have already considered the distinction among terms like 'teaching,' 'initiation', and 'indoctrination', etc. and come to the conclusion that 'teaching' can be made one or the other under pre-determined conditions. Indeed, there is a hierarchy among all these terms and concepts out of which 'teaching' emerges at the top.

Teaching has as a pre-condition the presence of a learner whether motivated or otherwise, a teacher, whether aware of his true role or ignorant of the same and also a definite body of information whether defined or undefined but ready to be transmitted all the same. In simple terms the process could be described:

Teacher+ A Body of Knowledge

↓

Transmission (The act of teaching) ↓ — ↓ Learner

Fig. 1

On its own no knowledge can be transmitted because the matter in which form knowledge is present, is inert. Dynamism is an additional input. In fact, this dynamism is what one may like to call an external agent. Unless one takes pains or undertakes the 'effort', knowledge, irrespective of its form and content, will remain static. 'Effort' is something common both to the learner and the teacher. Knowledge possesses no chemistry which may make it self-propelling. Without' 'effort' knowledge will remain an unknown phenomena or material, not unlike the movement of galaxies, which, on their own, do not ensure their thrust on one's awareness or become part of common knowledge.

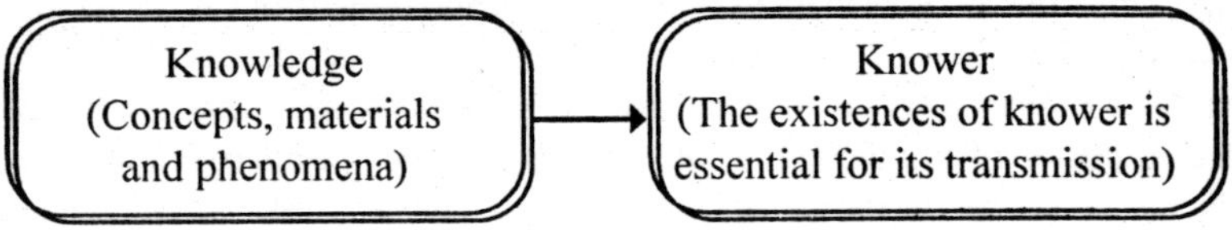

Fig. 2

Knowledge exists whether or not there is a knower. The existence of knower does not determine the existence of knowledge. Knowledge exists in the form of material, phenomena or concepts even without being known and transmitted. Taking the example of the life in the galaxies, we know that it may or may not exist. We have no means of knowing its exact form or extent. Only on the basis of our experience of life on this earth and of planets beyond earth, we can surmise that life may exist elsewhere as well. In other words, there is no one on earth who knows for sure what is or is non existent in the galaxies. We simply do not know what we may know with 'effort'. Of course, even 'effort' is of no avail in several cases. It should be of interest to realize that despite infinite capabilities, the human mind has limitations, imposed upon it biologically. These infinite abilities and possibilities are restricted by our sensory perception. We have a life span, unless the decaying process is controlled. It is further limited by the structures or frames it has created for understanding anything. Mind codes and decodes in terms of structures, needed for developing understanding. Knowledge exists beyond these decoded structures as well but it cannot be known or if known it can be done only partially which again is tantamount to not knowing wholly. We shall attempt to answer questions like these: (i) Does knowledge have categories/qualities and attributes? (ii) Is knowledge discovered? (iii) Can knowledge be created? (iv) Is knowledge transient or perennial? (v) Is it purposive or value-free?

Perhaps we may add a few more pertinent questions:

Can the ultimate in knowledge be known? How does one know, if one knows that the ultimate in knowledge is knowable? If one can answer some of these questions one may try answering these as well: Is knowledge whole, part or relative? How can we be sure that knowledge is intuition, confrontation or mere awareness? Can knowledge be 'collective'? Can it transcend itself, i.e. be Para-knowledge?

The reason why at least some of these questions need to be answered is that teaching can not be conceived of 'without understanding the nature of knowledge besides the limitations of its source: Knowledge by itself does not appear to have any categories or qualities. The latter are attributes in which we understand it because without structuring our brain will not comprehend anything. Brain has limitations of its own and only through these limitations can it appreciate the dimensions or the extent of knowledge it can possess. Brain like our stomach cannot chew or eat everything and neither can it do it as a whole. It must accept food (in the case of brain of knowledge) in a form and at a time when it can be digested. Knowledge exists as an external Reality-the true nature of which we perhaps can never understand. In Srimad Bhagwat Gita Lord Krishna deals with this aspect of the problem when he tells Arjuna that the latter con not see even a fraction of the Divine Reality because of the limitations of his physical eye. In order to perceive the Divine, Arjuna was granted by Lord Krishna a third eye which had no such limitations. The entire episode as presented in Chapter XI and Verse VIII of the Gita endorses our contention that knowledge—the Real one—exists beyond our immediate physical powers of comprehension. If we do not know that, it does not mean that it does not exist. We, however, cannot invent it. We can only discover it by a process in which we must raise our stature and powers of comprehension, and this is why Yoga was suggested as a remedy to this limitation. Thus we are sure the knowledge an ordinary human being can acquire must be of a transient nature. It can't be value-free as well. Man is acquiring daily ever new knowledge and is using it for this or that purpose. This, in fact, cannot be true for the knowledge Lord Krishna was talking about.

The entire Upanishadic literature is concerned with the question of the Ultimate in knowledge. Janak, the king of Videha, desired Yagnavalkya to tell him about it-and the latter replied "By the purified mind alone is Brahman perceived. In Brahman there is no diversity. He who sees diversity goes from death to death."

Brahman can be apprehended only as knowledge in itself—a knowledge, that is one with reality, inseparable from it. For he is beyond all proof, beyond all instruments of thought. The eternal—Brahman is pure unborn, subtler than the subtlest, greater than the greatest. The eternal glory of the knower of Brahman, beginning and end, revealed by divine knowledge, is neither increased nor decreased by deeds. Let a man, therefore, seek to obtain it, since having obtained it he can never be touched by evil."

In Brihadaranykaya Upanishad not only does Yagyavalkya teach Janak what real knowledge is, he also teaches him how to attain it. The methods of learning he suggested are: self-control and meditation. For attaining the same goal at a different place in the same Upanishad to the gods, Prajapati taught them to apply self-control, to the men he asked to be charitable and to the demons he enjoined upon them to be compassionate. In other words no single method is good enough for all.

According to the Upanishads it is possible to acquire the ultimate knowledge provided one opts for the right methods which are self-control and meditation. Sadhana is what one may try to achieve this goal with.

There remain several questions in this regard that cannot be answered so easily. Whether knowledge is whole or part depends on who is looking at what. If comfort is all that a common man seeks in life, attainment of the riches will be his objective. To a saint these riches will mean nothing and nor will the comforts have any meaning for him. For him peace and tranquility hold the ultimate charms and to this end he may seek Divine Bliss. Knowledge by itself has a use because it has a purpose. It is this purpose; which will define and structure it. For example, if a student proposes to become a surgeon, the knowledge he will like to possess should be related to this end and no other knowledge will be of any use to him. There is no limit to the perfection one may acquire in one's branch of study which· means surgeons will tend to be graded according to the level and degree of knowledge they possess. In each, case the last word in the possession of knowledge will be dependent upon the capacity of a surgeon to attain and master that knowledge. Like Aakash (sky) knowledge *per se* has no limit and neither does it like Vayu (wind/air) have any definite abode. Therefore, it is possible to acquire it through intuition and self-study, through confronting: other learned scholars, etc. Just as it is not possible to store all the water in the world at one place, knowledge too cannot be collected or even put in a collective form. Similarly, there may be gradations and types in the acquisition of knowledge but knowledge as such cannot transcend itself. What we can acquire through our senses is mere vidya (external/bookish) but gyan (inner/insightful) can be comprehended only through reason, analysis and intellect. One may teach vidya in a classroom because it is both structured and arranged but gyan one has to acquire. It is the latter which can help an individual become free and liberated.

Bertrand Russell made a distinction between 'knowledge by acquaintance' and 'knowledge by description'. Teachers are already familiar with acquainting students with their environment through direct experience. Therefore whether in history, political science or the physical or geological sciences they want their children to learn through practical projects like surveys, experiments, problem-solving methods, etc. The idea is to give knowledge in action. The other method of learning is by reading about the background of the "knowledge in action". After all, there is an enormous amount of knowledge already stored up in books which is called knowledge by description. Russell did not regard knowledge as 'inert'. Whatever manner a person pursues to acquire knowledge before assimilation one has to be actively acquainted with it.

There are both western and eastern theories about knowledge. There is a school of thought in both India and the West which holds that knowledge already exists in its complete form, and one has to acquire the wherewithal of mastering it. The Kantians and the Upanishadic philosophers agree with this school and the 'idealists' as they are, they lay emphasis on developing powers of mind and eye to learn about it. This group of philosophers who go much beyond what already exists in statements-of common sense, history and science, etc. There is another school like that of the existentialists, who hold that knowledge comes through personal participation and decisions, the knowledge which one person has of another, the 'knowledge' of good and evil, the knowledge of God. (See, *Ways of Knowledge and Experience* by Louis A. Reid, Allen and Unwin, London, 1961)

As one will sees it will not be easy to find answers for these queries. There are several ways of answering these questions. Due to limitations of time and space I should like to give illustrations both from the western philosophy and the Indian standpoint. In both these cases illustrations *are arbitrary as no single, philosophical system represents* entirely the West or India. The choice, therefore, will be made of the systems that are apparently close enough to be regarded as representative. My illustrations are from Plato, Descartes and Kant in the West and the Vedanta from India. The reader may like to add or delete these illustrations or even deny or refute their validity. But for our purpose they are very useful. They explain the nature of the content for transmission in a teaching situation.

For illustrating the Western standpoint on 'knowledge,' I have depended solely on Bertrand Russell's *History of' Western Philosophy*

(Unwin University Books, 1974) and used his terminology. To begin with, for Plato there is only one world, not many. In fact, there cannot be many as it is a created copy designed to accord as closely as possible with the eternal original apprehended by God. Everything in the world has been created by God after the pattern of eternal. He wanted everything to be like Himself. God made first the soul, then the body. The soul is compounded of the indivisible unchallengeable. In essence it is the third and intermediate kind. There are two types of causes. There are intelligent ones, and those that being moved by others are in turn forced to move others. The former are endowed with mind and are the workers of things fair and good, while the latter produce chance effects without order or design. As both make up the creation, both are to be studied.

"Earth, air, fire and water are not the first principles or letters or elements, they are not even syllables or first -compounds. Fire, for instance, should not be called thus but such that is to say, it is not a substance, but rather a state of substance. At this point, the question is raised: Are intelligible essences only names? The answer turns, we are told, on whether mind is or is not the same thing as true opinion. If it is not, knowledge must be knowledge of essences, and, therefore, essences cannot be names. Now mind and true opinion certainly differ. For one is implanted by instruction, the other by persuasion: one is accompanied by true reason, the other is not; all men share in true opinion, but mind is the attribute of the Gods and of a very few among men" (Russell; p. 159)

For Plato there is nothing worthy of being called 'knowledge' if derived by senses. The real knowledge has to do with concepts. Plato proposes to define 'knowledge' in Theactetus but according to Russell he ends his quest without advancing any satisfactory proposition. Plato argues that knowledge and perception are two different things. For example, sounds and colors are unlike but we possess no sense organs that can perceive both. "There is no special, organ for 'existence and non-existence, likeness and unlikeness, sameness and differences, and also unity and numbers in general". Plato argues to hold that the proposition 'knowledge is perception' must be modified to 'knowledge is judgments of perception' in order to be grammatically correct. The only formal knowledge not derived from perception is logic and mathematics. The rest by implication' is not true knowledge. Plato caricatures the doctrine of universal flux. He applies to processes of continuous change, such logical oppositions as perceiving and non-perceiving,~knowing and not-knowing. Russell is, however, critical of the application of logical opposition of these contexts as they were invented for our convenience and not in these situations wherein something like a quantitative apparatus is applied. Even so it is interesting to note e g. the moon gradually being enveloped by dark clouds and becoming invisible passes through an intermediate state of doubt.

The founder of modern European philosophy, Descartes, in his *Discourses on Method* (1637) and *The Meditations* (1642), which largely overlap each other had also tried to advance his theory of knowledge. He begins with skepticism with regard to the senses. Hallucinations and dreams can make anyone feel what is not real. According to Descartes, arithmetic and geometry are more certain than physics and astronomy as they are not concerned with particular things. Doubt is possible even with regard to arithmetic and geometry. Some Divine or Evil power may lead us to count the sides of a square or add 2 and 3. The only thing which one cannot doubt is the presence of thought. Even body may not exist i.e. I may have no body but thought is quite different. "While I wanted to think everything false, it must necessarily be that I who thought was something; and remarking that this truth, *"I think therefore I am*", was so solid and so certain that all the most extravagant suppositions of the skeptics were incapable of upsetting it. I judged that I could receive it without scruple as the first principle of the philosophy that I sought". The statement "I think therefore, I am" makes mind more certain than matter and my mind as against the minds of others. This philosophy is the very basis of subjectivism and modern idealism.

'Thinking' for Descartes includes a thing that doubts, understands, conceives, affirms, denies, "ills, imagines and feels because feeling, as it occurs in dreams, is a form of thinking". Since thought is the essence of mind even during sleep mind must think. Descartes while talking of the knowledge of bodies holds that certain things are apparent to the senses. He takes the example of wax. The sense tastes honey. It smells flowers, sees some size and shape, feels hot and cold, and if struck emits a sound. This wax, however, changes 'qualities' if put near fire. True, wax persists but what we had earlier seen was not the wax itself. The wax itself is constituted by extension, flexibility, and motion which are understood by mind and not by imagination. The perception of the wax 'is not a vision or touch or imagination but an inspection of the mind'. I do not see the wax, any more than I see men in the street when I see hats and coats. "I understand by the sole power of judgment, which resides in my mind, that I thought I saw with my eyes". Knowledge according to Descartes is confused if derived from senses—something we share with animals. "I can perceive wax-stripped of its clothes. From my sensibly seeing the wax my own existence follows with certainty, but not that of the wax". Knowledge of external things must be seen by the mind, not by the senses. Ideas, he holds, are of three types: (I) those that are innate, (2) those that are foreign and come from without, {3) those that are invented by me. The commonest error constitutes of ideas in the second category. The fact that there are ideas which are involuntary is no argument; for dreams are also involuntary although they come from within. The reason for supposing that ideas of sense come from without is also not conclusive. One can have two different ideas of the same external object, for example, the sun as it appears to the senses and the sun which is an object to an astronomer. The both cannot be the sun but the one that comes to us as a result of experience must be less like it of these two.

These considerations do not dispose of the skeptical arguments which throw doubt on the existence of the external world. This can only be done by first proving the existence of God. For our purpose which is important is the conclusion that the Cartesian system presents two parallel but independent Worlds: that of the mind and that of matter, each of which can be studied without reference to the other. That the mind does not move the body was a new idea.

To the question: Why does mind feel 'sorrow' when the body feels 'thirsty'? Descartes in his *The Meditations* holds that the body and mind are like two clocks and that one indicates 'sorrow' and the other 'thirst'

The Cartesian theory of material world is deterministic. Both dead matter and the living organisms are governed by the laws of physics. There is no need to explain the growth of organisms and the movements of animals. The only exception is human soul which can, by volition, alter the direction through not the quantity of the motion of the vital spirits. Cartesian theory does have a genuine difficulty of explaining 'Will'.

The same problem is attempted by Kant to be resolved although both Plato and Kant are more than 2000 years apart. *The Critique of Pure Reason* is Kant's important book. According to him our knowledge can transcend experience. It is, nevertheless, in part *a priori* and not inferred inductively from experience. The *a priori* knowledge is not merely logical but much that cannot be included in logic or deduced from it. Kant distinguishes between the 'analytic' and 'synthetic' propositions on the one hand, and on the other, he outlines the distinction between 'a priori' and 'empirical' propositions.

Examples of each are relevant because if 'teaching' has anything to do with the methodology of transmission of knowledge and also with the quest for true knowledge, we must know what propositions really are. An 'analytic' proposition is one in which the predicate is part of the subject;

for example, 'a tall man is a man, a dark woman is a woman'. Such propositions follow the law of contradiction. In this case if a tall man or a dark woman is not a man or a woman" respectively, it will be a contradiction. All propositions that we know only through experience are 'synthetic'. For example, we do not discover truths by a mere analysis of concepts. 'Akbar was a great king' and 'Buddha was a great sage' are parts of experience.

Kant, however, is not prepared to agree that all synthetic propositions are only known through experience. An 'empirical' proposition is one which we know with the help of sense-perception either our own or that of someone else, whose testimony we regard authentic. The facts of history and geography are of this sort; so are the laws of science. Any knowledge of a proposition's truth which is dependent on observational data will be an 'empirical' proposition. An *a priori* proposition may be edited by experience but its basis is not experience. For a child learning arithmetic may require the experience of adding two marbles with another two marbles. But once he grasps the general principle 'two and two make four' he no longer needs a confirmation. Here the proposition is a certainty which induction cannot ever give in the form of a general law. Pure mathematics is in this sense *'a priori'* to the question: How are synthetic judgments *a priori*? Kant presents his Copernican revolution in the shape of *The Critique of Pure Reason*. He has claimed in the first edition; "I venture to assert that there is not a single metaphor or problem which has not been solved or for the solution of which the key at least has not been supplied." The outer world, for Kant, causes only the matter of sensation, but our own mental apparatus orders this matter in space and time and supplies the concepts by means of which we understand experience. 'Things in themselves'—the causes of our sensation-are unknowable. These 'things-in-themselves' are not in space and time, they are not substances, nor can they be described by any of those other concepts called 'categories'. Space and time being parts of our apparatus of perception are subjective. But just because of this we can be sure that whatever we experience will exhibit the characteristics dealt with by geometry and the science of time.

For Kant space and time are not 'concepts' but forms of intuition. There are *a priori* concepts and there are twelve 'categories', which are divisible into four sets of three: (i) of quantity': unity, plurality, totality, (ii) of quality: realism, negation, limitation, (iii) of relation: substance-and-accident, cause-and-effect, reciprocity, (iv) of modalities: possibility, existence, necessity. These are subjective in the sense that time and space are part of mental constitution but these are not applicable on 'things-in-themselves.'

Whenever one applies space and time or the categories to things that are not experienced, one is likely to be troubled with 'antinomies'. Antinomies are contradictory propositions which in each of the propositions can be apparently proved, but of the four we may take up one as an example of time, and is also limited as regards space. The anti-thesis says: 'The world has no beginning in time, and no limits in space, it is infinite as regards both time and space'.

From our standpoint Kant's views on space and time are of specific interest. Kant holds that the immediate objects of perception are partly due to external things and partly due to our perceptive apparatus. For him even the primary qualities are subjective. Kant does not question that our sensations have causes, which he calls 'things-in-themselves', or Noumena. What appears to us in perception, which he calls a 'phenomenon', consists of two parts: sensation and our apparatus—the latter causes the manifold to be ordered in certain relations. The latter part he calls the form of the phenomenon. This part by itself is not sensation, and, therefore, not dependent upon the accident of environment. It is *a priori*, i.e. unchanging and not dependent on experience. Kant holds that space and time are *a priori* for us. This can be proved both by metaphysical and transcendental arguments. The former class of arguments is taken directly from the nature of space and time, the latter indirectly from the possibility of pure mathematics.

(A)

We have thus far tried to consider the major components of the major philosophies of the West. In so doing I have been merely attempting to establish that it is not easy to say that what the teacher teaches is true knowledge because. most of his knowledge is based on perceptions or experiences through senses. Reason is perhaps a step higher than perception or experience. But at a given range even Reason is of no avail. We shall, however, come back a little later to discuss our difficulty in transmitting partial knowledge which in turn is seldom fully received.

Let us now have a view of the major Indian philosophy: the Vedanta. Here I have principally depended upon 'Surendra Nath Sengupta's *A History of Indian Philosophy* (Vol. I and 2, Cambridge University Press, 1957).

'The Upanishads, forming the concluding part of revealed Vedic literature, are known as the Vedanta. Though Upanishads continued to be written long after the arrival of Islam in India, the important ones (ten in number) had been written by 500 B.C. The entire matrix of Indian philosophy constitutes the Upanishads. Whether to refute or support any argument, Indians have invariably to refer to the Upanishads for the simple reason that 'germs of diverse kinds of thoughts': are found scattered over there. The Vedanta is generally 'identified with Sankar's interpretation of the Upanishads, though there are many other systems that claim to be true 'Vedanta' doctrines. Sengupta himself holds the view that the Upanishads should be regarded as a repository of diverse currents of thought and be not identified with any single interpretation (p. 4). The Upanishads have one fundamental idea running through them, viz. underlying the *exterior world there is an unchangeable reality,* which in turn is identical with the essence in man. Vedanta is one long quest to unravel the Reality—Brahman. The substance of the Upanishad teaching is that Atman is the same as Brahman. The definition of Atman is a negative one. Yajnavalkaya says: "He the Atman is not this, nor this (neti-neti)." He is inconceivable, for He cannot be conceived, and is unchangeable, for He is not changed, untouched, for nothing touches Him, he cannot suffer by a stroke of the sword. He cannot suffer any injury" either.(Brihadarankya, IV. 5.15). The Bhagwad Gita uses the same language to define Atman. In Chhandogya Upanishad Prajapati says: "The Self' (Atman) which is free from sin, free from old age, from death and grief, hunger and thirst, whose desires are true, whose cogitations are true, that is to be searched for, that is to be enquired, he gets all his desires and all worlds who knows that Self'. The inmost essence has been described as pure subject-objectless consciousness, the reality and the' bliss'. He is the seer of all seeing, the hearer of all hearing and the knower of all knowledge. He sees but is not seen, hears but is not heard, knows but is not known. The state of Brahman is like a dreamless sleep. He who reaches this state is beyond fear. That is the state in which the' finite-infinite' (the Atman that dwells the body) ceases to be' limited. *When a man finds his peace, his fearless support is that invisible, support less, inexpressible. unspeakable* one,. it is then that he attains peace.

I am not trying to highlight the Vedanta as the principal philosophy of this country but merely wish to point out that the ancients held firmly to the idea that senses elude reality. The reality can be witnessed only through Sadhana, i.e. training of the senses, so that they may go beyond their limitations and help one to realize that only Mind can conceptualize the reality and only thus can Atman transcend physical boundary and merge in the ultimate Reality. Restraining and keeping the senses under control is one major refrain of the Indian philosophy and 'looking within' or 'Atmam Vid' the main objective of life.

According to Sankara the external world has been referred to in the Upanishads and accorded reality so that its relative reality is exposed as soon as Brahman is known. The external phenomenon has its own claims, but only so long as the Brahman is not known.

The world is composed of organic and inorganic things. All organic things like plants, animals or men have souls. Brahman willed to be many so he created fire (tejas), water (ap) and earth (ksiti). It is, therefore, the self-existent Brahman entered into these three, and it is by their combination that all other bodies are formed. This is the three-fold division of the primitive elements, which leads to the later distinction of the pure, infinitesimal substances and gross elements, and the theory that each gross substance is composed of the atoms of the primary elements.

Sankara has given a theory of causation too, though the Upanishads have nothing concrete to say about it. Citing the *Chhandogya Upanishad* (VI.1), Sankara talks about the clay as the material cause; and pots and jars as empty distinctions of name and form. Irrespective of the name and form, the earth is the essence. Similarly, the self-existent Brahman, despite the three manifestations, viz. fire, water and earth, is the ultimate reality and the rest is illusion. What the senses see is form and name but that is the point up to which they would go. So Soul as the Self identifies itself with its desires. He wills and acts according to them and consequently reaps the fruits in the present and the future. As and when the Self comes to know that He is the highest essence and principle of the universe, the immortal and the infinite, it ceases to desire. Man is the epitome of the universe. He holds within himself the constituents of the gross body (annamaya kosa), the vital functions (pranamaya kosa) of' life, the will and desire (manomaya) and thoughts and ideas (vijnanamaya), and so long as he keeps himself in these spheres and passes through a series of experiences in the' present' life and in other lives to come, these experiences are willed by him and to that extent also created by him. He suffers pains, pleasures, diseases and death. But if he retires from these into his true unchangeable being, he is freed from all these pains and pleasures, etc. and experiences neither change nor movement. This state is beyond the descriptive ability of anyone in the world. The true self manifests itself in all the processes of our phenomenal experiences. Eventually when it retires back to itself, it can no longer be found in them.

It may be interesting to note "that by regarding Brahman as both the material and efficient Cause of the world Vedanta reduces Causality to the principle of ground and consequence". Sankara's position is as follows:

"Consciousness is Reality as being what never can be contradicted or falsified. Objects as other than consciousness are other than Reality and in this sense merely appearances." (*The Main Problems of Philosophy*, S. K. Maitra, Calcutta, Progressive publishers, 1962, p. 20)

It is what appears that can be contradicted or falsified, 'what never appears, such as a barren mother, a square circle, or a sky flower, is incapable of being falsified or ever thrown. There is no difference between objects qua objects as regards liability to falsification and rejection. In this respect the illusory object and the object that passes as real in normal waking experience sail in the same boat. In other words, their liability to correction and eventually rejection as false is the same in both.

(B)

Israel Schaffler says that "Many philosophers in recent times have argued that once certainty is given up as a condition of knowing, truth must also be given up, at least in the absolute sense in which every statement is unequivocally true or false, irrespective of time, place, person, and circumstance. The motivations for this argument are various and complex-but the main common purpose has been to bring epistemology into line with scientific practice, in which ideas are treated as fallible hypotheses, subject always to future test. The moral has been drawn that there is, in science, no absolute truth just because there is, in science, no pretension to certainty at any given time. Theories are radically altered in the course of scientific inquiry, and then truth must, therefore, always be construed as relative to the data and assumptions of the scientific *community at a given time"*.(*Conditions of Knowledge*: Scott, Foreman. & Co., Illinois, 1965)

We raised a few questions in the initial stages of this chapter. It may appear that neither in the West nor in India do we have any positive answers to them. Depending on which philosopher one was talking about the nature of true knowledge one will take on that form and language. It obviously leads one to the conclusion that knowledge varies in interpretation and that 'true knowledge' is hard to define or identify.

Knowing as we do that we have very limited ways of knowing the reality, the content of teaching will to that extent remain affected. What we generally teach is appearance. Even in the laws of physical sciences there is only a relative degree of certainty. What we regard as certain today becomes so uncertain and naive tomorrow. We perhaps live more by faith than knowledge.

Schaffler faced with similar questions, has tried to react to them. The question, "Granted they found out, but did they really know", does not strike us as immediately relevant or natural. Those educators who stress so-called discovery and problem-solving methods in schooling may, in. fact, be operating upon the general presumption that such methods lead to strong knowing as an outcome. And emphasis on teaching, with its distinctive connotations of rational explanation and critical dialogue, may have the same point to develop a sort of learning in which the student will be capable of backing his beliefs by appropriate and sufficient means.

He also stresses the intentional part of teaching. When one is engaged in the activity (and not process) of teaching it clearly means that some kind of goal or intention is also implied in it. On this point, Schaffler states "obviously an appropriate bit of learning". In other words, he is not. prepared to conceive of teaching as an end in itself, or teaching as a goal-is activity–something which is there and can't be helped. Goal, intention or purpose is, therefore, an implied corollary of the activity called teaching. It is not a process because teaching is so specific an activity. A process may or may not be that specific. An activity *terminates at a given point, i.e. when the aim is achieved,* but the process does not; as it is continuous. Schaffler will be quite willing to concede that teaching can be auto teaching or agree that the state of activity in which a skill or knowledge is being transferred, there comes a point when it has to be transmuted before it is transferred. In case this does happen, and I think it does, knowledge or its part can be the first casualty. One cannot be sure as to the nature of knowledge that is transferred and how much—does it change in the process of transfer. We have already seen that it is a near rarity in which what is intended to be transferred or communicated is fully transferred or communicated. The other aspect of this communication has also been noted. According to Schaffler: "Any teaching is geared to what the teacher takes to be true; and his aim is not merely that his students learn what he takes to be true but that he be able to support it by criteria of proper backing taken to be authoritative". He comes to making almost the same point as I have done: "In so far as the teacher is teaching, he is, in any event, risking his own particular truth judgments, for he is exposing them to the general critique of these criteria and to the free critical judgment of the students' mind".

In fact, not only it is possible that the student may not agree with the judgment of the teacher, he may appreciate it only partially. Indeed, what I am trying to say is that the student may even colour the entire understanding given to him by his own lack of it. In the case of skill the student may learn it imperfectly or improve upon the imperfect skill, given to him by his teacher. The same may happen in the case of knowledge as well, besides a skill.

Perhaps it is in this sense that a student may question the belief of the teacher. His belief in the knowledge, communicated to him, can be at variance with that of the teacher. There may exist many reasons why this will happen. A strong puritanical family may attach a value to a ritual which both according to the teacher and the student's own reasoning may not stand the test of logic. It is quite possible that the student who may otherwise be very logical in *approach and very reasonable* may suspend his judgment wherein it has been believed "that knowing and believing are related forms of mental activity, the present idea leads us to differentiate sharply between them, in denying that knowing is simply a mental or psychological affair". (*op cit.* 1)

To know, therefore, is not the same as to believe it. Austin holds that we normally ask, "How do you know?" and "Why do you believe?" and not vice-versa. R. M. Chishold writes, "We must not think of knowing as being, in any sense, a 'species' of believing or accepting. A man can be said to believe firmly, or reluctantly, or hesitatingly, but no one can be said to know firmly, or reluctantly or hesitatingly". This should indicate very clearly that what we believe in or at times even know may not be correct. For example, we need not believe that Alexander the Great was really great. We are not sure of the truth that while teaching a problem in geometry, the solution given in the textbook is true. We assume it is; although we teach both these facts, we neither know their truth nor do we believe in what we teach.

While we are trying to understand the meaning and nature of the term teaching without its corresponding relationship with learning, Schaffler, not unlike many others, does not limit his area or inquiry in this sense. I would prefer to think of the activity before it tries to have a bearing. On 'learning' this is one reason I am distinguishing between pre-conditions and post-conditions. The intermediate state is that of teaching-learning— an activity in which the actual transfer takes place. If looked at in the context of' education, the intermediate stage is the most important one. If considered in terms of outcomes, the post-condition should be significant as it is measurable. But for a philosopher, I think, all are equally important, the first being a little more than the other two.

In my view the intermediate stage is of transfer of' knowledge, or information. It may appear that nothing like transfer of items of furniture or goods takes place in teaching and learning. I have indicated in the first chapter that out of several possibilities knowledge as a whole does get transferred in the shape of learning only very rarely. Normally either it falls short of the requirement or it goes wide of the mark. Also some other types of changes occur in this stage which one may liken to chemical changes, which may lead to a dilution or reinforcement of the material taught. Perhaps I would make this point clear with an example. Suppose I have an earthen jar with me and I show it to my pupils and say, "This is that jar which Emperor Ashok used for drinking water". Even if my pupil knows the significance of an antique and has the imagination to travel back in time by a few thousand years, this jar may strike to him like any other jar available in an Indian village. In other words, his conception of the antique jar may be quite different from the idea I intend to communicate with its help. These gaps may not be due merely to lack of information or experience or the age and competence of my pupil but his imagination will also interfere with it. In a dream as I talk to my old friend, I tend to overlook the gap in my recent knowledge about him and imagine him to be as old as he once was-as if Time has been static in his case. The earthen jar of Ashokan times may look like another jar which the pupil may imagine, is readily available in Indian villages. The real worth of this jar, though not lost to the teacher, may not appear all that important to the pupil. The antiquity of this jar to me as a teacher will always remain as an important factor in teaching because I have learnt it once that way but the pupil will take time to reach my level of attaching the same degree of importance to it as I do now. I am not suggesting that this degree of incapability in learning about the antiquity or uniqueness of the jar is due to my pupil's lack of maturity, but surely I am saying that his imagination lacks training.

Is it likely that my experience in teaching about an antique may be repeated if I am teaching an experiment in any of the physical sciences? I think the answer will be in the affirmative. In chemistry lab if a teacher demonstrates the properties of a chemical, the pupil will certainly learn all that, given the level of maturity to understand it. But beyond a point he will fail to grasp the significance of that experiment or its relevance in daily life, because the: latter requires a certain degree of maturation and experience.

Even as our perception is affected by the normalcy or otherwise of our naked eye and the manner in which retina adjusts itself to focus 'the vision and mind decodes the message into an object, the transfer of knowledge undergoes a process very similar to it. This is that stage of transfer which I have given the name 'intermediate stage'. It is here that the belief of the teacher may result in a very different type of belief in the pupil, something completely unanticipated or imagined. It is quite possible that the teacher's belief that 'cow is a sacred animal' may result in a violent disbelief in the pupil although the teacher is trying to do his duty which in turn is to expose his own beliefs also to a critical examination by his pupil. How one's sincere belief can lead to this kind of reaction is not easy to imagine yet it does so happen very commonly. In most cases the cause can be traced to a radical difference in the conditioning of the children and their teacher.

(D)

In the pre-conditions of teaching, one may as well consider the type of other variables that affect teaching. To a very large extent this consideration will be important if we think we can have positive answers to questions like: (1) Does the teacher have a 'free' will to change the content of teaching? (2) Can the teacher be allowed to teach his beliefs including prejudices?

We will agree to the creation of chaos if and when we hold that the teacher has a right to change the content of teaching. His personal likes and dislikes can both distort facts and try to set wrong things right. In any case the moment the teacher exercises his freedom to deviate, the results will legally and ethically be wrong. Legally in the sense that society hires the teacher to teach a given textbook and not something quite different from it. His freedom can also be ethically unjustified, because the teacher may, in the exercise of his right to deviate, teach immorality or even lead to revolution. The major problem in this case will be: Who will correct the inaccuracies whether factual or otherwise? A board of textbook can do that but that takes time. Therefore, what happens in the meanwhile? Does the teacher break law and be unethical or remain loyal and teach knowingly inaccurate facts?

We will also not easily concede that the teacher has any right to teach his belief. Perhaps under certain conditions we may permit that, e.g. in a seminar a teacher has the freedom to discuss his belief but before a class of small kids he can not be allowed to do so because these kids may not know how to distinguish between the teacher's belief and the untruth. Whether one liked or not teacher does color the facts presented by him either through emphasis, repetition, commission or by his own maturity or otherwise.

The corollary to this will be that if the teacher does not have the freedom to teach his prejudices or beliefs how societies will progress or change? Does that imply that the teacher is the vanguard of new ideas? We have now entered a very sensitive area of discussion. No society formally appoints teachers to teach revolution or permits indirect instigation against its own survival. If these things still happen and a few teachers are involved in it, this surely does not either betray a society's intentions or signify that the event is correct. Only a few revolutions have partially been justified by history. The teacher obviously enough does not occupy the position of a potential revolutionary or an agent of change. Changes occur despite teaching *status quo* and highly unimaginative and repetitive teaching.

(E)

I do not think I have any answers to the questions: Can knowledge be created? Is knowledge transient?

The alloys made in laboratories may suggest to us that knowledge of these alloys is something new, and since it did not exist before, it has been created This should lead us to hold the view that knowledge is being manufactured or created almost daily. The discovery of new information implies that knowledge about this fact did exist, but it had not been discovered until a certain date. A new chemical, paste, alloy, or a design is examples of knowledge created with effort. Their utility is, however, discovered much later. The purpose for which a chemical is created or prepared may prove to be wide of the mark because in actual practice, its usages may be found to be many and varied yet quite different from the original intended purpose. The earlier was the goal and the latter a discovery. At all this knowledge of a chemical or a product was created, the discovery of its usages is not unimportant. In a state like this we cannot be quite sure whether this knowledge is created or discovered.

In social sciences it is difficult to suggest that any knowledge has ever been created or could be created. The facts are found; they are collected, compared and shifted until a law operating underneath is discovered. These laws may or may not meet any particular need but even these laws are in fact discovered and not created because in a nebulous form things did happen, only they had never been systematically put. Rivers follow a course, the oceans hide within themselves an untold wealth of materials, people live and die, these facts are known but to put them logically so that these facts are explained in the 'whys' and 'hows' of information, is mere discovery of a law.

Even if one denies a determinist, it will not be correct to hold that any knowledge may be created. We may create a new instrument, we will know that this was also a discovery. An invention is no more a creation than a discovery. The invention is also a form of discovery. Whereas discovery is the consequence of a goal-directed hard work, an invention has insight as an additional constituent.

Knowledge under the circumstances is transient because it is relative. Knowledge in its absolute form must be one single whole. The old knowledge as known absorbs and systematizes new knowledge. It obliterates the newness and soon enough makes it indistinguishable from its old self. The new knowledge remains new until it is absorbed and made part of the old knowledge. This phase is so transient that at times it has been suggested that this is not so. The transitoriness of knowledge appears perennial even as the spokes in a fly-wheel in motion appear non-existent.

(F)

Knowledge as already stated is relative. We know a little less or more than the other person. Absolute and complete information is possible only to the Prime Mover, who was and is the Beginning and the End. For everyone else partial knowledge like partial blindness is the only reality.

(G)

To the question 'how does one know if one knows that knowledge is knowable?' we may consider the Indian standpoint. In his work titled *Indian Theory of Knowledge*, Dr. Bijalwan (Heritage Publisher, New Delhi, 1977, p. 60) has provided us with a readymade classification. The Indian philosophy differs on the major point from the Western philosophy while the Western philosophy accepts only two modes of acquiring knowledge, (a) perception and (b) inference, the Indian philosophy holds a divergent view on this matter. Different schools of Indian philosophy view the modes of acquiring knowledge differently. It is thus quite logical to hold that under each of these schools acquiring of knowledge, the processes of both learning and teaching, will, have to be considered separately.

On one extreme we find the Carvakas who recognize only one form of pramana (evidence or proof), viz. the pratyaksha, i.e. the direct perception; and on the other extreme are the Pauranikas who accept all of the seven pramanas. The Indians, unlike the Westerners, have a wide variety of available choices as far as 'proof' or evidence is concerned.

Before we describe the analysis of this classification we must make it clear that the role of the teacher is confined to being a catalytic agent in the process called 'learning'. This act of being a catalytic agent is guided and purposive, guided in the ·sense that the goal is clear to one or the both and purposive in the sense that the selection of the tool of service is made carefully by weighing all pros and cons. The teacher is supposed to be extremely "careful in helping a child appreciate the value of pramana (proof) and the utility of the proof has to be guided:

1.	Carvaka	p
2.	Vaisesika and Buddhist	p a
3.	Samkhya and Yoga	p a s
4.	Nyaya	p a s u
5.	Prabhakara	p a s u ar
6.	Bhatta and Vedanta	p a s u ar an
7.	Pauranika	p a s u ar an sam ai

Incidentally, we have not questioned the validity of the need for a teacher in this process. One may tend to hold out that as knowledge can as well be self-evident, one need not have a teacher. And once, it is assumed or asserted that an external agent like a teacher (the knower) is needed, to that extent the abilities of the learner have been put under a doubt. Because the need has been caused as (i) the learner is inherently incompetent to learn himself, (ii) the knowledge exists in such a form that its logical and proper handling is possible by some other person alone, and (iii) the knowledge is not self-evident and is not readily comprehensible to all or to a few. Our premises are therefore different.

We accept the existing criteria or the means of knowledge of both the Indian and the Western. Indeed, ours is a limited purpose, i.e. the examination of the relationship between conditions of truth and criteria of assessing evidence. Involved in that is the activity which happens to be our principal concern.

We present definitions of each of these terms given in the code so that we could determine which one hopefully or possibly may be involved in the process of teaching.

(a) *Prataksha*: The term is supposed to be equivalent of perception, i.e. what can be seen and shown to be seen. In Sanksrit it is a combination of prati (near to or related to) and aksha (eye). In certain conditions "seeing may not be believing'" as a stick in water though straight is perceived as crooked or bent. But here perception is regarded as illusion-free

(b) *Anuman*: That is what may be inferred. According to Jayantha, the process of anumana includes: (1) Perception of the reason, (2) The remembrance of the universal concomitance, (3) Judgment that to the subject of inference contains the problems, (4) Knowledge of the consequence, and finally' (5) Judgment that the consequence is worthy of being accepted or rejected.

(c) *Sabda*: Or the verbal testimony if based on the statement of a trustworthy person or to the perception, if it corresponds to a statement. Etymologically Sabda (*sabdyati*) signifies sound (dhvani), literally it stands for word (pada) and epistemologically it refers to source of knowledge namely "verbal testimony".

(d) *Upmana*: Or comparison is based on the well-known fact of resemblance between two cognitions, wherein upmana is a means and upmati the result.

(e) *Arthapatti*: Or presumption has been accepted as a distinct source of knowing, more particularly when there is conflict, it is resolved through the presumption of a fact and not of words.

(f) *Sambhava*: Is interpreted as the cognizance of a 'part' from the knowledge of a 'whole' with which it is inseparably connected; for example, we cognize number 'hundred' from the number one 'thousand'.

(g) *Aitihya*: It is held as a succession of rumours or the tradition spreading from generation to generation and emanating from unknown speakers. Ghost on a tree is one such example.

As the present study does not seek to examine the viabilities of each of these sources of knowledge nor hold out any opinion, we too shall content ourselves remarking that not all these categories need be taught to a student. It would be interesting to observe that for such content area or what we call subject-matter, one or more sources and evidences of knowledge may be found necessary. Also, we have reached a stage of technological development in which most of these sources of knowledge are 'impersonally' available.

We are considering here knowledge (K) or its variant (k) (the appearance of K) as that which exists outside of us, and also that needs to be cognized. This need may be spiritual or material but a need must surely exist as a precondition to that something must be cognized or else we will remain indifferent to knowledge in any form. In the absence of this 'need' or 'requirement', even the greatest object of beauty, valour or cognition will go absolutely unnoticed or at best be indifferently or casually noticed.

In the following diagram we give an improved version of the earlier diagram.

Pre-conditions to Teaching	*Teaching to enable Cognition*	*Resultant behavior*
(a) Learner	Interaction between them take place	(a)&(d) for (b)
(b) Knowledge (K or k)		
(c) Need		
(d) Situation under which these conditions can operate i.e. teaching can take place		

What we have so far been trying to describe is the resultant behaviour as a result of interaction between several variables.

(H)

We have now reached yet another important stage in our discussion. Teaching as an activity with precise goals must lead to a conclusion, not very different from that which was originally intended. Goals as we all know can be the result of auto-selection or selected by others like the society. There may or may not exist any choice in this regard on the part of the learner. For instance, in the 'closed' societies these choices are normally absent. Be that as it may, the outcome has to be judged in the light of goals alone—no matter how and who decides these goals.

"How much transmission of knowledge or skill is possible?" is a question we have already been answered. Skill as compared with knowledge has greater chances of being transmitted. Skill is manual and is dependent on our senses. Knowledge is basically theoretical and is based on certain principles. A skilled teacher may enable his students to becoming as clever and skilled as he himself is. It is doubtful if the same can be said of a knowledgeable teacher. If put to use, skill usually improves and shines. This improvement takes place because of its constant repetition. But knowledge by repetition does not grow likewise. It grows with further additions of a similar genre of knowledge. Knowledge even before it is put to use implies that the owner of that knowledge *knows what he knows.* Any addition or subtraction takes place only by further Knowledge. But in the case of skill, the improved performance is principally due to repetition leading to efficiency. Efficiency in this case will mean dropping out of those components of skill that reduce its show in performance and adding those that help its achievements.

In order that the activity of teaching terminates—that too 'successfully—the post-condition, i.e. transmission of skill or knowledge is essential. It will be useful if we use two different terms for these two different concepts—(a) skill and (b) knowledge. For skill 'instruction' is more suitable and for the transmission of knowledge the term 'teaching' is more appropriate. With regard to skill, the transmission of a skill could be ascertained, evaluated and even graded. If a child learns to walk or speak properly, one can say 'instruction' in these skills has been successful. Instruction is purely mechanical i.e., how to put fingers on the key-board of a typewriter will be called 'instruction' which also partakes of the basic character of teaching. Drill, repetition and non-deviation from the given instruction are parts of skill transmission. However, in the case of knowledge one cannot be very sure about the outcome for the simple reason that the knowledge being given is only relatively true. Therefore, what we give is not some thing quantifiable but which is vague and only marginally positive. For example, what we will regard as 'good' or 'effective' teaching vis-à-vis knowledge is not the transmission of a measurable quantum but an attitude which may enable the taught to add or subtract what he has learnt. What we call 'teaching' has for its end-product rationality, an acquaintance with the tools of acquiring knowledge, the ability to distinguish between good and bad. Indeed, teaching as an outcome has education as the ideal, though both are neither 'synonyms nor even similar'.

In a way the post-condition must be similar to what 'Gardner Murphy' (*Freeing Intelligence through Teaching*, Harper &Bros. 1968; pp. 59-60) says:

'Can the teacher teach rationality? My answer will be 'yes', under five conditions, which assume that there is: (1) freedom from demoralizing fear; that rationality is not an object of terror for the learner; that the ego strength is adequate to accept and to use constructively the normal range of daily anxieties and challenges; (2) a love of the subject-matter and of the system of knowledge and skill and world order of which it is a part; there must be cathexis upon subject-matter, the process of confronting it; and the meanings which emerge from masterly of it; (3) cathexis, too, upon the very methods themselves, by which such rationality is sought; a love of learning in Spinoza's sense; (4) underneath such a process, acceptance of one's own self, cathexis upon the self as seeker, knower, lover of reality, and finally, (5) in every relation between teacher and taught a full transaction, the teacher being taught, the student teaching, the two learning and teaching in reciprocity.

19

Conditions of Teaching: Goal-Setting

THE ASSUMPTIONS

TEACHING being a purposive act has to be defined in terms of assumptions, goals, and conditions. Teaching qua teaching is an absurdity. If it does not meet certain requirements, its need will be seriously jeopardized. The important fact to remember is that knowledge is seldom imparted to be an end in itself. As already indicated, teaching is intended to equip one to become rational. In turn rationality must enable one to discriminate and distinguish between good and bad. A rational person should be able to pick and choose his own information and content area, i.e. knowledge, which means he can perceive the need for furthering knowledge. In this sense teaching activates a process which terminates only with one's final departure from this world. By itself teaching is a specific activity with a long-range goal called rationality. Teaching, a skill in this sense, is quite distinct from teaching knowledge.

If we assume that teaching leads to rationality, the imparting of a sense of discrimination, we can not be certain that rationality is an absolute value. To be rational is not necessarily to be good. Also rationality has its limitations as well. There are several difficulties in this regard. For example, we all know our stay on this earth is brief and not always happy People take birth, live for a spell of time and finally die. So death like birth is a small event and one should neither be depressed at the news of someone's death nor feel elated at the birth of a child. If this rationality is to be applied to news of the death of someone very close to us, society will condemn us for the callousness of our attitude and behavior. In this case rationality will invite either criticism or equal indifference when a similar occasion comes in one's life.

Similar problems are encountered even when the intention is remarkably guileless. We may have a belief, for example, in helping others and acting good Samaritans. We may also believe that no one is a born criminal, and that relationships like that of father or son, etc. cannot be denied. Acting on this belief we may as well help a thief while decamping with someone else's property. For example, we see someone not being able to lift a load of material. We help this person in his effort. Later on we come to realize that we had helped a thief in his actual act of thievery. In this case, however, we may have acted unknowingly. But knowingly we help our parents in all their activities, even if they are not always legal. While we show a sense of obligation toward our parents we are accessories to a criminal act. Therefore we decide: (a) unless we knew why a person needed assistance in lifting some material, we would not risk a bad conscience in future, or become accessories to an act of crime, (b) our obligation to our parents can be shown in several ways, not necessarily by helping them dodge the State or breaking the law of the land. Therefore, as soon as we come to know that our parents are law-breakers we approach the police and inform them against the law-breaking. In both cases the knowledge of a fact prevents us from discharging a moral obligation A prostitute's daughter cannot walk out of the profession her mother follows just because the daughter thinks otherwise. In any case if ignorance leads to disastrous results, knowledge also does not help much.

Let us take a more innocuous example by helping a deer we can prevent a lion from his rightful meal. The belief that the weak must be helped does not always lead to social justice. In India the Naxalites did come close to seeing that social justice was achieved, even if that meant the death of a few unwanted rich people. We cannot be too sure that social justice is an achievable goal by the mere knowledge that it is a good goal. No sooner do we start acting on our knowledge or belief than we become ourselves law-breakers.

The sanctity of law itself is doubtful. If a law holds that acquiring of property is an inherent right and fails to regulate the process of such an acquisition, its own sanctity becomes highly suspicious. Therefore, even while we are taught that the state is the final authority and ultimate power with regard to adjudging values like good or bad the state being run by a government and objectified in laws can itself be immoral. We may, in fact, be quite justified in overthrowing a dictator although this dictator may have reached his status by extremely legal means.

In other words, our rationality comes constantly in conflict with the actual social, political and economic set-up and fails to help us even in our daily behavior. If a woman falls in love with another man while she is still living with her husband, it gives rise to a social as well as an ethical problem. Whichever way the ultimate solution lies, the fact is that rationality is quite frequently clouded over by our emotional ties and behavior.

(A)

In the matter of writing textual material all kinds of problems arise before the authors. The achievement of goals set in this case becomes so complicated that the end-result is. invariably a hotchpotch of compromises:

Let us take a concrete case: A board of authors has been told that their material must be 'secular' in approach. Even the term 'secular' has. been defined. They will be hard put to it to writing sensibly on the question of cow protection law or on controversial topics in Medieval India. The question that must always bother them is: "How secular is the term 'secular'?" While being what they cannot be, the authors are being disloyal either to their community or unfaithful to their task. Their belief in regard to one can come in conflict with their knowledge about the work they are doing.

In fact no society can ever anticipate and, therefore, resolve the problems of conscience. Consequently, a kind of straight-jacket policy is pursued. The boards of textbooks are informed of the nature of activity which in turn is governed by the nature of society, its political system and values which they cherish. Within this frame which is as vague as their work, authors write and become acceptable. Marked deviations, conflicting with any existing laws or practice or even common beliefs, are avoided. For example, in order that a child ceases to be superstitious we teach him the distinction between the real and the unreal and equip him with what is commonly termed as 'scientific temper'. This we assume will be more lasting armour for meeting the dangers of superstitions than debunking each and every superstition individually. In brief, we arm the child with anti-superstition equipment and not kill the superstitions for him.

The problems of conscience are also dealt with at the same level. Society helps its citizens to develop a conscience which is thoroughly conditioned to suit its own purpose. A monolithic society, for example, will underplay teaching of logic and talking of unrestrained freedom. The chances are that in these societies 'anti-social behavior' will tend to be more neatly defined than the approved one. In such societies the positive is known only by the condemnation and elimination of the undesirable, which means the 'undesirable' is that which is not sanctioned or approved in the interest of rulers. Similarly, what can help them remain in power and position will by definition qualify to be called 'positive'. In other words, those that continue to be troubled by a live anti-social conscience either end up in jails or become revolution's successful heroes. As the majority consists of those who follow 'middle of the road' policy, they become models of conscience-keeping and ethical conduct. One may call them 'time-servers' or insensate pigs but it is these doormats that eventually govern the educational system. They develop a conscience-free organism with a sort of single channel receiving set. The mess created by the NCTE, which is basically governed and run by professionals, is an example how ethic-free their behaviour is. While claiming to work in the interest of the teaching profession, they have brought the level of teacher preparation to a level from where it cannot go down any further. A basically unimaginative system has been made to yield before those who should have never been permitted to enter the system in the first place. Consequently, what we see on the ground is a reality which cannot be called a teacher education system.

(B)

The question of values has been answered in several different ways. A distinction is sought to be made between the universal and the particular. We are told that the particular must always be subjected to the universal. The good of all is the highest value and perhaps the most impersonal one. The ancient Indian scriptures also support the modern view that the State must look after the *welfare of all* its citizens. We are told that merit alone must be the criterion of selection in almost every walk of life. A brilliant student should not be permitted to languish for want of monetary support. Schools should be so run that besides talent the common, average student also does not suffer. We have so far not been able to define and identify 'brilliance' because the limited number of studies that we have, suggest that the brightness of students is generally limited to those who come from professional class homes. In other words, 'brilliance' is a socially definable term. This means we wish the system to support those that need no support and justify our claim by citing examples of financially weak students who outshine others after they have been helped. The rare is made to look universal. The logic in this case is so twisted that an educational system eventually betrays the worst example of monopoly perpetuation, and yet the facade retains the innocence that gives rise to a feeling of worship. With all the incense-burning and bells ringing we have no fear or suspicion that the temple is in fact a sacrificial altar.

Similarly, we have so far not evolved any tools to 'identify the types of talent children can have, and yet offer a variety of choices in the shape of vocational and professional studies. The limited number of options being currently provided is defended on devious grounds. The values attached to professional studies far outweigh the ones associated with vocational choices. We come across several vocations which have high financial rewards, e.g. confectioners, dry fruit sellers, jewellers, etc. but one considered them inferior to a medical practitioner's or a lawyer's work, etc. It is interesting to observe that financial return itself is a value which we want to accord a high degree of priority. Still we are, however, prevented from acknowledging this fact quite openly, though in private this is one value which one hears so often mentioned. It is not surprising that teachers, doctors, lawyers, engineers and even the saintly religious practitioners adopt short-cuts to amassing wealth. In other words, we quietly permit the public hypocrisy of declaring a profession superior to a vocation yet compromise on the sly to a value; even its pursuit may endanger the values attached to the profession which we avowedly cherish so much. The imposition of limits to define the perimeters of their practice is openly flouted.

What I am hinting at is that there is an inherent contradiction between what we do and what we declare we are doing for. These levels and shades of hypocrisy have their built-in mechanisms of rationalization to guide our actions. Over a period of time hypocrisy has been socially sanctified. For example, the entire examination system is socially discriminatory. It is beside the point that no one has any respect for it. We know that the teachers discriminate while awarding: marks or hardly bother to examine for the real purpose of evaluation. Students cram and present bits of information as knowledge. Majority of students will prefer a more honest system than the one we have, yet succumb to the machinations of a small group interested in the perpetuation of a thoroughly y discredited system. Favours bestowed on students carry with them their own price tags. Objectivity, fairness and commitment to higher goals like learning for learning's sake, etc. are the first victims of a class-oriented rigmarole called admission test of an examination for grading. So thoroughly has this game been debunked that no employer now seriously considers a candidate's fitness for a position on the strength of a university certificate alone. Private business goes by efficiency' on the job and contacts but the public sector while trying to be more objective than its private counterpart, scrupulously follows Peter's Principles.

Under the circumstance even a talk about values like honesty and decency in public life exposes one to ridicule. There are no fog lights or light-houses available which means that values themselves stand compromised. No one could imagine of receiving~ potable water out of a jungle of drain pipes.

(C)

D.G.O, Conoor (See, *Philosophy and Education*, op. cit., pp., 1-9) lists the aims of education and then goes on to examine each one separately for their real worth.

1. To provide men and women with a minimum of the skills necessary for them: (a) to take their place in society and (b) to seek further knowledge;
2. To provide them with a vocational training that will *enable them to be self-supporting;*
3. To awaken an interest in and a taste for knowledge;
4. To make them critical; and
5. To put them in touch with and train them to appreciate the cultural and moral achievements of mankind.

For O'Connor "such a list as this may seem merely one more of the edifying platitudes that are so apt to occur in writings on education". This is one of those lists that one cannot also ignore to consider because in all societies such a list is readily furnished for discussion. On a close examination one can not really substantiate what one meant by each of these listed aims. He finds all of them vague but reserves his special comments for 4 and 5.

"Since to make men critical is only to teach them to proportion the degree of their various beliefs to the weight of the evidence in their favour. It is difficult to understand how it can properly be deprecated as an educational aim... its neglect in practice leads us to suppose that, like most moral rules, it is more inspiring and comforting as an unrealized ideal than as a way of life.

"That educated men and women should have some knowledge and appreciation of what is best in literature, art, music, science, and the rest of the apparatus of higher civilization is an educational platitude so banal that it seems hardly worth recording".

The purpose of citing O'Connor is to illustrate the point that aims of education if one goes by consensus will be as banal as we have seen they are, or will be so controversial that only an unthinking conformist may support a few of them. Education, not unlike the society to which it owes its existence and survival, attempts to keep away from controversies, and if a few are floated it merely shows that they are more in the nature of complaints than anything serious. In other words, a few complaints, are registered so that on the next available opportunity some compromises can also be made. For example, if a train can carry only a limited number of passengers and one comes across complaints about the limit or the manner of booking, it indicates that a few *more bogies be added to the train or else the introduction of* a new train will become absolutely necessary. Complaints against the educational system have no more meaning than the ones we come across being registered against any public enterprise. Only a few demand the total abolition of an undertaking whereas the majority would agree to small adjustment in the face of a public uproar. Persons like Everett Reimer or Ivan Illych are no more radicals than Naxalites who want the peasant to fight for his perceived demands. Illych and others hold that the present system is corrupt and crumbling, therefore its replacement is necessary. They do not say that no replacement is needed. While replacing the present, a compromised plan should be implemented. Education by its very nature does not preach revolutions. Even when one talks of according status to radical demands; one merely implies that one may be heard and, if possible, respected. Radicalism like an exotic taste is tolerated. It provides variety to a rich man's drawing room.

(D)

Hirst and Peters (*The Logic of Education, op cit.*, p. 86) conclude their discussion on teaching by stating: "the education processes are those processes of learning, which may be stimulated by teaching, out of which desirable states of mind, involving knowledge and understanding, develop". They imply that education is a process in which learning may or may not necessarily take place. We have already examined this aspect of their definition and agree with them. They hold further that teaching stimulates learning. This view can only very partially be correct because we have tried to show that teaching and learning do not have one-to-one correspondence. If we were to accept the view that teaching stimulates learning, it may mean: (a) in order that learning takes place, stimulation is essential, i.e. it is a pre-condition, (b) if stimulation is something like ice-cubes in a drink, then it means it makes the effort pleasant, or (c) teaching refreshes the act of learning. It does not seem quite likely that teaching does any of these things. Of the variety of teaching specific things be they of skill, knowledge or information, learning is picked up according to one's taste, competence, level of maturity and the ability of the teacher to communicate. Mere stimulating teaching will not. Level of maturity or the ability of the teacher to communicate, one hopes, is implied.

Hirst and Peters also hold the view that the outcomes of teaching are: (a) desirable states of mind and (b) desirable states of mind are qualified by knowledge: and understanding. This means they are suggesting that learning is a value which teaching attempts to transmit. If one examins this value and sees how it is acquired, one will immediately conclude that values are linked to time and space, and although there is a suggestion of Absoluteness about a few of them, yet on examination this claim is found to be hollow. For example, the year 1857 of Indian history will be taught differently in India and Great Britain. Of course, teaching in either country can merely interpret the sequence of happenings on the Indian sub-continent differently, but 1857 by itself will remain what it is—something of an objective reality and therefore free from any partisan view.

We know by now that what we teach is not real knowledge but its appearance. Fragments of knowledge or its partial communication will, if at all, result in partial understanding only. The learning which Hirst and Peters: suggest will indeed be only partial learning.

The processes of education are said to be the processes of learning, which I doubt is really the case unless we hold that education and learning are one and the same thing. This we by now know is not true. Education covers the whole gamut—society and its ethos, teacher, curriculum, and learner, etc. along with a desire to learn, out of which a qualified learning is the only positive outcome. Beyond that we could not justify any statement.

(E)

It is commonly agreed that through education we do not 'insist on the transmission of knowledge alone but what we try is to equip the learner with a set of skills—for instance, reading, writing, etc. that may enable him learn more. This also means that we ourselves do not attach any degree of finality about teaching any definite sets of skills or knowledge for the simple reason that we know there cannot be any such finality. Reasons for this state of affairs can be: (a) knowledge itself, which is neither definitive nor final. It grows changes and develops, (b) scholar's abilities and potentialities are so indefinite; and/or (c) tomorrow's needs cannot be easily anticipated. Additionally, we doubt that any teacher can hopefully perform this job.

We have already cited Gardiner Murphy in an earlier chapter, who says that rationality is teachable. Of course, there are a few conditions and within whose frame it should be possible to do so. Schaffler defines 'teaching' as "connoting an initiation into the rational life, a life in which the critical quest for reasons is a dominant and integrating motive". (*Conditions of Knowledge, op cit.*, p. 107)

In other words, both Schaffler and Murphy are agreed that rationality should be the aim of education as a process and teaching as an activity. There is no reason to deny the desirability of such a goal. Our difficulties arise as soon as we start looking for material and equipment which can help achieve our goal. We are here overlooking our discussion at the beginning of the chapter for the time being.

How does one teach rationality? How can intellect be initiated into a perpetual rational frame? As we notice there is considerable difference between teaching rationality for a given goal and the rationality which is global in outlook and operates in all walks of life, ranging from our love to our children and accepting or rejecting the hypotheses regarding the theory of expansion of the Universe. As an objective, rational behaviour is an ideal which not only 'teaching' but social life itself should demand to be fulfilled. Also, we should not be rational in one thing and irrational in another. Rationality like brick and mortar must build the entire edifice of our personal and social life. It should run through every idea, dream or action that we attempt to cherish. How does one teach? Rationality is as difficult a question as viewing the galaxies without the help of a telescope. Thereafter to see that if at all this rationality has been acquired it must guide all our actions and behaviors.

We must restrict our discussion by considering only a limited number of examples: (a) can language help in teaching rationality? (b) can any of the social sciences be of a particular use in this regard? (c) Does the teaching of basic sciences help?

Language does not show that it has itself been developed on very rational grounds. The names and structures of things have been fixed arbitrarily in the course of its development. Language does not always perform the job it has been developed for. Not only do we notice that it falls short of expressing shades of meaning but it could only help communicate the stereotypes. For example, we express our 'regrets' for anything, ranging from our inability to help another person to being critical of any event of international importance. "I regret to say that I am not in a position to help you" to "The 'Government of India regrets to say that it cannot endorse the U. S. policy on nuclear control." Both are regrets but of a different genre. It merely illustrates that 'regret' is a term which is both particular and universal. Since this is so no teacher can limit its usage or demonstrate with any degree of exactness the type of structures it can fit into. The rationality behind the structures may be explainable but the limits to the pliability of words must also be explained. We have seen that the latter is not easy to attempt.

Out of several subject-areas in social sciences we select history to examine the possibility of its being fit for teaching rationality. History teaches us the development of ideas and institutions, reasons for social mobility and declines and falls of empires as also of individuals. It has explanation for every thing. If a king was no good, the reasons for his being so are traced to his defective education, his incompatibility with time, his inefficient friendly relations with the neighboring countries, etc. while no formula exists to guide the actions of a king, no genetic technology has so far been evolved to see that kings can be any different from ordinary mortals. Similarly, while no one will say that benevolence is a bad trait, a benevolent king in turbulent times will be as great a national hazard as an autocrat during peace. If autocracies decline because of their excesses and irrationality, democracies also succumb to their weaknesses. Indian history can easily illustrate both these statements. Can we find a similar pattern in all countries, and if not, why not? Can we say that neither democracy nor autocracy is suited to India?

There are no reasons to explain why India or Africa would have been subjected to foreign rule for so long unless we say that Indians had no strong identity of their own, which is to contradict that Indians are Indians and not someone quite different. The maximum that we can do by teaching history is to present facts objectively, and let the students draw their own morals. Since these morals will be different for different students (or else there will be no controversies) it shows that each one of the students has his own perception and set of value-judgments, which the subject cannot really determine or control. Obviously then rationality of a subject area can be distorted or restored according to the whim or perception of a student or may be of a teacher. This clearly establishes that rationality does not govern the organization of subject-matter.

We now come to the third aspect of this discussion, i.e. should the rationality be global or specific? I have no doubt people will vote for the Global rationality because specific will be too narrow a goal to restore any order in its application. Besides the fact that this kind of rationality is an impossible target to achieve, it cannot be considered even desirable. Two reasons why I will condemn it for being desirable are: (1) it will turn human beings into automatons, and (2) the gaiety of life which is ascribable to irrationality will vanish, leaving life unbearably boring. We feel sorry on the death of anyone but more when the dead was dear to us. The intensity increases corresponding to the degree of closeness. The loss of a wife or a child is even more intensely felt than the death of a national leader. Is one's wife more important than the national leader? Perhaps not, then why do we feel so sorry about it? The reasons are purely personal and emotional. Both grounds are indefensible. Does that matter?' Yes, it does; because we are globally rational. The moment we apply this level of rationality to our daily lives, we will lose most of the charm in living. Also emotionality is dependent on closeness, usefulness, familiarity and similarity of tastes. We will, however, not like to admit that irrationality is also a desirable goal.

It is one of the tragedies of life that language is a great handicap in communication. But the greater tragedy lies in the fact that even when we want to say something, have also the necessary equipment to say, we do not express ourselves frankly. Indeed, we do not wish to express ourselves at times for certain considerations, which are purely social or personal in nature. For example, we never tell our host that the dishes served by him did not measured up to the standard of their formal preparation or they have not shited to our palate. This kind of suppression of our judgment constitutes 'etiquette', which is another term for hypocrisy or lying. A lie to keep someone in the dark is not too bad. In fact, it is socially permitted. Where is the rationale for this? Hurting someone's feeling is no good but exposing him behind his back is also not, or is it? Or, should one hope that every time an individual is served his favourite dish in an unfamiliar flavor, his taste must also undergo change correspondingly.

(F)

Earl C. Kelly (*Education for what is Real*, pp. 15-22, Harper Row, N. Y. 1947) has detailed the assumptions why education is considered a value. He says:

1. We assume that the child goes to school to acquire knowledge, and that knowledge is something which has existed for a long time and is handed down on authority.
2. We assume that subject-matter taken on authority is education in itself.
3. We assume that the best way to set subject-matter is in unassociated fragments or parcels.

4. We assume that a fragment or parcel of subject-matter is the same to the learner as to the teacher.
5. We assume that education is supplementary to and preparatory to life, not life itself.
6. We assume that since education is not present living, it has no social aspects.
7. We assume that the teacher can and should furnish the purpose needed for the acquiring of knowledge.
8. We assume that working or tasks devoid of purpose or interest is *good* discipline.
9. We assume that the answer to the problem is more important than the process.
10. We assume that it is more important to measure what *has been learnt than it is to learn.*

We would consider a few of these assumptions against the light of discussions contained in this paper. It is true that knowledge is the principal reason why a child goes to school. Implied in this assumption are two more minor assumptions, viz. (a) knowledge has a direct correlation with formal schooling, and (b) knowledge exists as an object which it is possible to neatly pack and transmit. We hardly need to respect these assumptions because they are not based on reality. Knowledge is relatively transient and the means of acquiring it equally uncertain. We also know that formal schooling is only one of the several agencies and not a very effective one at that. We have also seen that knowledge does not get transmitted like pieces of furniture but gets changed in the process. The knowledge that teacher has can be fragmented and parceled, which means that the fragments when re-assembled do not make the whole. Even within the given frame, Plato of teacher's understanding is not the same Plato that the students know of, whereas the teacher may know a little more than what he is prepared to explain to a student and, therefore, the two may differ in the real knowledge of Plato. There may be several other reasons equally valid for explaining the differences in knowledge which the teacher and his taught have.

A few of the assumptions Kelly enumerates have lost their relevance. For example, very few would uphold the medieval theory of disciplining Mind by feeding it with understanding data. Even the *Grammarians' Funeral* is a thing of the past. Similarly, we do not subscribe to the view that a teacher can and should furnish the purpose needed for the acquiring of knowledge. It is, in fact, not a very valid assumption. Not only can the teacher not furnish the purpose, he also must not, because in that case the teacher will cease to be an agent of society and become the society itself. A teacher can be given certain authority but not an Absolute one No sooner do we do that, then the school will be transformed into a penitentiary, which surely it is not. The dullness of the classrooms marked by indifferent teaching and listless learning does sometimes give this impression that we do after all consider schooling a punishment But a large-scale denial of this state of affairs does indicate this kind of dullness. It is true that a search for answers to these problems is given undue importance as compared with the process which may in the ultimate analysis turn out to yield better results. Mistaken as we are with regard to this problem, we are not less dense to give precedence to measuring what has been learnt over what it is that could be learnt. To put it crudely, examination has ·become the solitary important goal of education.

(G)

Before we close this part of our examination, let us see 'whether the purpose of 'teaching' is 'education'. Why does any one wish to teach?

It should be of some interest to note that 'teaching has for its end a purpose and this purpose is to enable the person or persons being taught to learn'. According to Schemer: "what distinguishes teaching is its special connection in the rational ·explanation and critical dialogue with the enterprise of giving ·honest reasons and welcoming radical questions. The person engaged in teaching does not merely want to bring about belief, but to bring it about through the exercise of free-rational judgment by the student. This is what distinguishes teaching from propaganda or debating. ... 'One would like: to agree with Schemer about his assumption that teaching and rationality have one-to-one correspondence and, therefore, ·teaching and propaganda are different. If one extends this logic a bit further, this will mean that a society which proposes to educate all of its citizens will know nothing of terms like "propaganda", "proselytization", etc. and life in such conditions will be ideal.

One will appreciate the reason why Schemer relates teaching to rationality and radical questions. He belongs to an open society where only that teaching is permitted which can answer radical questions and is based on reason. Unfortunately, for him there are societies that are not all that open, even as the medieval societies were mostly not. It will be difficult to hold that teaching does not take place in such societies, even if teaching/ education is not always very welcome. Also in a highly structured society teacher occupies a high status and is not questioned. He also does not like to give reasons for his beliefs. Still teaching continues.

Edward de Bono in his book *Teaching-Thinking* holds on a political level that many countries enjoy or seem to enjoy democratic system. It doesn't really matter whether the party machines allow those elected to be truly representative of the electorate. What does matter is that once they are in power, the politicians do have to pay heed to the opinions, attitudes and preferences of the electorate in order to keep· themselves in power. It should be the Individual thinking of the electors that determines their attitudes. If they do not think so then habit or party line or instant television persuasion is the only available substitutes. At either extreme of the political spectrum we have elitism ill which the self designated elite class determines the thinking of the rest, who cannot be trusted to think for themselves. A left-wing teacher once said that "he did not approve of a programme to teach every-one to think because in a diversified society some people were going to do the thinking and the rest would follow". True, de Bono (*Teaching-Thinking* Penguin Books, 1978, p. 19) does not agree with that left-wing view of the teacher but he does find his logic agreeable enough to attract his attention. For us the situation itself provides a contrast to what Schaffler holds as a pre-condition to teaching. Besides being an impossibility, the way Schaffler says teaching must be conducted because there is so much arbitrariness about everything, including the view that democracy is good for everybody or that two and two make four or that teacher has an answer to all questions or that what teacher teaches he knows it or believes it to be true, etc. Teaching itself is an imposition whether self-invited or decided upon by someone else.

Of all the other relationships teaching may have with education, the latter itself is a learned behavior. Teaching is conducted to produce consciously certain changes or modifications in the behaviour of the person undergoing teaching. If this were not so, society would not pay for it. Since society pays for it, the proposed modified behaviour has its tacit approval. Therefore, logically enough, the nature of teaching will vary corresponding to the nature of society. It is inconceivable to view teaching as independent of the nature and 'will' of society. In a closed society, e.g. the reasoning of the teacher can not be questioned in the classroom, until the teacher comes directly in conflict with the state. Radical questioning, a welcome proposition in an open society, will thus be an anathema of this society. Thus teaching and education will vary according to the nature of' society, yet their exact relationship will remain as unclear as ever.

20

Teaching: An Analysis

(A)

Peters likens 'educating' to a term 'gardening', which ·covers such specific activities like digging, or hocking, or pruning, etc. and holds that "gardening does not exist apart from them." He further says: "'Education' is similar in this respect, though it seems to be an even more abstract term. We say quite naturally that we spent the morning gardening or cooking, but it seems odd to say we spent it 'educating', or to say 'Go and get on with your educating.' 'Educate' like 'reform', 'improve', 'ameliorate' and other such words seems to draw attention only to the standards to which this class of activities must conform and which give them their principle of unity." We, therefore, have "a group of activities related at this very high level in that they all contribute somehow to achieving the general end of an educated person".

We have come to a point where we can state: (a) Teaching leads to learning, (b) Teaching, however, does not always lead to learning, and (c) Learning can take place without any conscious teaching as well. We can also say that a teacher may teach without believing in what he teaches, and similarly a student may learn something without having any faith in it. In other words, teaching itself is value-free and deals with knowledge in a very non-committal manner. Although in normal circumstances, teaching as a process is helpful in educating a person, in others it may not be all that helpful. Indeed, teaching may help one get de-educated as well. Therefore, terms like 'progressive teaching' or even 'progressive methods' of teaching are extremely inadequate and explain almost nothing. Indeed, Peters is right when he says "It certainly is not a conceptual truth that either 'learning' or 'education' implies 'teaching'".

Teaching is normally associated with classroom activities, which have a positive intention of effecting bits of learning whether as part of jigsaw puzzle where only the teacher knows the final answer or the state knows what students 'ought' to learn or the parent wishes to buy him learning. We have already discussed that in a formal situation teaching evokes the image of a teacher teaching something with lot of planning and effort so that he is able to achieve his objective. Teaching in such circumstances is seen merely as a valuable activity in which all the parties-parents/society, pupil, teacher and the school climate—are cooperating in their own given manner. Teaching, if such is the case, is known to be a necessity, a requirement, a pre-condition for the specific purpose of achieving the goal 'learning'. Or else, we can not enact laws to risk schooling company.

As can be seen, the acts or actions which constitute teaching in a classroom are very artificially repeated or perhaps they are more mechanical than natural. A teacher is conditioned to start teaching with the going off the bell and terminates or winds up his activities called teaching with the next bell. This artificial arrangement may be responsible for the mechanization of the activities but then teaching is not to be confused with classroom teaching alone. It is a generic term which is both general and specific.

It is true that teaching is not 'initiation', 'indoctrination', 'proselytization', 'propaganda', 'preaching', etc. but all of these terms and activities do partake of a good deal of teaching. A priest 'initiates' or a mystic initiates a disciple into a ritual but while doing so he does explain his purpose. The pupil has a ready state of mind and also perhaps has a motivation. To a large extent these conditions are, if not exactly identical, similar to a 'teaching' situation. Whereas it is possible that classroom teaching may not have 'belief' as a necessary adjunct of 'learning', but in the other case, it is the first condition. There is *also an element of willing submission to the act of 'initi*ation' but this may not be true of any other activity, be it 'indoctrination' or 'proselytization'. It may be stated that in the case of latter activities, the 'effort' of teaching has no necessary concomitant like 'learning' or 'belief', and perhaps also that 'effort' is mostly one-sided. In the majority of cases, the result of extremely clever 'propaganda' might result or might not result in 'belief' in the taught content but little or no similar commitment on the part of the listeners is possible in the act of teaching. This activity is not participatory and in democratic countries it is taken as part of larger purpose of letting everyone have the right to express an opinion. Indeed, one should not be surprised that the right to express an opinion is also propaganda because everybody may not have an opinion on every subject, and even if one has an opinion one may not like to express or share it with others. Only a few in any society do take it upon themselves as their right to speak out their opinions and hold that they are true. The truth in their case can be as far away as it may be in the case of a classroom teacher. The teacher may still teach something which he may neither be able to explain, nor believe to be true. Such, however, will not be the case with a man engaged in 'propaganda', or 'indoctrination', etc. The latter either holds that what he believes is true or knows how to explain his way in

We thus have a negative definition of teaching. 'Teaching' is not 'propaganda', it is not 'proselytization' and it is also not 'indoctrination'. There is some similarity between 'teaching' and 'initiation' but then the distinction between the two is also very clear. Whereas teaching can take place without being accompanied by learning, in the case of a student-initiate this will not be so. A person being taught may be an unwilling participant in the learning activity but not the 'initiate'. Therefore, 'teaching' and 'initiation' are also not identical. Indeed, there is no other term which comes close to 'Teaching' except 'teachings'. Teachings are crystallized forms of experiences, handed down in terms of time by a 'person who comes to be accepted as a great teacher. Such teachers have followers or disciples. These teachers are not always physically present—only their recorded sentences are, which means, these teachers have extra-legal authority. The students of these teachers are generally highly motivated, informed and discriminating. They normally will not accept the authority of the teacher without any question. These questions are, to use Schaffler's terms, likely to be 'radical questions'.

This obviously is not what we mean by a teacher or teaching in ordinary parlance. A teacher in this case is not a self-appointed person and obviously has no legal or moral sanctions to exceed his limits either in terms of subject matter or time or place. For example, a chemistry teacher of Class X will teach only chemistry and not physics and he must take his class at the appointed hour only. In most cases he has no authority to go beyond his text or period. In subjects like literature or history where interpretations are permitted, he has little or no authority to offer an interpretation that is contrary to social approval. For example, no teacher has a right to discuss the sex life of any of the socially accepted Saints or Fakirs or even Kings like Akbar, Ashok or Alexander unless the course of study so requires.

In the ordinary sense of the term teaching is identified with classroom teaching although the latter does not necessarily mean the former. Indeed, teaching can not be as restricted a concept as classroom teaching is. It is a little more than that. Only if the classroom teacher has the moral sanction of society to exceed his limits, he can share 'teaching' with several others like mother who 'trains' the child in bowel movement or father who 'explains' household gadgets or peers or siblings who 'acquaint' him with their class norms, besides a whole host of teachers who like air and water are abundantly available all over the child's immediate neighborhood.

In fact, what all these people are doing all the time is to inform the child or adult on matters that concern him here and now, or what his future concerns will be. No matter what a teacher does and no matter who the teacher is, the child is gathering information. This information he shares with others, makes it a point to test the validity of the information and after he finds it useful and reliable he repeats it in action or words. We are running into the danger of equating 'propaganda' or 'indoctrination' with teaching because the former is also concerned with communicating information. "Propaganda' is somehow taken to mean convincing of an audience which does not readily accept the viewpoint being propagated. 'Indoctrination' is little more subtle than 'propaganda' and is so pervasive, repetitive and convincing that the indoctrinated person ceases to use his own brain or his powers of discrimination. Such a person cannot use his information either discreetly or ably. Perhaps on this point alone we find that teaching is slightly different, if not exactly better than 'indoctrination' because it enables or seeks to enable its recipient to use information both competently and discriminately. This teaching is also distinguishable from 'training in a skill'. In training there is a lot of its component which is axiomatic, something which forms a part without it being questioned, and also training leads to a kind of conditioning represented in S—R terms. The limitation of' training is that it cannot be transferred easily and universally. Consequently, a skilled person cannot always exceed his skill. However, this supposedly will not happen in the case of a well-taught person because he will be able to match his wits according to the situation or in other words change his strategies according to the need of the time. Still it may appear that 'teaching' and 'training' are siblings of the same parents, i.e. they have a genetic relationship. In so many ways they can be taken as identical—twins. One is to discover later on and after a bit of thinking that they are merely close relations. We have no wish to go into these details here because the 'distinctions' are quite well-known.

Teaching is thus a unique concept which does not resemble any other. From 'teaching' to 'indoctrination' there is a range of activities—one being as distinctly different from the other, not merely in purpose but in design and the layout as well. We can perhaps say that these terms are not so different after all except in the value-system attached to each. 'Propaganda' is less subtle than 'indoctrination' because the latter is perhaps more sinister than the former. 'Training' is an 'inferior' activity in comparison to 'teaching', because the latter involves some degree of the understanding of the philosophical basis of the subject being taught. These unspoken and at times unsuspected values come to distinguish these terms.

We may at this point consider the possibility of identifying 'teaching' as distinct from rumour-mongering. We can argue that teaching is value-free. The transport itself makes no choices of its owners. Teaching is an activity which goes on unmindful of the end-result, although where it ends, its purposes have a direct correlation or a one-to-one correspondence with activity that can be categorized in a hierarchical manner, which means that the activity that achieves in full the purpose for which it was set in motion is superior to the one which does not achieve or achieves but partially the goals set. In fact, what is being suggested here is an 'effective', 'ineffective' or 'partially effective' mode of achievement. Let us take an example.

Teaching has a purpose to achieve because we know that it can not be without one. The purpose is to enable a child learn French or solve an equation. The child is either able to learn French, or learn it perfunctorily or not at all. It is possible to have several more categories or degrees of this achievement. Teaching as an activity thus must belong to one of the several grades of achievement but whether effective, efficient or not, teaching retains its character and nomenclature so long as the conditions of teaching remain in evidence. The teacher, the learner and the knowledge or skill to acquire: are all preconditions for any activity like 'teaching' to start with. The rest are mere grades and qualities of one or of any of the three. A 'foolish' or 'inexperienced' teacher will also teach irrespective of the results, provided a society allows him to perform this duty. His 'foolishness' and 'inexperience' do not take away the meaning from the activity called 'teaching' with its real purport. Similarly, whether the knowledge is true or false must not influence the subject, that is to be communicated. Whether the learner learns or does not, has no bearing on the 'will' of the teacher who intends to teach.

It is quite interesting to see whether a rumour or an inaccurate inference may also be taught with impunity. Can such knowledge form a valid part of the teaching activity? A teacher is supposedly not allowed to teach a rumour or an inaccurate inference. But if he has no evidence to refute a rumour, does it become 'accurate' knowledge; perhaps not. If we have no evidence to say that Mohammed Tughluq was an able and wise ruler; does it mean that we can say that he was not? The opinion or the will of a teacher should not interfere in this matter. Let the society or the boards of textbook writers decide about it. The teacher may keep his opinion in reserve. We have thus tried to say that a teacher has no right—since it has nowhere been decided that he has such a right to teach inaccurate inferences or falsehood. In matters where the teacher has a doubt about the veracity of information or there is lack of proper evidence, he must refrain from crossing his marked limits. A teacher does not have a moral right to rumour-mongering, though quite possibly he may be doing so unconsciously or unintentionally. If a teacher keeps on saying that "Chinese are superior to Indians and can defeat them any time" it is an opinion with no proofs or valid evidence and, therefore, a teacher, unless he happens to be a spy and is paid to teach inaccuracies will not say so.

But we keep on coming across numerous examples everyday wherein a teacher does nothing but sanctify rumour and accord it the status of knowledge worthy of being learnt. He fails to apply his reason before stating the partial truth as true. There is, however, a danger that if for lack of evidence we do not teach something, we may not have proofs enough to teach anything, For example, there may come a day when the sun may not rise in the East or it may not rise at all. We have evidence to state the daily occurrence but not the possibilities. The possibility is a mere inference and inferences need not be true or valid. But if they are, we are denying our children the knowledge of the possible truth, the axiomatic truth and the inferential truth.

Even the Carvaka who holds that only that is true which has direct and valid evidence for support, but will not say that two and two do not make four. No one denies the possibility that one day the sun may grow cold and earth may become uninhabitable. Yet today we do not teach it because it is a distant possibility and our only ground to say so is that "Nothing is Eternal on this Earth". The Cosmos is Eternal, the matter changes form and yet the sun may not grow cold after all. There is, however, a very indistinct line between the Truths that have evidence and the possibility which has support in an inference. Who decides these matters? Surely the teacher is not the arbiter. If we agree that even peers teach besides parents and perhaps learning in that case is the most effective, we do not and obviously cannot prevent these teachers from exceeding their boundary lines, and that they must always support their statement with valid evidences. As this does not happen, rumours would continue to be in circulation-and also look respectable.

Also as we distinguish between 'teaching' and 'training (while teaching 'knowledge' or 'training' in skill, what means have we to say that a smuggler who lectures upon the advantages of smuggling, is not actually 'teaching'. He will cease to be a teacher if he starts 'training' in the art of smuggling but so long as he lectures or teaches, he is not performing his job in any different manner than a Socrates or Sai Baba does. We can therefore summarize:

1. 'Teaching' and 'training' are different concepts.
2. While 'teaching' axioms and inferences may be taught but the moment there is a possibility that the universal laws and the laws of earth are in conflict, teacher may not broach that matter.
3. Rumors are unsupported, baseless, proofless statements, the authenticity of which is clouded. Whether 'motivated ' or innocuous rumours form part of our daily life and must be tested before one accepts them. But unfortunately to find a proper evidence to support a rumour is difficult. Teaching rumour may be unethical but the question is: Is it possible to avoid it? This inability to overcome a rumour does not justify its teaching.
4. 'Teaching' of political science, is no different from 'teaching' of smuggling or 'pick-pocketing' except that the end-result of one may be so different from that of another. 'Teaching' pick-pocketing may not be respectable or ethical or honorable but it remains 'teaching' all the same for the simple reason it meets alt the requirements of a 'teaching' situation. We need not go into the reasons why political science is more respectable than 'smuggling' because these matters do not directly come within our purview. No society permits an individual or a group of individuals to destroy the very fabric on which it stands. Smuggling; or pick-pocketing, therefore, do not pass that test, whereas political science does.

(C)

Is' 'teaching' an activity or a process does an activity constitute an isolated act of teaching or it has an end and a beginning with something like a gamut of activities thrown in between to give 'teaching' a distinctive feature of its own? Can one conceive of teaching as an independent act long before it starts to have repercussions of its own, i.e. learning; achieving, etc.?

There are no easy answers to these questions. 'Teaching' is an activity and also a series of activities that end up in attempting to help someone learn. It becomes a process when 'teaching' is viewed in broader terms to cover 'education' and towards achieving this end teaching must be conducted in consonance with the noble and positive aspects of social behaviour. A master-cheat despite his university degrees cannot be called a cultivated man or a person who has been well-taught. *Education is a positive value.* A cheat like this one may be obviously very 'well-initiated' or 'well-instructed' but not 'educated'. Education must reflect itself in the positive behaviour of an individual which is not in this cheat's case. A cheat like a professor of philosophy may be dependent on his wits to make his both ends meet whereas one has no social sanction, while the other one has. What is being suggested here is that the nominal resemblances do not necessarily make this action or concept alike? Therefore, if someone starts a school of cheating with courses of study-being taught by competent cheats who were well-versed both in the theory and practice of cheating, this school can never make the grades of a 'school of medicine' or a 'school of dancing. The missing points in the school of cheating are: 'social sanction' and 'positive purpose' or noble ends. But in all other respects this school will be like any other. Therefore what differentiates 'education' with anti-social activity is the moral purpose of the content and design in both. To use the same illustration further: cheating is helpful in making one person live off the income of others. Surely this is exploitation and using of unfair means to sustain oneself and it can never be regarded as the goal of education or 'teaching'—a means of achieving it.

But if one does not take into account the 'moral' or 'social -sanction' angle, teaching in the 'school of cheating' will in no way appear very different from teaching in the 'school of medicine'. Both may employ qualified, skilled teachers, both may require a rigorous training of around five years and both may give practical training and a certificate. While teaching -surgery or cheating the use of video-tape or audio-visual aids may come in handy. It is, therefore, interesting to observe that the activity or process of teaching in either case does not vary at all. They are identical. This should help us to summarise that teaching leads to education within a moral frame. 'Teaching' per se is a value activity and has moral binding. We have suggested earlier that teaching is value-free but it is not true or else we will have to equate cheating with teaching.

Even the tools and modes of 'teaching' stand approved, or otherwise only to the extent they lead to social good which implies personal good. In the 'school of cheating' the individual was aiming to benefit at the expense of society and, therefore, although teaching in that school has all the attributes and paraphernalia of being regarded 'teaching', it falls 'short of the moral requirement'.

There is one more consideration in this regard. If the content of teaching has no 'moral' implications, will teaching in that case pass muster? Perhaps 'yes'; perhaps 'no'. For example, we may talk of Cosmos in a manner as if it were ·the property of Earthlings. Obviously human beings on this Earth may not regard this viewpoint as immoral. On second thought we may discover that we have no such right. Or, we may teach physics or chemistry without realizing that the ultimate in either can give an individual or a nation such power that it may keep every other nation or the entire human race under constant threat of annihilation. No one will say that teaching chemistry is bad but he will surely condemn an individual inventing or discovering a gas that may hold everybody else in terror. In terms of purposes also we may never be sure that what has the approval and moral sanction today, may not stand up to our original assessment.

To be on the safe side it is for better to conclude that "teaching' must at least handle only that content", which is socially approved.

Teaching also appears to be a process having its origins in a series of activities. What appears more plausible is that even the purpose of each activity may not be known to either the teacher or the taught. These purposes can remain hidden, implied or unclear to the teacher. For example, mathematics develops reasoning or teaching terse materials enables one to develop memory. There may be highly questionable assumptions but then they are there. Even a very elaborate study will not succeed in dislodging mathematics from its pedestal or make all teaching very interesting. Teaching as an activity continues and the process of learning mathematics for a very unclear aim may never terminate.

Indeed, teaching continues as a process, preparing and educating generations of people in insufficiently clear subject materials. But just as no mother will refrain from teaching her child the arts of walking and running for the fear that in near future this walking or running may be utilized for smuggling or robbery. Teaching is an activity which can not be stopped in order to guard oneself against a future possibility of its content being misused. In fact, we come across almost everyday people misusing their education in one manner or the other whether deliberately or otherwise, but that has not made the society reconsider its continued unquestioned support to it. Had this been done the folly of society would have been so inexcusable. After all, the misuse is disproportionately small as compared to the same being put to good use or at least this is what one hopes it should be like.

(D)

Perhaps we ought to relate 'teaching' to 'quality' of life. We have already tried to examine 'teaching' as a concept both independent of learning and ethical values. We have also seen how an activity—an isolated act of teaching a skill or knowledge acquires the status of 'process'. Such a seemingly neutral concept and medium as 'teaching' may or may not have any bearing on the 'quality' of life. In fact, I am entering an entirely new area altogether when I am trying to define 'quality' of life. Beyond economic standards and etiquettes we do have a quality in life which can be measured and defined. For quality of life of a businessman will be different from the quality of life of a poor Indian farmer. Both may be equally honest, i.e. may not come in conflict with the law of the land. The 'quality' of life in this respect will be class 'quality', dependent on several conditions such as the level of education, the type of ambitions and their ethics and also perhaps the time and type of place they live in, etc. But surely the quality of life in essence suggests the inner peace of mind and a right kind of relationship with the society around. This obviously means that a thief or a cheat, howsoever clever he may be, will never be able to establish either this relationship and also can never have the kind of peace which our businessman or our farmer generally has. The quality is thus a class and society bound term which may encompass a bit of ambition as well, i.e. the poor farmer may like to become a rich farmer and a small businessman a big businessman, but the moment one wishes to become the other that is the farmer proposes to become a businessman he ceases to have his usual relationship with the world around himself. The resultant disequilibrium will seriously jeopardize his earlier 'quality' of life.

What I am trying to say is that when teaching is conducted, whether orally or otherwise, it must have some near relationship with the 'quality' of life of the person attempting to learn. We cannot conceive of a 'teaching' which seeks to drive its recipient mad or crazy, or for that matter so ambitious or depressed that he is 'ill at ease' with the world, around himself. 'Teaching' thus has something to do with a life style that is not torn apart because of the content it transmits to the learner. 'Teaching' may help one grow and not get uprooted or alienated. Teaching cannot in this sense be ever revolutionary. It merely helps one enrich one's life and understanding.

This view is, however, disputed by Neil Postman and Charles Weingartner (*Penguin Education Specials*, p. 13, 1976) who hold that "change-constant accelerating, ubiquitous is the most striking characteristic of the world we live in and that our educational system has not yet recognized this fact. "They recognize that "most criticism of the old education, and of the old concepts it conserves and transmits, from Paul Goodman to John Gardner, makes the point that the students who endure it come out as passive, acquiescent, dogmatic, intolerant, authoritarian, inflexible, conservative personalities who desperately need to resist change in an effort to keep their illusion of certainty intact". Therefore, while suggesting strategies for survival they plead for a school where new education is offered which "consists of having students use the concepts most appropriate to the world in which we all must live. All of these concepts constitute the dynamics of the question-questioning, meaning - making process that can be called "learning how to learn". This comprises a posture of stability from which to deal fruitfully with change. The purpose is to help all students develop built-in, shockproof crap detectors as basic equipment in their survival kits".

Interestingly enough, even these supposedly radical authors timidly agree with the basic function of teaching that I have been trying to say. Teaching merely helps one "to learn how to learn" so that he adjusts in the world around himself. Life changes, so does teaching and its content but the latter cannot ever stop the former.

This standpoint can be proved to be logical even through Indian religious philosophy. Life is Eternal. God is life giver and sustainer. Therefore, changes take place only when God wills. He Himself helps people to get insight into the mysteries of his Creation. God is Eternal, beyond Beginning and End, He is sublime consciousness.

Says Taittiriya Upanishad, "He who knows the joy of Brahman, which words cannot express and the mind cannot reach, is free from fear. He is not distressed by the thought, "why did 1 not do what is right? Why did I do what is wrong?" He who knows the joy of Brahman, knowing both good and evil, transcends both.

OM

May Brahman protect us, and Aurobindo also teaches knowing full well that they never qualified in the sense the former do. In this respect what we mean by teaching is the instruction, which modifies our moral behavior. Whereas an ordinary classroom teacher deals with partial truths, half-knowledge, resemblances and matter-of-fact information, the real teacher transcends these limitations. For him teaching is not information-mongering. He hesitates to regard his role as a vendor of knowledge. In fact he takes upon himself the role of a teacher because of his perception that the people around him need his help. He interprets knowledge available to him in the language of his people. Life, however, does not restrict himself to any limits imposed by geography. Therefore, while such a teacher addresses people of his own area, his 'teachings' transcend ordinary boundaries and concern themselves with the universal truths. This Teacher can also be called *seer*, who through his word and deed attempts to affect the life-styles of his followers. These teachers command respect because of their dedication and· work. Most of their work consists in convincing their audience that they need to urgently modify their behavior.

We may cite an example: Communal disturbances are endemic to our society. We teach secularism in our classrooms and political leaders never tire of talking about it. Both in their own ways attempt to convince people that secular behaviour is the only way-out for a multi-religious society till riots take place. Only a Gandhi could demonstrate that secularism was good behaviour or non-violence was a superior weapon to violence. In the former situation a teacher merely defines secularism as given in the textbooks and a politician exhorts people to adopt secularism because he regards that as superior way of life. A Gandhi sees the moral of secularism and lives it. Therefore what a teacher teaches in the classroom is mere information transmission but a Gandhi interprets 'secularism' and lives it. From the Indian standpoint a teacher should not only know what he teaches but must also be able to live it. Teaching, therefore, either as a process or end-product cannot absolve itself of the moral content of textual material.

Bibliography

Archambault, R.D., *Philosophical Analysis and Education,* London: Routledge & Kegan Paul, 1965.

Bennet, Neville, *Teaching Styles and Pupil Progress*, London: Open Books, 1976.

Bijalwan, *Indian Theory of Knowledge*, New Delhi, Heritage Publishers, 1977.

Brubecher, J.S., *Eclectic Philosophy of Education*, Englewood Cliffs, New Jersey: Prentice Hall, 1951.

Chisholm, Roderick M., *Theory of knowledge*, New Delhi: Prentice Hall of India, 1977.

Connor, D.J., *An Introduction to the Philosophy of Education,* London: Routledge & Kegan Paul, 1965.

Dearden, R.F. Hirst, P.H. and Peters, R.S. (Eds.) *A Critique of Current Educational Aims,* London: Routledge & Kegan Paul 1952.

Dearden, R.F., Hirst, P.H. and Peters, R.S. (Eds.) *Reason,* London: Routledge & Kegan Paul, 1972.

Hare, R.M. *The Language of Morals*, New York: Oxford University Press, 1952.

Hirst, P.H. and Peters, R.S. *The Logic of Education,* London: Routledge & Kegan Paul. 1974.

Hirst, P.H., *Knowledge and the Curriculum.* London: Routledge& Kegan Paul, 1974.

Illych, Ivan D., *De-Schooling Society.* London: Calder and Boyars, Penguin, 1971.

Kant, *Education*, Ann Arbor Paperbacks, 1960.

Kelly, Earl C., *Education for what is Real.* New York: Harper Row, 1947.

Langford, Glenn and O'Connor, D.J., *New Essay in the Philosophy of Education*, London: Routledge & Kegan Paul, 1973.

Maitra, S.K. *The Main Problems of Philosophy,* Calcutta: Progressive Publishers, 1962.

Murphy, Garden, *Freeing Intelligence through Teaching,* New York: Harper & Bros, 1961.

Nyberg, David (Ed.) *The Philosophy of Open Education*, London: Routledge & Kegan Paul, 1975.

O'Neill, Reginald, R.S.J., *Theories of Knowledge,* Englewood Cliffs, N.J.: Prentice-Hall India, 1959.

Peters, R.S., *Ethics and Education*, London: George Allen & Unwin Ltd., 1966.

Postman, Neil and Weingartner, Charles, *Teaching as a Subversive Activity* Penguin Education Specials, 1976.

Prabhavanand, Swami and Fredrick, Manchester. (Trans.) *The Upanishads* A Mentor Religious Classic, 1957.

Radhakrishan, S., *True Knowledge*, New Delhi: Orient Paperbacks, 1978.

Russell, Bertrand, *History of Western Philosophy,* Unwin University Books, 1974.

Ryle, G., *The Concept of Mind,* London: Hutchinson House, 1957.

Schaffler, Israel, *Conditions of Knowledge,* Illinois: Scott, Foreman & Co., 1965.

Sengupta, *A History of Indian Ohilosophy (Vol. I and II),* Cambridge University Press, 1957.

Taxonomy of Educational Objectives (Bloom). Handbook: Cognitive Domain London: Longman Green & Co., 1996.

Terry, G., Thomas, S.B. and Marshall, A.R., *International Dictionary of Education*, London: Kogan Page, Nicholas Publishing, New York, 1977.

Woolzey, A.D., *Theory of Knowledge*. London: Hutchinson University Library, 1949.

Yolton, John W. *Theory of Knowledge*. New York: The Macmillan Co. 1965.

Index

Acquisition of General Knowledge, 41
Adult education programmes, 95, 140
AIR, 113-14, 132-33, 145
Alberta, 127
Alphabets knowledge, 59, 97
AMCEE, 124
Ancient & Medieval India, 97
Archaic
  scripts, 163
  society, 39
Aristotle, 33, 81-83
Arithmetic, 91, 97, 235
Asian Countries, 182-83
Asian Programme of Educational Innovation for Development, 133
Association for Media-based Continuing Education, 124
Atharvaveda, 25, 96, 97, 150, 157
Atkinson, 215-16
Audio-Visual Research Centers, 141, 154, 186
Autonomy, 134, 148, 151
Awareness programmes, 178

B.Ed., 77, 79, 107
Basu, Aparna, 161
BBC, 113, 123, 150-51
Best Educational Programme, 184
Beteille, Andre, 18
Bhatt, Kumaril, 52
Borrowed knowledge, 67, 200
Brahman, 14, 24, 25, 231-32, 239-40, 276
British education, 30
Buddhists, 37, 96, 97, 248

Caste system, 7, 16, 43
CBSE students, 65, 198
CCTU, 125
Center for Educational Technology, 134, 151
Centers of Mass Communication and Educational Technology, 135
Central Institute of Educational Technology, 141
Child marriages, 7, 38, 45, 47, 48
Civilizations, 51, 88, 124, 163, 257
Classroom
  instruction, 62-64, 69, 78, 101, 109, 112, 185, 203, 223
  teaching, 71, 108, 111, 113-15, 267-68
Co-education institutions, 77
Colonial India, 8, 12, 27, 40
Common knowledge, 38, 50, 162, 230
Community programmes, 114, 130
Computer literacy programmes, 142
Computer-education modules, 142
  Integration of, 142
Consortium for Educational Communications, 144, 151, 181

Content analysis, 173-74
Content quality, 107, 109
Conventional universities, 123, 125
Countries enrichment programmes, 119
Courseware, 156
Curricula-based education, 143
Curricular programmes, 119
CWCR, 148-51, 162-64, 177, 189, 192

Development of ideas, 103, 261
Disabled child, 219
Dissemination of educational programmes, 145
Distance education institution, 125
Distance learning, 145, 174
Doctoral research, 69, 202
Doordarshan, 117, 132-33, 145, 167, 181, 191
Dubbed programmes, 131, 182

East India Company, 4-6, 11, 12, 26, 37, 90, 92
Education Codes, 209
Education
- adult, 114, 162, 164
- college, 40
- compulsory, 47
- defective, 261
- distance, 124, 143, 146-47, 164
- elementary, 46, 47
- experimental, 164
- female, 40, 42
- formal, 42, 117, 119
- goals of, 83, 98, 99
- history of, 6, 139
- indigenous, 22
- in-service, 77
- logic of, 258
- medieval, 97
- modern, 38, 40, 88, 94, 98
- monastic, 92
- non-formal, 164-65
- physical, 47, 82
- primary, 100, 116
- secondary, 94, 95, 100
- stages of, 95, 98
- syllabus-based, 118
- university, 98, 172
- vocational, 164

Educational advancement, 99
Educational broadcasting, 133-34, 151, 176
Educational films, 140
Educational Information, 142
Educational material, 145, 147
Educational psychology, 226
Educational research, 49, 64, 69, 140, 202
Educational software, 137, 141
Educational Technology, 130, 132-34, 137, 140, 143, 151
Educational Video Competition, 181, 184
Educational Video Programme, 182-83
Enrichment programmes, 117, 120, 144, 162, 164-65
Environment education, 77, 165
ETV, 113, 115, 117, 119-21, 124, 126-27, 139-40, 142-43, 151, 155
European education, 30, 94
Examination system, 87, 256

Feedback, 110, 114, 123, 145, 173-74, 186, 188
Fellowship programme, 172
Financing of education, 101
Formal
- schooling, 118, 214, 263
- system, 95, 215

Formative research, 145, 147, 174, 182-83

General enrichment programmes, 140
Global society, 99
Grounded theory, 60

Hakluyt, Richard, 4
Health Education Scheme, 46
Heisenberg effect, 60
Higher education, 46, 49, 50, 64, 94, 95, 98, 100, 108-9, 135, 139, 141, 164-66, 194-95, 198
Hindustan Times, 32, 33, 36, 65, 194, 199

Iconography, 42
ICT, 13, 77
Indian Adult Education Association, 114
Indian Constitution, 11, 34, 46, 77
Indian Satellite Experiment, 131
Indian Space Agency, 129
Indian Space Research Organization (ISRO), 116-17, 130, 178-79
Information Age, 98, 150, 194
INSAT, 132-34, 138-40, 144, 151
Instructional television, 118
Islam, 10, 18, 27, 28, 30, 33, 34, 92, 97, 238
Islamic education, 29, 30

Jains, 22, 28
Japan, 63, 119, 127
Joshi, Ila, 176-78

Kindergarten, 94, 95, 98
Knowledge Commission, 198
Knowledge
- defining, 229
- digitalized, 111
- divine, 91, 232
- formal, 234
- human, 54
- modern, 8, 27, 94
- modes of, 247
- packaged, 78
- sacred, 92
- specialized, 49
- spiritual, 97
- transmission of, 225, 236, 250-51, 259
- ultimate, 158, 232

Lastrucchi, Carlo, 53
Lecture-based programmes, 178

M.Ed, 63, 66, 199
Macaulay, 3, 8-10, 12, 13, 23, 57, 58, 90
Madrassas, 7, 20, 22, 27, 29, 94, 96, 97
Management skills, 67, 201
Mass Communication and Educational Technology, 135
Mass Communication Research Center, 154
Media library, 196-97
Media-based Continuing Education, 123
Millennium Learning System, 79
Ministry of Education, 125, 132-33

National Center for Educational Media, 138
National Council of Educational Research and Training (NCERT), 21, 59, 117, 131-33, 140-41
National Fundamental Education Center, 114
National Policy on Education, 45, 139
Nature of Learning, 164
Nature of Teaching, 164, 205, 207

NCTE, 63-66, 68, 79, 107, 199, 202, 255
Neurath, Paul, 115
Non-commercial broadcasting, 117
Non-Formal system, 95, 133
NSS, 39
Nuclear Science Center, 144, 151
Nutrition, 46, 130

Panchayats, 84
Philosophy, branches of, 212
Plato, 33, 81-83, 224, 233-34, 236, 263
Prasar Bharati, 155
Pre-recorded programmes, 179
Professional Education, 97
Proselytization, 264, 267-68
Proto-type programmes, 130
Provincial Education Bureaus, 125
Psychology of Education, 70, 204
Public Schools, 95, 107
Quality Assurance in Educational Research, 49
Quality education, 89
Quality management in Education, 75
Quality of life, 25, 120, 196, 223, 275

Radical questions, 264, 268
Radio programme, 140-41
Reith, Lord, 150-51
Research Cell, 166, 176
Rig-Veda, 10, 37, 41, 48, 81, 91, 97, 157
Rumour-mongering, 270-71
Russell, Bertrand, 233-34

Sachchar Panel, 32
Samaveda, 96, 97, 157
Sanskrit universities, 13, 17, 96
Sarabhai, Vikram, 116, 152
Satellite communication, 143-44, 151
Schaffler, 215, 242-43, 260, 265
Schools
  co-educational, 47
  educational, 76
  elementary, 142
  formal, 92, 100
  secondary, 46, 95, 114, 121, 140-42
Self-financed colleges, 66, 68, 200-1
Sex education, 47, 121, 162
Siddiqui, I.H., 161
SITE, 116-17, 129-30, 134
Skill transmission, 251
Skilled teachers, 250, 273
Skinner, B.F., 110
Social justice, 253
Social life, 44, 260
Social sanctions, 220, 273
Social system, 84, 218
Socialist party, 17
Societal functions, 84
Socrates, 81, 82, 272
Space Application Center, 132
Student-teacher relationship, 127
Subject expert, 179, 181, 184
Subject-based programmes, 156
Subject-oriented programmes, 160
Syllabus-oriented courses, 133

Talkback facilities, 178-79
Teacher trainees, 47, 77
Teaching machines, 110
Tech-centered learning programs, 79
Technical Teacher Training Institutions, 141
Tech-Savvy Teachers, 65
Teleconferencing, 179
Teleteach, 141
Television programmes, 126, 130, 132, 172, 186

regular educational, 114
syllabus-based, 172
Theory of Education, 212

UGC, 46, 49, 50, 89, 99, 132, 138, 143-46, 148, 151-53, 156, 166-67, 172, 178-81, 187-89, 191-93
UNESCO, 34, 113, 116, 133
Upanishads, 209, 232, 238-40
Urban child, 218

Value system, 214, 220-21
Values education, 164
Vedanta, 233, 238-39, 248
Vedas, 13, 25, 36, 37, 41, 42, 48, 49, 51, 81, 84, 85, 96, 97, 112, 157
Verbal testimony, 249
Vernacular Education, 7
Video lectures, 155, 160-61
Video-centered distance learning courses, 124
Vocational training programmes, 46
Vyas Channel, 154, 195-96

Western education, 8, 11, 16, 17, 21, 22, 40
Western knowledge, 8, 159
Women Studies, 46

Yajurveda, 25, 37, 49, 80, 91, 97, 157
Yash Pal, 171-72